Linnaeus

The Man and His Work

Linnaeus
The Man and His Work

edited by   *with contributions by*

TORE FRÄNGSMYR   STEN LINDROTH
GUNNAR ERIKSSON
GUNNAR BROBERG

UNIVERSITY OF CALIFORNIA PRESS
Berkeley Los Angeles London

University of California Press
Berkeley and Los Angeles, California
University of California Press, Ltd.
London, England

© 1983 by
The Regents of the University of California

Printed in the United States of America

1 2 3 4 5 6 7 8 9

Library of Congress Cataloging in Publication Data
Main entry under title:

Linnaeus, the man and his work.

Includes index.
1. Linné, Carl von, 1707–1778.   2. Naturalists—
Sweden—Biography.   I. Frängsmyr, Tore, 1938–
II. Lindroth, Sten.   III. Eriksson, Gunnar, 1931–
IV. Broberg, Gunnar, 1942–
QH44.L56   580′.92′4 [B]   82-2044
ISBN 0-520-04568-8   AACR2

Contents

Editor's Introduction

Whether seen from an international or a national viewpoint, Linnaeus (Carl von Linné) is in many ways a very Swedish figure. Abroad, he is one of the few really well-known Swedes. He was not only a scientist of genius, but also heir to the general optimism and belief in progress which characterized science in the eighteenth century.

But for Swedes, too, Linnaeus is "Swedish" to an unusually high degree. It may even be that he has played a crucial part in creating something which we consider typically Swedish—the feeling for nature, the sense of discovery inspired by the Swedish countryside, the clear literary style. For Swedes, Linnaeus has become something of a guide to Sweden.

The Swedish idea of Linnaeus was formed during the Romantic period of the early nineteenth century, and Linnaeus himself played no small part in painting the picture. It was the custom for members of the Royal Swedish Academy of Sciences to write their own *curricula vitae,* so that the material for a biography was there when the time came. Linnaeus was vain; he cared for the judgment of posterity. As the years went by, he wrote four such autobiographies. They were published in 1824 and came to constitute the essence of the Swedish view of Linnaeus. He himself called attention to his achievements quite without modesty. The Swedish Romantics did the rest. And thus arose the picture of the gentle Prince of Botany, surrounded by friends: "God created, and Linnaeus classified."

Linnaeus became a national figure, and botany gained the rank of a sort of national favorite subject. Generations of Swedish schoolboys had to arrange herbaria and learn Linnaean taxonomy. The homage reached its peak with the Linnaean anniversary celebrations of 1907 (the bicentenary of his birth), when the University of Uppsala, in particular, turned out to commemorate the memory of its great son.

At that time the history of science was not yet established as a university discipline. Linnaeus's achievements in various fields were described by representatives of those fields. Linnaeus as a physician was portrayed by a physician, Linnaeus as a botanist, by a botanist, Linnaeus as a zoologist, by a zoologist, and so on. All of these studies had many merits. Nevertheless, a more unifying perspective was lacking, that of Linnaeus as a cultural figure, as a part of the general history of science.

Not until 1932 was a chair in the history of science set up at Uppsala, and when it was, the orientation differed from that in other countries. It is significant that the subject was called the "history of science and ideas," marking an approach that was more humanistic than strictly scientific. The first incumbent of this chair, Professor Johan Nordström, came originally from the history of literature, and his outlook was humanistic in the broad sense. It was not, therefore, a question of studying the internal history of the sciences but one of seeing the development of science in the context of Swedish cultural history. This approach was decisive. The history of science became one of the humanities from the outset, and Nordström quickly gathered a brilliant group of historians.

Naturally, these pioneers in the subject soon became interested in the figure of Linnaeus. There was much to be done. Linnaeus occupied, after all, such a central position in the eighteenth century. But there were also obstacles. These historians were dealing with a Swedish national figure, with all that this entailed in the way of admiration and respect.

Outside Sweden, a more objective view of Linnaeus prevailed. Both his trailblazing achievements and his limitations had been recognized early. At the same time, something was missing from the appraisal, something which was perhaps connected with Linnaeus's Swedish background. There is room for evaluations and judgments which perhaps only a Swede, steeped in the cultural climate of Sweden, can supply.

Professor Sten Lindroth, Nordström's successor as professor of the history of science and ideas at the University of Uppsala, has dealt with the task of giving an overall portrait of Linnaeus as a scientist and as a man. In particular, he has wished to correct the picture of Linnaeus, the gentle Prince of Botany, presented by Swedish Romanticism. Linnaeus was a perceptive observer of the world of nature and its processes, but he was also in many ways a troubled individual with a deeply pessimistic outlook on life. His secure Christian childhood has to be set against the demand for empiricism and rationalism which could be made of a natural historian in the intellectual controversies of the eighteenth century. Linnaeus's concentration on classification and taxonomy may have obscured other important aspects of natural history.

The other studies in this volume consider various aspects of Linnaeus's vast field of activity. Professor Gunnar Eriksson has examined the background to *Systema Naturae*, the ideas which inspired Linnaeus to undertake this huge work of classification, what he took from his predecessors, and what was the product of his own mind.

Linnaeus's views on cosmology and geology are discussed in a study by Tore Frängsmyr. The question at issue is how Linnaeus saw the biblical story of the Creation in the light of empirical discoveries which had been made about the history of the earth. Linnaeus was caught between two fires: he tried to compromise between the Bible and empiricism. He very much wanted to retain his Christian beliefs, but he could not close his eyes to the observations and findings which were, in fact, at hand.

The fourth study, by Gunnar Broberg, examines Linnaeus's view of man. It was, of course, Linnaeus who coined the term *Homo sapiens*. With this he defined man as a thinking being; he wished to define the nature of the human species and give it a place in the larger global perspective. Linnaeus's conception has undoubtedly had a major influence, both positive and negative, on our view of man as a biological and cultural being.

It is hoped that this volume will throw new light on Linnaeus both as a man and as a scientist. The specifically Swedish angle may perhaps be able to bring out more prominently the outstanding but far from uncomplicated natural historian that Linnaeus was.

Contributions to the translation and publication expenses have been given by the Swedish Council for the Humanities and Social Sciences, and from Längmanska kulturfonden.

For permission to use quotations and manuscripts we want to thank The Linnean Society of London and the University Library in Uppsala. Loeb Classical Library has been kind enough to let us quote Ovid's *Metamorphoses* (1944) and Horace's *Epodes* (1946), and Great Books of the Western World has kindly let us quote Newton's *Principia* from the 1952 edition, vol. 34.

Contributors

STEN LINDROTH (1914–1980) became Professor of the History of Science and Ideas at Uppsala University in 1957. He established a reputation as a leading authority on the science and learning of the seventeenth and eighteenth centuries in particular. His dissertation dealt with Paracelsism in Sweden, *Paracelsismen i Sverige till 1600-talets mitt* (1943). He is the author of an exhaustive work describing mining and copper production in Sweden prior to 1800, *Gruvbrytning och kopparhantering vid Stora Kopparberget* (2 vols., 1955). In addition to a series of special studies, he has written the history of the Royal Swedish Academy of Sciences from the start to the time of Berzelius, *Kungl. Svenska Vetenskapsakademiens historia 1739–1818* (3 vols., 1967), and he was, at his death, working on the first Swedish history of learning, *Svensk lärdomshistoria* (3 vols., 1975–1978, a fourth volume posthumously published in 1981). From 1950 Lindroth was editor of *Lychnos*, the yearbook of the Swedish History of Science Society, and of its series of publications, *Lychnos-Bibliotek*. He was also a member of a number of academies and scientific societies, including the Royal Swedish Academy of Sciences and the Swedish Academy. The essay in this volume has previously been published in Swedish, in *Lychnos* 1965/66.

GUNNAR ERIKSSON, b. 1931, became Professor of the History of Ideas at Umeå University in 1970, and since 1981 he has been Professor of the History of Science and Ideas at Uppsala University. He defended a thesis on the Swedish botanist Elias Fries and the Romantic movement, *Elias Fries och den romantiska biologien* (1962). His published works since then have included a history of Swedish botany up to 1800, *Botanikens historia i Sverige intill år 1800* (1970), and a book on the connection between science and industrialism in Sweden, *Kartläggarna* (1978). The chapter on Linnaeus in the present volume is a translation of a part of his history of botany.

TORE FRÄNGSMYR, b. 1938, became Associate Professor of the History of Science and Ideas at Uppsala University in 1969 and in 1981 Professor in a Program in Technology and Social Change at Linköping University. In 1982 he was appointed Research Professor in History of Science at Uppsala. His dissertation was on the subject of geology and the doctrine of Creation in the eighteenth century, *Geologi och skapelsetro* (1969), from which the chapter in this book has been taken. Since then he has written on, among other subjects, the emergence of Wolffianism in Uppsala 1720–1760, *Wolffianismens genombrott i Uppsala* (1972), and on the role of the glacial theory in the geological discussion in Sweden in the nineteenth century, *Upptäckten av istiden* (1976). He has also published a study on utopias and other visions of the future, *Framsteg eller förfall* (1980). A study on Sarton and the Positivist tradition was published in *Lychnos* 1973–74.

GUNNAR BROBERG, b. 1942, has been Assistant Professor of the History of Science and Ideas at Uppsala University since 1976. His dissertation was entitled *Homo sapiens L.* (1976) and contained studies of Linnaeus's interpretation of nature and anthropology. His contribution to the present volume comes from that book. Since 1977 he has been the editor of the year book of the Swedish Linnaeus Society, *Svenska Linnésällskapets Årsskrift*, and he has edited a Commemorative Volume of the bicentenary conference in 1978, *Linnaeus: Progress and Prospects in Linnean Research* (1980). Broberg is at present engaged in an examination of racial controversy in Sweden in the beginning of the twentieth century.

MICHAEL SRIGLEY, B.A., English lecturer at Uppsala University, has translated Lindroth's essay.

BERNARD VOWLES, B.A., translator and living in Gothenburg, has translated all the other papers.

STEN LINDROTH

The Two Faces of Linnaeus

Without doubt, Carl von Linné, known in the English-speaking world as Linnaeus, is the greatest figure in Swedish natural science. Even during his lifetime he was acclaimed by the whole world, and his writings became peerless books of law. Within the domain of natural history, he reigned supreme, just as Newton did within the exact sciences. Certainly there existed impenitent foreigners who refused to bow before the authority of the Swedish botanist, especially in France, but his influence only increased with the years, and his reformation of the most lovable of the sciences became general property. Even today, several of Linnaeus's works remain indispensable tools for the biological investigator.

But what is remarkable and unique about Linnaeus's posthumous reputation is the influence he has exercised on his native country. It is without parallel. We know of no other example where a great scientist has become part of a whole people's national consciousness, a patriotic symbol. There exists, or at least has existed, a Swedish Linnaeus legend, piously tended by those who considered themselves to be the guardians of the memory of Linnaeus. Its founder, it could be claimed, was Linnaeus himself. With his nervous and overwrought self-awareness, he described and commented on the extraordinary destiny of his life and his incomparable greatness as a scientist. But it was not until a little way into the nineteenth century, with the full development of Romanticism, that Linnaeus first became the object of a national cult. His person and work were regarded with reverent awe, and under the sign of the new sensitivity Linnaeus became the Prince of

1

Flowers, pointing the way to the sanctum of the mysteries of Nature. This picture of Linnaeus was bequeathed to coming generations. The delicate *Linnaea* was made his symbol, soon to be embroidered on the collars of the uniforms worn by members of the medical profession. It was as an incarnation of all the loveliness of the short Nordic summer that Linnaeus gained his prestige. Meadows and groves sang his praises, and Linnaean botany, the science of herbaria, has remained down to our own generation a sort of Swedish national asset, a joy or a vexation to generations of schoolboys.

The cult of Linnaeus, the native reverence for Linnaeus and things Linnaean, has naturally stimulated efforts at research in depth. Modern Swedish research on Linnaeus started in the decades about the turn of this century, during the period of the Linnaean jubilee festivals. An inventory of the extant manuscripts was made and texts were published. In 1903 there appeared Thore Magnus Fries's monumental biography, and just fifteen years later the Swedish Linnaean Society was founded. Linnaeus's life, his environment, and aspects of his work were becoming known in the minutest detail. But still, the traditional attitude of awe and wonder was maintained. Linnaeus's saintly halo shone with greater clarity than ever. He belonged to the Swedish people, and it was not fitting to make a critical evaluation of his person and his scientific accomplishment. Since then, matters have improved. Through the research of the last decades we know that the man Linnaeus was other than the one of the Romantic legend—the sweet and sentimental elements have vanished. His inner world also contained dark tones of depression and despair, at least in his later years. Linnaeus now emerges as more complicated than had previously been suspected. This applies also to his work, primarily his biological view of nature and his religious outlook, which have been the object of increasingly penetrating studies.

Thus the revision of the current picture of Linnaeus proceeds. But there still remains much to be done; one is never really finished with a man like Linnaeus. There are great and important questions that research has scarcely touched. And perhaps the Romantic Linnaeus legend still lives on in certain respects, preventing an impartial interpretation of Linnaean botany and the man behind it. We must have the right to invite Linnaeus to step down from his pedestal and to put some searching questions to him; his limitations and failures cast a clearer light over the incomparable quality of his genius. To the best of one's ability, and with his works as a guide, it is a matter of separating the light from the shadows; an attempt in this direction will be made in the following pages.

There is good reason for beginning with what is well known and undisputed.

The World of the Senses

The natural, almost obvious, point of entry into Linnaeus and things Linnaean is provided by a theme that can be called "Linnaeus and the world of the senses," which is fundamental to Linnaeus as an investigator and as a man. He was a brilliant observer; nothing escaped him. Linnaeus experienced the diversity of species and forms in the empirical world around him with exceptional intensity: the beetles on the road, the herbs in the meadow, the shells in the chalk hills. He was, Linnaeus rightly said of himself, "one of the keenest observers we ever had."[1] It is with good reason that there has been talk of Linnaeus's eye, of Linnaeus as a visual genius. Delicately, and to the point, Göran Wahlenberg develops the subject in an essay on Linnaeus and his science, which is still readable today. Linnaeus, says Wahlenberg, took in the life of nature through his eyes; he was one of "nature's voluptuaries," driven by his hunger for sensual images.[2] With the lack of modesty that distinguishes him, Linnaeus spoke of his "brown, quick, sharp eyes," and he was right.[3] His eyes were exceptionally beautiful—his portraits confirm this (we know also that when Linnaeus was going to say something naughty he made one of his eyes considerably smaller than the other). The eye is the most wonderful of all our organs, and the Creator granted us sight in order that we might observe the beauty of His work.

No one observed nature more sedulously than Linnaeus. He had an inspired gift for the sensual, a hypersensitivity to visual impressions. When he sits down in Holland writing his Lapland flora, he remembers the "ilagräs" of his childhood—the marsh lily, *Narthecium*—in the moss-beds of Småland: those wonderful flowers enthralled him, "turned his eyes to them."[4] With what pleasure, and at the same time how exactly, he noticed in the same *Flora Lapponica* the fragile, unearthly beauty of chickweed in the somber light of the woods: the white flower seemed in some way to "bewitch" the observer. Odd as it may seem, Linnaeus was not a good draughtsman; his sketches of the countryside, plants, and other things, which we can study mainly in his *Journey to Lapland*, have the necessary precision but are very fumbling in execution. The more miraculous, therefore, is his gift of rendering what he sees in words; of conveying his sensual joy. Linnaeus's feelings are incessantly in play; in spirit and in fact he was a lover ("Tantus amor florum"), whose words vibrate with the happiness of

---

1. *Vita Caroli Linnaei*, ed. E. Malmeström and A. Hj. Uggla (Stockholm, 1957), 145.
2. G. Wahlenberg, "Linné och hans veterskap," *Svea* (1822), 96.
3. *Vita*, 144.
4. *Flora Lapponica* (Amsterdam, 1737), 99, 104.

visual contemplation. He is amazed, carried away, "reels" before Nature's richness; he is like a wide-eyed child among brand-new toys; and—naive at bottom—he gives full rein to his pleasure.

Linnaeus was thus an empiricist. As an observer and a describer of objects of the senses he has had few if any equals. He belongs to the great empirical tradition of the West. Along with Aristotle, his forerunner and teacher in natural history, Linnaeus saw in the cognitive process an outflow of pictures from things; nothing existed in the intellect that had not previously existed in the senses. His *Fundamenta Botanica* begins with a quotation from Francis Bacon, the admired prophet of the modern philosophy of experience. The investigator who abandons nature, the evidence of the senses, is lost. The truth, says the young Linnaeus in one of his extravagant accounts of his program of research, should be derived from "the object itself."[5] Again and again he preaches the majesty and necessity of the empirical study of nature—"to know the thing itself" (*res ipsas nosce*) was one of Linnaeus's many slogans. He, if anyone, knew nature's things, surrounded as he was by herbaria and natural objects from all corners of the world. The hunger for reality which gave his whole being its basic note could only be satisfied by natural history.

It is this Linnaeus, the brilliant observer, that we have all learned to love. We see him before us, a master surrounded by his disciples, on his unforgettable excursions into the countryside around Uppsala. It is a June day, and he sits down under the oaks at Gottsunda; the students bring insects, stones, and herbs; he lectures on them, gives the right names, and interprets the greatness of creation. Inimitable and living, we meet him in his Swedish writings, in the journeys into the provinces, in his speeches. They are packed with observations, with wonderful facts that pursue each other in dizzying procession over the pages. Everything is remarkable, worth a quick glance and a note. In the same breath Linnaeus speaks of the age of carp, the herb *Hypochoeris* on the beach, a runestone at a church, and how the farmers of Skåne season their steak with thyme. Perhaps the originality of the Linnaean travel-diaries has been overestimated, at least as a literary genre. Here as elsewhere he could be linked up with the Uppsala tradition; his old teacher, Lars Roberg, for whom Linnaeus always felt the highest respect, has written a diary of a journey to Väddö, which in its general tone is Linnaean, filled as it is with information about natural objects and folklife.[6] But Linnaeus's quickness and sharp eye, his appetite for facts, give his travel-diaries their undeniable character. But, of course, he is at his most supreme and most free in his famous public speeches, where he was able to

5. *Carl von Linnés ungdomsskrifter*, ed. E. Ährling, vol. 1 (Stockholm, 1888), 93.
6. "Lars Robergs Resa till Väddö 1712," ed. Å Dintler, *Lychnos* (1950–1951), 182 ff.

arrange the mass of material after his own taste. The first of them—the presidential address to the Academy of Sciences, *On Wonderful Things Among Insects*—took the shape of an enthusiastic account of the wonders he discovered among the smallest creatures. It is an encomium to the eye. "Behold ... behold ... behold ..." exclaims Linnaeus, like an ecstatic exhibitor of attractions. What in the whole of creation is more remarkable than the evening mosquito as it performs a jig above the marsh? Or the spider, which launches itself from the wall, catches a fly, and is drawn back to the wall by its own thread?

It is as if Nature itself has entered the pages. All this finds its brilliant reflection in Linnaeus's artistic style. A great deal has been written about it, and there is little that can be added. His style follows his swift glance. It is short, quick, muscular, and has an extremely rapid beat. There is the description of the Lapp to whom Linnaeus showed some of his drawings from his notebook: "He became afraid, took off his cap, bowed, turned his head to one side, and beat his hand against his breast, mumbled a little, as though with deep veneration."[7] Not a redundant word: the thing itself, the bare observation, is everything. When Linnaeus read his student Kalm's long-winded prose, he suffered. For Linnaeus the important thing was to accommodate in the smallest possible space the utmost possible truth.[8] This nervous staccato rhythm, the asyndetic arrangement, could well cause the reader difficulties. No less a person than the great Condorcet, in his commemorative speech on Linnaeus, spoke, half complainingly, of the "extreme laconism" in his writings, so alien to the Gallic eloquence that had its most brilliant exponent in his opponent Buffon.[9] It is undeniable that Linnaeus's love of pithiness in more demanding theoretical contexts can make him hard to understand. It happens that his words become oracular riddles which conceal more than they reveal. Anyone who has attempted to penetrate the obscure maxims of his principal medical work, *Clavis Medicinae*, will know this. Linnaeus had a fondness for conciseness that made him a coiner of aphorisms; *Nemesis Divina* provides fine examples. He himself liked the term—it was in aphorisms, "aphoristice," that he dealt with human life in his youthful notes on *Diaeta naturalis*, and with the fundamentals of plant science in *Fundamenta Botanica*.

Sometimes, when faced by Nature's inexhaustible riches, Linnaeus broke out in ecstatic, half-lyrical cataloging. There is the famous opening to his *Journey to Skåne*: the swans are swimming in Öresund, the storks stroll about on their long legs, the larks hover over the cornfields trilling, frogs

---

7. *Iter Lapponicum*, ed. Th. M. Fries (*Skrifter* 5, Uppsala, 1913), 133.
8. Suggested by W. T. Stearn, London.
9. Condorcet, "Éloge de M. de Linné," *Acad. des Sciences, Histoire* (Paris, 1778), 66 ff.

ring and boom in the ponds. Such a listing, which is found in the most unlikely contexts, is an infallible sign of Linnaeus's enthusiasm. He is never more refreshing than when, in the best of spirits, he examines his recruits in the teeming army of the Flora and Fauna. His dissertation *Flora Capensis*, not otherwise among the gayer of his works, captures at lightning speed the living wonders of Africa: lions and mighty elephants, rhinoceroses and hippopotamuses, countless jackals, civet-cats, gazelles, cobras, ostriches, and crocodiles by the rivers, as well as strange human creatures such as thick-lipped Negroes, troglodytes, satyrs, bushmen, hamadryads.[10] In the Proceedings of the Academy of Sciences (*Vetenskaps-akademiens Handlingar*), Linnaeus sets out the central theme of natural science as the basis of husbandry, and there follows a rapid inventory of nature's three kingdoms, which almost leaves the reader breathless. When he is most engaged, there result masterpieces in which each word pulls its weight. The dissertation *Calendarium Florae* sings the praises of the seasons of the year by means of simple lists of nature's signs: aspen-buds open, at night the walls in the house crack, horse dung eats into the ice, the mosquitoes dance.[11] The most original examples are certainly offered by his speeches: there Linnaeus's mastery of the catalog style reaches virtuosity with its sudden changes and unexpected comparisons. All this did not come to him perhaps as spontaneously as is usually claimed. In an interesting study, Sixten Belfrage has shown how Linnaeus reworked and labored with his dedication of the *Journey to Skåne* so as to achieve a maximum of condensed expressiveness.[12] But however self-conscious he may have been as an author, the power of the original experience remained undiminished; all is fresh and vital as it was on the first day of creation. And as was Linnaeus's style, so was his person. He has characterized himself in his autobiography as objectively as if he had been a natural object and certainly not one of the lowest—"little, flurried, rushed, nimble"; sluggishness made him desperate.[13]

Empirical reality, the object, was everything for Linnaeus. But the zeal with which he contemplated nature caused him to put something of himself into his descriptions of it. This is primarily true of the Swedish writings, where he was addressing a wider circle of readers and felt unconstrained. His humor has free play; he goes to extremes and is drastic; his concrete fantasy is ever ready for the farthest flight. Linnaeus, it has rightly been

---

10. *Amoenitates Academicae seu Dissertationes Variae* (hereafter called *Amoen.*), 10 vols. (Stockholm, etc., 1749–1790); here vol. 5, 353.

11. *Amoen.* 4, 395 f.

12. S. Belfrage, "Dedikationen i Linné Skånska resa," *Svenska Linnésällskapets Årsskrift* (hereafter *SLÅ*) (1944), 1 ff.

13. *Vita*, 97.

said, had a poet's need of magnifying and dramatizing.[14] Every reader of his works will know of examples. The fly-tormented reindeer "run and jump," tails in the air, "like the fleetest deer."[15] The hordes of insects come in swarms, frightened of nothing; they alight on the king's nose and stain his crown; uninvited, they come to the feast and sip from the goblet; they leave nothing untouched.[16] Brilliant in its orgiastically mounting realism is the description of the stages of drunkenness in the dissertation on intoxicating liquids, *Inebriantia;* earlier Swedish poets, such as Stiernheim and Lucidor, have stood as godfathers to this, but the touches of color and details are Linnaeus's own.[17] The animal man also belonged to natural history, and his follies, his unnaturalness in the straitjacket of civilization, caused Linnaeus's drastic stylistic art to flourish in lectures and notes on what he called the natural diet. And there are the many letters—Linnaeus, in nightgown and slippers, pouring out his heart to his bosom friend, Abraham Bäck, or to Secretary Wargentin—filled with irresistible superlatives. Linnaeus "rejoices down to his little toe"; his disciple Anton Martin had "frozen to a block of ice" at Spitzbergen; Rolander's discoveries about a certain kind of beetle were so incredible that no mortal had heard anything like it; dear brother, tell me something about the big wide world that "we gape at like cows at a barn door."

Not least, Linnaeus, when he was in the humor, loved to humanize, to describe nature and its inhabitants in anthropomorphic terms. He meant nothing in particular by it, but did it out of pure pleasure and because he always wished to be concrete in the highest degree. Naturally, zoology gave him the best opportunities; sometimes we find ourselves close to the world of saga and animal fables. The celebrated description of the raccoon, "Sjupp," in the Proceedings of the Academy of Sciences, is a character sketch according to the rules of art: Sjupp was as stubborn as a knife-grinder; he went through the pockets of visitors like a customs officer after smuggled goods; if he grew vicious, he protested with curses, threats, and "harsh mumbling."[18] When the ants' wedding is over, Linnaeus told his rapt listeners at the Academy of Sciences, then "father and mother are shown the door."[19] This is fairy-tale style, and the same sovereign grasp is found in the portrait of the Arctic Skua, the Elof of the fishermen of Bohuslän, Linnaeus's "Black Lawrence," the cossack who collects taxes

14. K. Hagberg, *Carl Linnaeus* (Stockholm, 1957), 78.
15. "Om renarnas brömskulor," *Vetenskapsakademiens Handlingar* (1739), 121.
16. *Pandora Insectorum* (1758), in *Amoen*. 5, 240.
17. *Amoen*. 6, 189 ff.
18. *Vetenskapsakademiens Handlingar* (1747), 277 ff.
19. "Tal, om märkvärdigheter uti insecterna," *Fyra valda skrifter*, ed. A. Hj. Uggla (Uppsala, 1964), 24.

from the seagulls.[20] The high point in this naive and demanding genre was reached by Linnaeus in his later years, in the highly original oration that he called *Deliciae Naturae*, the delights of nature. Here nature becomes a copy of human society with its military and civil classes. There is the light cavalry of birds in uniforms of colored down and with military music of pipes, the ugly, naked pedestrians of the reptiles, fish that are sailors and oarsmen with oars and steering wheels as banners, insects "for land and for horse" with different sorts of uniforms, and plants—the grass that is the downtrodden and tormented peasantry, the herbs or nobility in gaudy attire, the straggling mob of mushrooms. Not only is this witty; these vivid comparisons etch themselves into the memory and fulfill their didactic role.

In addition, there are Linnaeus's excursions into mythology, his use of classical authorities. Although during his school years at Växjö he may have nodded during the Latin lessons, he loved the great poetry of Rome, and Virgil and Ovid were his constant companions. He quotes them as often as he can, most profusely perhaps in his earlier years when the world still had its comeliness, and living was a joy. No dissertation is too learned for Linnaeus to enliven with a few quotations from his favorite poets, preferably as mottoes or as a sort of indication of key. In *Calendarium Florae*, Ovid, Virgil, Horace, and their fellow poets are made to bear witness to the changes of the seasons; in the dissertation on arboreal culture, *Arboretum Svecicum*, the Virgil who wrote the *Georgics* is responsible for the poetic essence. With his playful imagination Linnaeus was always ready to clothe the facts of natural history in gracious mythological robes. The Latin trivial names provide a host of examples. On occasions the result can be an awkward little masquerade, as when he groups and names the gaudy butterflies after figures from classical myth and history. Here we meet "knights," the muses (*heliconii*), the danaids, nymphs, plebeians, the species of knights in their turn distributed into Trojans and Achaians after the Homeric heroes, and named after them: *Papilio Priamus, P. Hector, P. Agamemnon*, and so on.[21] These learned allusions are, it might be thought, always artificial; but they also delight a modern reader who has lost the familiarity with the classical world once possessed by any educated person. Even in the titles of Linnaeus's works the fountainhead of myth is flowing; there are Flora and Fauna, *Pan Suecus*, and *Pandora Insectorum*. He deals with the art of gardening, and immediately there appear before his inner eye the Elysian landscape and divinities of the classical authorities: Pomona, or the orchard, the eternal winter-green trees of the Hesperides, the hanging gardens of Semiramis (plants in hanging pots!), Adonis, or the

20. *Västgötaresa* (Stockholm, 1747), 182 f.
21. *Fundamenta Entomologiae* (1767), in *Amoen.* 7, 157 f., and *Systema Naturae*, ed. XIII (Stockholm, 1758–1759), vol. 1, 744 ff.

little window garden.[22] When he received from South Carolina a curious little amphibian with two hands, a fish-tail, and a querulous voice like a duckling, he baptized it *Siren lacertina* and opened his description with notes on the finely singing sirens of the Greeks and other fabulous creatures.[23] Classical mythology gave him inspiration for his pleasure in personifying nature in playful joy, as it were, doubly exposing them. The most beautiful example is provided by his celebrated description, dating from his youth, of the wild plant *Andromeda* in the Lapland marshes, bound to a tuft of grass like the chained maiden of the story from whom it received its name, bowing its head in sorrow.[24]

In this way Linnaeus gives external reality a new dimension of poetry and mystery. But he can also bewitch us when he only paints with facts. Linnaeus describes the arrival of night after a long summer's day: dusk fell, and the high pine woods could be seen as a wall twice as high because of the darkness; sheet lightning flashed like ghostly lights, without thunder; horses kicked and struck fire from the stones; the nightjar spun like a spinning-wheel; in the distance blacksmiths, "Vulcan's pale shirt-lads," thundered and hammered. This from the *Journey to Västergötland*.[25] Linnaeus's lyrical word-painting never reaches greater heights than in passages like these that deal with times of the day and changes in weather; such passages are found in the diaries of his journeys to the provinces, otherwise a little prosier than is usually thought. In the same way Linnaeus raises the tone, becomes a poet, when following the example of the Roman poets he speaks of primitive man in his untouched environment. We find examples in the *Flora Lapponica*, the most personal of his large works from the Holland years. The innocent bliss of the Lapps—a favorite theme of the young Linnaeus—is portrayed in light colors. Far away from taxes and the evil of the world, the Lapp pursued his tranquil life, free of problems, wandering like a bird through the woods and the grassy groves; crystal-clear water was his drink—Holy Innocence, was thy throne here among the fauns in the uttermost North?[26]

Linnaeus was happiest when confronted by the loveliness of the Nordic summer. He was giddy and confused; each spring was a new miracle. *O formosissima aestas*—O most delightful summer! Naturally, there have been Swedes before Linnaeus who have rejoiced at the arrival of the beautiful season; they have also given their pleasure literary form. The Caroline baroque poets sang the comeliness and love-play of the flowering season,

---

22. *Horticultura Academica* (1754), in *Amoen.* 4, 211 f.
23. *Siren Lacertina* (1766), in *Amoen.* 7, 311 ff.
24. *Iter Lapponicum*, 73 f.
25. *Västgötaresa*, 246.
26. *Flora Lapponica*, 269 f.

mainly in the amply flowing wedding poems, and the young Linnaeus's dependence upon them would be worth closer investigation. There Phoebus and Flora met him, grass and greenery, the whole unadorned erotic gospel. Where the ear hears, where the eye sees, intoned Johan Runius in a wedding poem, "everything is glad and gay, and smiles rather delightedly"; the fish play in the lake and the birds twitter. The lark's triumphant "tirili," which from the very beginning cast a shimmer over Linnaeus's *Journey to Lapland*, was a standard topic in the nature poetry of Sweden's Age of Greatness. In other ways, too, Linnaeus appears to be anchored, in a slightly old-fashioned way, in the style and feeling of the baroque. This applies to his taste for extreme conceits, abrupt changes and antitheses, not least in the way this taste breaks through in his cosmic philosophy, his thoughts inspired by the wisdom of the stoics on life and death and the cycle of nature. The fluttering butterfly is nothing but "flying earth."[27] At Frändefors churchyard he loses himself in contemplating the mighty power that transforms the virgin's clean pink cheek into the stinking henbane.[28]

But Linnaeus's hymns to summer always tremble with a sense of happiness that is his own; he could not have learned it out of books. In early writings and notes, which he never intended for publication, we find it at its most ornate, and yet as a revelation—an indication of the strength of his feelings. How close he stands to traditional wedding poetry in the admired opening to the dissertation on the nuptials of flowers, and how Linnaean it is! The insects emerge from their hiding places, the sun confers inexpressible joy on all life, love assails the very herbs.[29] The same applies to the actual message of the work, the description of copulation, the nuptials of flowers in matchless bridal beds. With his hot sensuousness the young Linnaeus was as though obsessed with love, the mysterious drive that kept all living things in motion. When Venus excites, fish from the bottom of the sea are cast on the shores, the birds become blind, "the trembling animals deaf and the innocent ones armed." Love is what everything most yearns for, most enjoys, "the most general, most inevitable"—it is almost a paraphrase of the Apostle's words.[30] The sexual act, Venus in the physiological sense, became for Linnaeus the essence of the mystery of the short Nordic summer. It was the season of reproduction: bees buzzed, and the fruit trees celebrated marriage in white gowns. Everything was renewed. "The trees shake their leaves and make a pleasant whisper; the birds concur with all sorts of fine songs; the whole vegetable kingdom releases a lovely scent. The insects fly about in the air, and alight here and there like ornaments; yes,

27. *De Curiositate Naturali* (1748), ed. K. Hagberg (Stockholm, 1962), 27.
28. *Västgötaresa*, 225 f.
29. "Blomstrens biläger," *Skrifter* 4, 8.
30. *Diaeta Naturalis 1733*, ed. A. Hj. Uggla (Stockholm, 1958), 111, 52.

everywhere one turns there are marks of the inexpressible Creator. A person would have to be a stone not to be invigorated by all such things."

Linnaeus was no stone; he was moved. To the last he was a priest singing the praises of nature's inexhaustible variety and beauty. His fact-filled arias are in reality hymns. In his rapt and most emotional moments neither the Roman poets nor the homespun wedding poets are enough; he turns to the Bible. The Book of Psalms and the dignified phrases of Ecclesiastes give his style elevation and grandeur; he works by repetition, parallels, and the powerful rhythm which, from his childhood in the Småland vicarage, he knew so well from the Bible's poetic books. Linnaeus achieved his master-pieces in this genre when he stood in the rostrum. There he was the preacher, filled with the spirit of the Bible, giving out the text on the Creator's miracle in nature.[31] His address on the marvels of the insect world is, it has been shown, a straightforward thematic sermon on some verses in the twelfth chapter of Job. The Bible's words gave vim and vigor to Linnaeus's writings, not least during the later years. O Lord, he exclaims with the Psalmist, how great and manifold are Thy works, wisely hast Thou created them all, and the earth is filled with Thy possessions—we meet these words at the beginning of his life's crowning work, the twelfth edition of *Systema Naturae*. With the prophets and holy men of the Old Testament, Linnaeus sang the praises of the miracles the Lord had vouch-safed him to witness, as in the magnificent final hymn to the *Dalecarlia Journey*: "Thou, mighty Creator and Preserver of all things, Who allowed us to come so high up in the mountains of Lapland, so deep down in the Falun mines . . . praise be to all that Thou has created, from the beginning to the end."[32]

The rare strength of feeling with which Linnaeus experienced nature led him to religion. His point of departure was always empirical, what the eye saw—without exception, after a burst of lyricism and mythological games, he ends by singing the omnipotence of the Creator. This is the real theme of his work.

Much has been written about Linnaeus's religious view of nature, pri-marily by Elis Malmeström, who has devoted considerable research to it. As a religious thinker Linnaeus does not lend himself to a ponderous treatment; he spoke spontaneously out of the fullness of his heart; and what he preached about God's wisdom in nature was only occasionally original. Linnaeus belonged to a time when all educated men glorified the miracle of creation as the safest way to a natural knowledge of God. So-called physico-theology was the fashion: the wonderful interrelatedness of natural things

---

31. Cf. J. Sahlgren, "Linné som predikant," *SLÅ* (1922), 40 ff.
32. *Dalaresa*, ed. A. Hj. Uggla (Stockholm, 1953), 150.

proved that an almighty and benevolent God had created them. The theme was preached in a rich literature. God's wisdom, exclaimed eighteenth-century entomologists, directing attention to a passage in Pliny, was "maxima in minimis," the greatest in the very smallest creatures such as plant-lice and mites, not to speak of the new world discovered by Leeuwenhoek under the microscope. English naturalists such as Ray and Derham spelled out this text in the most trivial detail. *The Wisdom of God Manifested in the Works of Creation* by the great biologist John Ray opens with the same quotation from the Book of Psalms as the later editions of Linnaeus's *Systema Naturae*. For both Ray and his younger countryman William Derham, whose *Physico-Theology* appeared in Swedish translation in 1736, it was a matter of fighting the detested atheists—Cartesians, materialists, and other blasphemers. Everything in creation witnessed its divine origin; the earth's swarms of living creatures struggled toward preordained goals that were hidden from themselves. In this best of all worlds everything was arranged in the most wonderful way; Derham especially gives vent to his gratitude in disarming language. What a wonderful and wise arrangement was Newtonian gravity; how "curiously" insects were composed; how much could be said of the wind's benefits and services in human life. The universe was a perfect harmony in which everything fitted together, link by link. The enlightened theology of the century was inspired by these thoughts and became, with the Wolffian doctrines imported from Germany, something of an official university philosophy, not least at Uppsala University.

Nothing was more natural than that Linnaeus should join the pious chorus. He was able to do this with greater knowledge than any other, and in inspired moments even more beautifully. I saw, he says in some famous lines, "the eternal, all-knowing, all-powerful God from the back when he advanced, and I became giddy! I tracked His footsteps over nature's fields and found in each one, even in those I could scarcely make out, an endless wisdom and power, an unsearchable perfection."[33] Natural science became for Linnaeus knowledge of God; research into nature—out in the field or in the herbarium—a religious service. Man's highest task, the real reason for his presence on earth, was to contemplate nature and praise its eternal Author; no science, therefore, was nobler than natural history. With the doggedness of a preacher, Linnaeus drums in his theme of the Creator's omnipotence in nature; this became something of a fixed rhetorical formula, not least as an opening to his Latin dissertations. He beheld in the minutest things, as in a vision, proof of God's majesty. At Luleå, he saw in the water innumerable newly hatched fry; they were transparent, the eyes

33. Introduction to the later editions of *Systema Naturae*.

biggest, "so that with wonder I had to admit the whole world was full of Thy glory."[34] All was signs, hints, portents—and everything had a meaning, a goal decided by the Creator. Every object, says Linnaeus in the dissertation *De Curiositate Naturali*, was created "for the sake of something else."[35] This formulation expresses the central thesis of the natural science of the period, its teleological basis. Everything created was linked together in an endless chain in which each creature had its mission in the service of the whole.

Inevitably, this philosophy, even in the formulations of Linnaeus, can sound commonplace to modern ears. This is particularly true of its application to man as the crown and lord of creation, whom the rest of nature served. When the woodpecker pecked for larvae in rotten tree-trunks, this was not only to feed himself; he also disintegrated the tree, "so that it no longer offered such a useless and depressing sight."[36] The herons of Egypt, claimed Linnaeus, had the task of eating up the land's many reptiles so that they would not frighten people with their terrible appearance[37]—snakes and lizards, the "ugly, unpleasant, naked crew," always aroused in Linnaeus intense revulsion; they challenged his optimism. But even in such anthropocentric interpretations he followed the conventional line, that of Derham and others; and by the standards of their own time they were not naive. God had not blundered in the work of creation, but had thought of everything, planned down to the smallest detail; it was the task of the investigator to detect His intentions. The physico-theological world view set out to find a meaning in nature, and this goal was not an unfruitful soil for the growth of scientific inquiry.

This was not least so, as we shall see, in Linnaeus's case. The dry pedantry that disgraced other adherents of natural theology is seldom to be found in him; he has his own note of wide-eyed wonder before the curiosities that he meets in nature and that waken his questing spirit. Without effort he finds the great, numinous words. One of the contributory factors is his exceptional self-confidence. Here we reach something highly specific to Linnaeus: his certainty of his vocation. It cannot be left out of the picture. Its moral structure must for the moment be left aside; here it interests us as a condition of his scientific activity. Linnaeus saw himself as a chosen interpreter of nature, one of the prophets called by God to reveal His work, for the present and for times to come. The decisive, oft-repeated passage appears in one of his autobiographies. It is magnificent and frightening. The Lord, Linnaeus declares, has allowed him to see more of the work of

34. *Iter Lapponicum*, 92.
35. *De Curiositate Naturali*, 33.
36. *Migrationes Avium* (1757), in *Amoen.* 4, 569.
37. *Fundamenta Ornithologica* (1765), in *Amoen.* 7, 124.

creation than any other mortal; He has given him the greatest insight into nature any human being has been granted, destroyed his enemies, and made him a great name "like unto the greatest on earth" (2 Sam. 2; 7–9; 1 Chron. 17:8).[38] Thus Linnaeus worked under the special protection of Jehovah, like the ancient prophets of Israel. It is not only his dogmatism, his naive confidence in himself as lawgiver to all botanists in the world that must be seen in the light of this biblically inspired certainty of vocation. Reasonably enough, it also confirmed him in the belief that he had penetrated more deeply into God's decrees than any other natural scientist before him, that he had mapped out the mysteries of creation. In all of this, as elsewhere, he is extraordinarily close to his great Swedish contemporary, also called by the Lord to be the interpreter of the selfsame secrets: the seer Swedenborg.

Linnaeus reached deepest into the work of creation with his pronouncement on the Law of Order in nature. In itself it was part and parcel of the times: in the Newtonian universe the heavenly bodies revolved and the stone fell to the ground according to immutable natural laws; there was no loophole for caprice. This might be said with confidence about dead things, the movements of which could be determined with mathematical rigor; but it was more difficult to find the divine orderliness in the organic world, where everything flowed, changed form, decayed, and was generated. Although it could never be convincingly demonstrated, Linnaeus experienced with the whole strength of his being, as a vision, the inexorable order in nature which was an outflowing of God's immutable law (*lex immutabilis Dei*). What we "usually call nature" is identical with the laws and decrees that are, that make up creation itself.[39] Living nature, too, followed the established rules of the game, and they allowed no exception: oats could *not* be changed into barley. Linnaeus was extremely indignant on God's behalf at this idea, which for some years caused an uproar in Sweden.

The eternal Law applied just as much to man, not only to his physical being, but to his moral being as well. To this theme Linnaeus devoted his well-known notes on *Nemesis Divina*, divine retribution in human life; strange and wonderful, perhaps, but at heart only an expression of his trust in a divine order beneath the surface confusion of the world. "You see everything moving confusedly . . . but here dwells a just God."[40] The Nemesis notes certainly have, therefore, a more optimistic tone than is usually thought; here, too, Linnaeus is displaying the balance and order that are the lever of creation, and its mystery.

But it cannot be denied that the matter also had another side. The deeper

38. *Vita*, 146.
39. Cf. *De Curiositate Naturali*, 25, and *Systema Naturae*, ed. XIII, 1, 11.
40. *Nemesis Divina*, ed. K. Hagberg (Stockholm, 1960), 7.

the aging Linnaeus penetrated the inner side of nature and of man, the more desolate did they show themselves to be. The chilling inhumanity in his Nemesis speculations cannot be explained away; it strikes us like a breath of cold air. And something similar is true, in the last analysis, of his view of nature. A grand cosmic whisper is always in evidence there, but this does not become fateful so long as the stage is filled with hosts of living organisms. It is only when Linnaeus rolls up the carpet of flowers and stands faced by the naked primeval ground, that the tone darkens. His most basic declaration of faith was given in the hymn already quoted under the heading *Imperium Naturae*, nature's empire, which opens the later editions of *Systema Naturae*. Its subject is Nature in nature, God, the upholder of everything, the Being of being and the Cause of causes, Who steers the changes of earthly life and the revolutions of the planets. He is everything; He is known under different names. "If you wish to call Him Fate, you are not mistaken, for everything hangs by His finger; if you wish to call Him Nature, neither are you mistaken, for everything has arisen from Him." He is Foresight, He is entirely Mind, entirely Vision, entirely Hearing; He is Soul and He is Unique. No human guessing can give Him any form; it suffices that He is an eternal and endlessly Divine Being (*Numen*), a Creator Who fills our eyes and Who escapes them; only thought, only the soul, has right of entry to the holy throne where He dwells.[41] This passage is, in fact, a mosaic of quotations from many sources; even so, or just because of this, it is far from being easy of interpretation. We can be certain that it hardly pleased the orthodox theologians of Uppsala. Linnaeus had already gotten into trouble with them; he was conscious of the fact that he was treading dangerous ground—the theologians, he told his students, "are complaining that we are confusing God with nature."[42] When we look at the sentences in the *Systema Naturae*, it is easy to understand them. Those obscure maxims on God as Being, Fate, and Nature were not irreproachable. They smacked of pagan thought, of Aristotle and the philosophy of fate of the ancient Stoics, which had earlier made an ineffaceable impression on Linnaeus; Seneca the Roman was one of his lifelong authorities. But one thinks also of Spinoza, persecuted and defamed, of whom Linnaeus had no doubt heard in Holland;[43] for him, spirit and matter, God and nature, were one and the same, the only indivisible being beyond man's desires and suffering.

Linnaeus had traveled a long way. Behind the nuptials of the flowers and the jubilant song of the birds he glimpsed the outlines of a harsh, un-

41. Ed. Hagberg (Stockholm, 1962), 166 ff.
42. *Lachesis Naturalis*, ed. A. O. Lindfors (Uppsala Universitets Årsskrift, 1907), 23.
43. Cf. Hagberg, *Carl Linnaeus*, 185 ff.

fathomable countenance—the sovereign, divine power in its pure, almost abstract majesty.

The Eternal Order in Nature

There are a few writings in which Linnaeus as the biological thinker applies the doctrine of eternal order in nature. This is particularly true of two or three Latin dissertations; the most important of them is entitled *Politia Naturae* and appeared in 1760. If we are to answer the question—perhaps all too seldom put—whether Linnaeus truly penetrated more deeply into the secret council-chamber of nature than any of his contemporaries, it is to these papers that we must turn first of all. There Linnaeus has constructed what might be called an "ecological theory" of astonishingly modern cast.

We know the general background already. According to the God-centered world view of this time, nature was filled with meaning; each creature played the role ordained by the Creator, as part of the whole. Harmony and balance were the central concepts in this view of nature, classical in type, so to speak. The universe was conceived of as packed with created beings, "full of forms" (*plenum formarum*), interrelated in hierarchical order from the lowest, lifeless matter through plants, animals, and man, to angels and spiritual substances.

During the eighteenth century this vision of the chain of creation, which ultimately goes back to Aristotle, became the common property of the educated.[44] Linnaeus had it constantly in mind: "The closer we get to know the creatures around us, the clearer is the understanding we obtain of the chain of nature, and its harmony and system, according to which all things appear to have been created."[45] In his *Systema Naturae*, Linnaeus wished to present the Creator's work "in an orderly chain."[46] There were no sharp boundaries; nature made no leaps; the mineral kingdom merges almost imperceptibly into the plant kingdom; between plants and animals there are intermediate forms. The systematist had to know all this if he was to classify the multiplicity of creatures and reconstruct the plan of creation.

But the chain of nature, *catena naturae*, could also be given another meaning. It did not just extend vertically like a cosmic ladder on which every created being had its fixed place. Nature was also at every moment alive and operative; its thronging creatures were dependent on each other in a network of reciprocal actions, and this interconnectedness—in width,

44. Cf. A. O. Lovejoy's classic book *The Great Chain of Being* (1936, new ed. New York, 1960).
45. *Taenia* (1748), in *Amoen.* 2, 59 f.
46. *Vita*, 135.

16

horizontally—was dynamic and biological. These two ways of looking at things complement each other, at least in Linnaeus's conceptual world. In an already classic study, *The Great Chain of Being,* A. O. Lovejoy showed how the doctrine of a hierarchically graded universe necessarily led to the conclusion that each separate link in the chain existed in order to make the series complete.[47] This was also Linnaeus's idea. But when he spoke as a biologist, he could put forward the opposing argument on equally good grounds—every single thing was "created for the sake of something else." No creature could live in isolation; the universe was so constituted that the one served the other as food and maintenance. In this connection, evidently, Linnaeus could certainly argue in the current hierarchical spirit. The lower existed for the higher; the mineral kingdom gave nourishment to the plants, and the plants to insects, birds, and cattle; on them, in turn, lived predatory animals and human beings.[48] But afterward everything returned to its origin in reversed order. The predatory animal was devoured by the bird of prey, the bird of prey by the worm, the worm by herbs, herbs by earth— "Yes, man, who turns all to his own need often becomes food for predatory animals, and fish, for worms, and the earth."[49] The biological chain was, in fact, endless, an eternal circulation of life and death, of eating and being eaten. With the whole of his being Linnaeus had experienced this trans- migration of bodies in Frändefors churchyard; it was one of the basic laws of nature and filled him with holy awe. "Thus does everything go round"— natural history was the doctrine of the metamorphoses of dust.

But this by no means exhausted the subject. In his dissertation on the order of nature, *Politia Naturae,* Linnaeus goes deeper in his investigations. The food-chain, its circulation, had a hidden significance. It was the instru- ment with which created beings were kept within their prescribed limits. There was a measure for each species of plant and animal not to be ex- ceeded, a balance that was identical with order itself; *Ordo*—a sort of moral order presided over by divine justice—was active in human life. When swarms of insects devoured plants, this was done primarily not to fill their stomachs but to prevent a catastrophic increase of certain species of plants. Linnaeus made a rough numerical estimate. If one tobacco plant in one year produced 40,320 seeds that were allowed to grow without hindrance, the earth would soon be full of tobacco plants; but this was against the world order of the Creator.[50] In the same way, insects had their enemies in the food chain, parasites and birds of prey that kept them in check; the insect-eating birds were devoured by the birds of prey. Every form of life

47. Lovejoy, 186.
48. *De Curiositate Naturali,* 31. Cf. ibid., 27 f.
49. "Tal, om märkvärdigheter uti insecterna," 13.
50. *Politia Naturae* (1760) 1962 ed., 73.

had its supervisor; the intricate interplay between the eaters and the eaten had as its goal the task of keeping the number of individuals in every species constant. Order in nature, what Linnaeus liked to call balance (*proportio*), had to be maintained. How easily this delicate balance could be disturbed—it needed no more than the removal of one link in the ecological chain for it to be broken to pieces. If all the small birds were wiped out, our parks would be devastated by grasshoppers and other insects.[51]

None of this was perceptible through superficial observation. The untrained eye saw only a jumble of eating, hunting, and chewing, as if everything occurred in the greatest confusion. Violent competition reigned in a nature full to the bursting point, a chaotic "war of all against all" (*bellum omnium inter omnes*). Nature, says Linnaeus in *Politia Naturae*, was a "butcher's block"; the spectacle might well appear repulsive and meaningless.[52] Only a person who had pierced the veil realized that the merciless struggle for existence was a prerequisite for the functioning of creation. Behind the seeming disorder one was met by a well-thought-out strategy that expressed divine Wisdom.

Linnaeus's thoughts on balance in nature were not altogether original. As a defense of divine world order it formed a natural part of the religious ideology of the time. From the common doctrine of a world full of a maximum number of organic forms, it was easy to draw the conclusion that they had to compete with each other. Linnaeus himself refers to William Derham.[53] Derham, too, saw in this balance—the due *proportio*—among the species of animals a proof of the harmony of creation, although he followed another line of argument in his *Physico-Theology*: animals that live long reproduce themselves sluggishly, and the reverse. The problem had, therefore, been posed by pious naturalists before Linnaeus. Even so, his *Politia Naturae* stands forth as one of his most personal works. None of his other writings gives such a modern impression—in it Linnaeus, as a biological thinker, has attained a remarkable insight into nature's hidden play of forces.

The value of this work was not lost on the future. Both of the Darwins, grandfather and grandson, devoted themselves to a study of *Politia Naturae* and closely related writings by Linnaeus, and to their great advantage. It seems undeniable that that unusual country doctor, Erasmus Darwin, was inspired by Linnaeus's writings in his thoughts on evolution. In his magnificent verse epic, *The Temple of Nature*, he draws a picture of the struggle among the species which seems to use Linnaeus's *Politia Naturae* as a

51. Ibid., 102.
52. Ibid., 218.
53. *Oeconomia Naturae* (1749), in *Amoen.* 2, 52. Derham's *Physico-theology* was translated into Swedish by A. Nicander in 1736.

model; he even uses the same term: the world as a bloody stage, "one large slaughter-house."[54] Moreover, we now know that Charles Darwin read Linnaeus's dissertations when he was working on his theory of the struggle for existence and natural selection; concepts such as natural order and balance in nature were fundamental to Darwin's way of thinking. Thus Linnaeus, even if in a different way than is normally thought, came to play a role in the early history of evolutionary theory.[55] One of the contributory factors in the writing of *On the Origin of Species* was Linnaeus's dramatic and graphic interpretation of nature.

But quite apart from this, when Linnaeus stood full of wonder before the wise arrangements of the Creator, he was able to penetrate into the hidden life of nature. Most rewarding of all are still his Latin dissertations—the "academic entertainments," *Amoenitates academicae,* as he himself called them. There we encounter his teaching on flowers and their dispersal, on climate and plant geography, and on the ecology of the individual life forms. He writes about the position of plant leaves in sleep—a discovery that filled him with rapture—and follows the seasonal changes of the Swedish flora; he notes the host plants of insects; and in a paper on *Taenia* he investigates the nature and habits of the remarkable tapeworm. In all of this, Linnaeus is a thoroughgoing empiricist; he stands in the midst of living nature and takes its pulse. He was a pioneer by virtue of his trained insight into the demands made by plants on their environment. He dealt with this theme time and again, also in the *Philosophia Botanica,* that great summation of his biological thinking. Each species of plant had closely defined requirements for climate and type of soil, and this determined the distribution of the species. Linnaeus culls examples and makes divisions according to his custom, above all in the dissertations *Stationes Plantarum* and *Horticultura Academica,* where, with a sure hand, he sets the boundaries to ecological and climatic plant regions. His goal, indicated as early as the introduction to the *Flora Lapponica,* with its famous description of the geographical plant-belts in Lapland, was to find the laws that governed the behavior of vegetation on the face of the earth. These regions also served, as he wrote in a brilliant section of *Politia Naturae,* the divine world order in a more intricate sense.[56] In its natural locality each plant was protected from competition with intruders with other environmental demands—intuitively, Linnaeus anticipates the modern biological concept of the so-called ecological niches in nature.

54. Erasmus Darwin, *The Temple of Nature* (London, 1830), 130 ff.
55. R. C. Stauffer, "Ecology in the Long Manuscript Version of Darwin's Origin of the Species and Linnaeus's Oeconomy of Nature," *Proceedings of the American Philosophical Society* 104:2 (1960).
56. *Politia Naturae,* 65 f.

Linnaeus put some of his best work into his investigation of fertilization and the dissemination of seeds. Nowhere else, it seemed, had the Creator constructed so many and such superlatively ingenious arrangements; here was a real playground for physico-theologians who wished to sing the praises of the divine architect; and it was not just Linnaeus who took advantage of the opportunity. But added to this was the fact that he was personally deeply engaged. The act of fertilization, through pistils and stamens, was for him a sort of sacrament, around which, ever since his youth, he had built up his botanical system. The study of this mechanism was a precondition of his reformation of botany. It is, above all, in his treatise *Sponsalia Plantarum* and the prize-winning answer to the questions of the St. Petersburg Academy, *De Sexu Plantarum* (1760), that Linnaeus has made important contributions to the sexual biology of plants. He describes different sorts of fertilizing arrangements; nature's capacity for variation in the matter of ensuring pollination for the various species of plants seemed to know no bounds. One of his finest dissertations, *Nectaria Florum*, was devoted to the morphology of the nectar glands and their role in fertilization through insects. With astonishment Linnaeus followed the career of the ripe seed and fruit out into the world. Here, also, he had forerunners, among them Derham yet again, who provided edifying examples of nature's methods of spreading plant seeds; but it was Linnaeus who gave the biology of dissemination a scientific form and fitted it into a broader context. These amazing feats of artistry (*stupenda artificia*) constituted so many pieces of evidence for the Creator's inventiveness. Seeds and fruit were borne through the air on wings or down; other species ejected their seeds from capsules; there were seeds equipped with claws that fastened in animal fur; berries were eaten by birds; other fruits or seeds were carried into the earth by earthworms and moles; fruit was washed down by floods, or carried across oceans.[57]

Living nature was inexhaustible, and Linnaeus was its prophet.

The Systematist

Linnaeus was nature's prophet, too, in the great works that established his world reputation—the *Systema Naturae* in its various editions, the *Philosophia Botanica*, and *Species Plantarum*. In these works Linnaeus wished to embrace the richness of creation and organize the multifarious forms. It was as a systematist that he made his epochal contribution; in his own opinion, and that of others, he was opening a new phase in the history of science in this way. So far, we have followed Linnaeus as the brilliant

---

57. Cf. *Oratio de Telluris Habitabilis Incremento* (1743), in *Amoen.* 2, 450 ff.

observer and the religiously inspired interpreter of nature's secrets. It now remains to pose the question of how, against this background, his true life's work, his botanical system in the first place, fits in the total picture. Here we turn a new corner and approach Linnaeus from another angle. It seems, at last, that we find ourselves faced by something resembling a paradox.

As an all-seeing empiricist and dogged tracker of God's miracles in nature, Linnaeus, one would think, had enough on his hands. We have seen how, working from such points of departure, he gained certain fundamental and fruitful insights. But these are only on the margin of his total lifework. Linnaeus did not pursue the course on which he had embarked. He could well have done so, even as a botanical systematist. Nothing could have been closer to hand for him than what—even at that time—was called the *natural* plant system. That system explored the extent of the Creator's plan link by link in the chain of the plant kingdom—the innumerable groups of plants in the spontaneous interrelatedness provided by nature. As clearly as anyone else, Linnaeus saw the urgency of the task. It is well known how time and again from his youth onward he insisted that a "natural" plant system was the real goal of botany, "the first and the last that should be sought in botany."[58] But Linnaeus considered, rightly it might be thought, that in practice nearly insuperable difficulties were encountered in the attempt to carry out this program; the whole enterprise demanded a knowledge of all the species of plants on earth, which not even he himself possessed. It is true that Linnaeus published a bare outline of a natural plant system in his *Classes Plantarum* and returned to the subject in private lectures later in his life. It was always his view that his own sexual system was only a provisional tool, a substitute for the natural method. But further he would not go. Linnaeus won his European reputation as the creator of the sexual system, a system that belonged basically to another kind of reasoning.

Linnaeus's way out of the dilemma was perhaps both wise and necessary. But without a doubt it implied that he abandoned that side of his nature that we have already come to know. As a systematist—and this is what he was above all—Linnaeus was forced to relinquish empiricism as his sole guide; he began to refashion nature. That he did this without any scruples requires some explanation.

There was the general condition of botany when the young Linnaeus set to work in the middle of the 1730s. It had become increasingly more difficult to maintain order among the hordes of trees and herbs. A little over a century before, the Swiss botanist Caspar Bauhin had listed six thousand species of plants in all; since then the number had increased without inter-

---

58. *Philosophia Botanica* (Stockholm, 1751), 27.

ruption. The national floras of Europe were becoming ever better known, and from distant lands, through increasing foreign trade and scientific expeditions, a stream of unknown plant forms poured into Europe. The botanical gardens in Holland, England, and France were filled with exotic seeds, roots, and bulbs. Leading botanists, especially John Ray and the Frenchman Tournefort, had done what they could to describe the new species and work out a comprehensive system for all the plants on earth, and Linnaeus accorded them deep respect, particularly Tournefort. But the situation within systematic botany was far from satisfactory. The different plant systems competed with each other; the descriptions of the species in Latin were long-winded and obscure—it was easy to lose your way in the botanical reference books. The situation pained Linnaeus, and he felt as if chaos were threatening. It was hard enough even to get a grip on the Swedish flora and the remnants of a more exotic splendor that he found in his student days in Rudbeck's gardens in Uppsala. It was precisely his very sensibility, the clarity with which he experienced the individual forms in nature, that threatened to overwhelm him in a sea of impressions. And surely it is here that the paradox lies. By virtue of his visual genius Linnaeus was compelled to hold fast to the concrete object, and so the matter of ordering, of systematizing, became for him of such supreme importance that other considerations had to give way—even his allegiance to nature. The only way out was to catalog and classify rapidly, to find some sort of system, a pattern, that would give the uncoordinated mass a structure. "Without the system," said Linnaeus, "chaos would reign."[59] He was an impetuous, temperamental being, who could, it is true, toil away at one and the same literary task for years that sometimes stretched into decades, but the work had to go quickly—patience in small things was not among his virtues. For this reason he was able, without too many scruples, to sacrifice natural relationships, so long as this was useful as a sorting principle. To an eminent degree Linnaeus had a practical knack for doing things, and he loved simplified solutions—one of the most instructive examples of this is offered by his binomial nomenclature. It was from these points of departure, therefore, that he created his handy but artificial botanical sexual system with its twenty-four classes, as well as his whole taxonomic life-work.

Here we must pause a while to consider another basic characteristic of the man Linnaeus. He was a born systematist. Throughout his whole life he felt a compulsion of almost demonic intensity to *arrange* everything—in groups, sections, and sub-sections, like troops on parade. "God created, Linnaeus ordered," said an admiring posterity.[60] His Danish disciple Fab-

59. *Fundamenta Botanica* (Amsterdam, 1736), 18.
60. Cf. D. H. Stoever, *Leben des Ritters Carl von Linné* I (Hamburg, 1792), title page.

ricius claimed, probably with justice, that Europe would hardly ever witness "a more systematic genius."[61] All who have read Linnaeus will recognize his curious passion for systematizing everything that came to hand. It is met with everywhere, sometimes raised to a controlled fury, even in letters and private effusions. He cataloged and divided, even when it was uncalled for, and the results can be strange. In the *Biblioteca Botanica* he provides a natural system for the botanical literature, with examination key and all. The class "describers" (*Descriptores*) is divided into the orders "forgotten," "used," "select," and "special" authors.[62] In the literary order "polemical" he elsewhere ranks wars fought by potentates on behalf of plants, such as when the cedar tree drove Hadrian to destroy Jerusalem. Curious parallels are presented in schematic form. He assigns the larval stage of insects to Hunger, the pupa represents Pain, and the fully-fledged imago Venus, Love. He was inspired above all by military ranks, which provided him with a hierarchical pattern that could be filled with biological content. "Linnaeus stood victorious amidst his flower-pennants," sang Tegnér and perhaps spoke more truth than he knew. It is as if the great Caroline army, whose triumphs and defeats cast their lights and shadows over his boyhood years, had been won over to living nature. New plants become "recruits" in Flora's immense army. Martial imagery is found in his speech on nature's delights, *Deliciae Naturae*. When Linnaeus in an extravagant mood made a list of all contemporary botanists in one of his autobiographies, it was done in strictly military terms: he himself is the commander-in-chief, and the Frenchman Bernard de Jussieu, second-in-command, while his deadly enemy, the German Siegesbeck, ends down at the bottom as a corporal.[63]

Such things were, of course, just fun and games, but quite revealing. Discipline and order were basic needs for Linnaeus; each thing had its place in the world. His drive to organize also took practical form. His famous botanical excursions with the students were as carefully organized as if they were military maneuvers: start at 7:00 A.M., meal-break at 2:00 P.M., short rest at 4:00 P.M., demonstration by the professor every half-hour, and special light clothing—the botanical uniform—for those taking part.[64] It is in essence the exceptional desire for clarity that constitutes the most characteristic feature of Linnaeus's writings. He was unable, he wrote to his French friend Sauvages, "to understand anything that is not systematically ordered."[65] Linnaeus belonged to the same spiritual climate as the

61. J. C. Fabricius in *Deutsches Museum*, vol. 1 (Leipzig, 1780), 433.
62. *Bibliotheca Botanica* (Stockholm, 1736), 24 ff., *Philosophia Botanica*, 11, *Pandora Insectorum*, 238 f.
63. *Vita*, 153 f.
64. *Philosophia Botanica*, 293.
65. "Lettres inédites de Linné à Sauvages," *Alais*, 1860, no. 9 (2 Nov. 1737).

great philosophic-system builders of the previous century, Descartes and others; in their muscular majesty his great systematic works resemble the fugues of Bach. Consistency and discipline were everything for him. At all costs he had to discover an Order in nature—if he did not find it, he would have to invent it himself. And in doing so, he did nature violence, forced it to obey the laws of logic. This characteristic, this mania, if you will, never caused him to turn his back on reality; but throughout his work there exists a tension between the demands of empiricism and the demands of order, and in situations of conflict it is nearly always order that is victorious. Linnaeus became a botanical legislator, with the sexual system as the crown of his work.

In this connection it is interesting to glance at his concept of species. Plant and animal species as unchangeable entities were the very core of the Linnaean mental world. They were the guarantees of order. There are the famous maxims in the *Systema Naturae* and the *Philosophia Botanica*.[66] The individual species had been created complete, once and for all, by God in the beginning. The invariability of species was the condition for order in nature (*unitas in omni specie ordinem ducit*), and hence for the system. Each living creature emerged from an egg or a seed and was, therefore, a copy of the first parents; the idea of spontaneous generation was always opposed by Linnaeus, because disorder would then reappear. It is well known, and does not need to be developed in more detail, that with the years Linnaeus began to weaken in his belief that no new species could emerge. It was something of a shock when he discovered, or believed he discovered, that new, true species could be created through hybridization. His world-picture threatened to collapse. With great openness of mind he accepted the consequences, and in his old age he worked out a theory, partly imaginary, according to which the multiplicity of organisms had arisen through hybridization among a limited number of original forms. But this did not mean turning his back on the past. The species, as much as ever, were fixed units, and in themselves just as sharply delimited as before. A species could never spontaneously, of itself, be changed into something else; such was the law of God and nature. With topical point Linnaeus laid stress on this during the controversies of the 1750s about the belief in the transformation of oats into rye, which he rejected "on the basis of the principles of botany," with reference to his own concept of species.[67] It is noteworthy that as a botanist he never concerned himself with varieties. They caused trouble, turned his beautiful order upside down; only gardeners and worthless botanists bothered their heads about them.

Linnaeus's dogmatic concept of species seems to fit in harmoniously with

---

66. *Philosophia Botanica*, 99; *Systema Naturae*, 1735 ed., "Observationes."
67. *Transmutatio Frumentorum* (1757), in *Amoen.* 5, 106 ff.

his general view of nature, but it contains certain problems, nevertheless. The ideas about the chain of creation and the hierarchy in nature, which were self-evident for Linnaeus and his contemporaries, might just as well have led to a repudiation of the species concept in its strict form. If link joined link, if "nature made no leaps" (as Linnaeus never tired of repeating), there ought not to have been any possibility of separating one species from another. The life-forms from the algae to the human being made up a continuum, where, also, the great systematic groups blended—but where did the corals and the other zoophytes belong, with the plants or the animals? In Europe there were scientists who were denying the existence of species on precisely these grounds, among them Buffon in his early work, and the Swiss philosopher and entomologist Charles Bonnet. Nature, argued Buffon, advanced by imperceptible degrees; the division among species and families did not correspond to the endless nuances of reality.[68] But Linnaeus refused to draw these conclusions. From the depths of his heart he detested flux and formlessness. He had come to the the world to tidy up and set in order. He, therefore, paid attention to differences; however close the innumerable forms in the created hierarchy might approach one another, they remained, nevertheless, logically definable entities in their own right, and upon them the Creator had impressed permanent stamps, or characters. The chain of creatures became for Linnaeus a proof of nature's multiplicity, not its connectedness. Species were joined to species as pearls in a necklace. Without a concept of fixed species Linnaeus was helpless. He could only think of nature as a system of unchangeable substances.

So the system, the arrangement of objects in nature according to certain prescribed norms, became for Linnaeus the most important and all-but-exclusive task of biology. He insists on this time and again. The key words are *divisio* and *denominatio*—division and denomination. Natural history, says Linnaeus categorically, is the same as arranging natural objects and baptizing them. What is a botanist? Simply, a person "qui nominibus noscit nominare," who can give the right names. The more species he knew, the greater he was as a botanist.[69] For Linnaeus, nature was an immense collection of natural objects which he himself walked around as superintendent, sticking on labels. He had a forerunner in this arduous task: Adam in Paradise. In the Garden of Eden—to be understood, according to Linnaeus, as an island on the equator—the first human being looked at the Creator's work "as if at an entirely complete collection of natural objects."[70] Linnaeus developed the theme in the foreword to *Fauna Svecica*. Adam sat in

68. Lovejoy, 227 f.
69. *Systema Naturae*, 1735 ed., "Observationes"; *Genera Plantarum* (1737), "Ratio operis"; *Philosophia Botanica*, 202.
70. *Museum Adolphi Friderici* (Stockholm, 1754), "Företal"; *Fauna Svecica* (Stockholm, 1746), "Praefatio."

Paradise, carrying out the two highest functions of science: he observed the creatures and named them with the aid of special signs, almost as though he had Linnaeus's writings to hand. Adam was the first Linnaean; and Linnaeus, a second Adam. Once again he had found a religious sanction for his scientific lifework; at least it was transfigured with something of the innocent early morning light of Paradise. For him, botanical gardens were, both in spirit and in fact, Edens, paradises. He liked to call them that and walked his own Eden on Svartbäcksgatan, inspecting the characters and distinguishing marks of plants, as once long ago our first parent did.

In this way Linnaeus narrowed down the field of botany greatly. He was monumentally one-sided—everything other than nomenclature and classification was scarcely accorded the rank of science. This does not mean that he was indifferent to contemporary advances in natural history in other branches. He kept up with research in physiological and anatomical writings and availed himself of the work of experimental scientists. Bonnet's sensational discovery of the parthenogenesis of the green-fly was absorbed by him into his entomological ideas. He repeated Stephen Hales's findings about the rise of sap in plants and was transported with joy at Trembley's discovery of the ability of the little water polyp to regenerate amputated parts.[71] Now and then he tried his luck, not always so successfully, with similar problems; one or two of these will be glanced at in what follows. By and large, it might be expected that Linnaeus, loyal to his religious convictions, would be captivated by physiological and anatomical questions. Where did God's omnipotence reveal itself more clearly than in the strange mechanisms found in organic life? But when it came down to it, he treated them casually. His heart was elsewhere, and it did happen that he would give extreme expression to his contempt for the work of anatomists. Pioneering plant anatomists, such as Malpighi and the Englishman Grew, were placed by him, along with Hales and other physiologists, in the group "botanophili," plant lovers; they did not deal with botanical science "in the true sense."[72] When in the dissertation *Incrementa Botanices* Linnaeus gave a short survey of the history of botany, it all had to do with systematizing and with the glorification of himself, with not a word about anatomical and experimental research. When logic demanded it, he could neglect his own excursions out into living nature. Both of the remarkable dissertations *Oeconomia Naturae* and *De Curiositate Naturali* were ranked by him under the bibliographical category *Oratores*, orators; they were only sermons, rhetorical exercises on the Creator's omnipotence.[73] The real and only goal of science was to identify objects in the three kingdoms of nature, and

71. *Sponsalia Plantarum* (1746), in *Amoen.* 1, 332; *Oratio de Telluris* . . . , 432.
72. *Philosophia Botanica*, 15.
73. Ibid., 10.

Linnaeus's great reform of botany consisted, finally, only in a new way of ordering and putting labels on the vast host of plants.

This was to be done according to certain rules worked out by Linnaeus himself. Heaven help the botanist who departed from them—he was a heretic, "heterodoxus," and Linnaeus spat him out. To be a Linnaean meant slavishly following the instructions laid down by the master in his great works *Systema Naturae*, *Philosophia Botanica*, and the others. These were the eternal guidelines. Linnaeus wished to force nature into a pre-constructed system of thought. Use of the "right" terms and concepts was the sign of a true botanist.

Linnaeus's use of the word "method," *Methodus,* is revealing. To work methodically and, therefore, scientifically meant to establish *a priori* certain rules and then apply them to the botanical material. A true method led rapidly to knowledge about the plant and its name. Without such a method a botanist was lost. If he had it, he could, with its help—and here once again we meet Linnaeus the general—distribute all the plants in the world in phalanxes, the phalanxes in centuries, the centuries in decuries. How helpless, Linnaeus continues in *Classes Plantarum*, is the pure empiricist when faced by an unknown flower. He tried to work out the family from its general appearance; he racked his memory for something similar that he might have seen before; he thumbed through his herbarium and searched night and day through books and engravings. But the person who had a method—or *the* method, for that of Linnaeus was the only one allowed—followed its regulations, beginning with the key determination of class and then working his way step by step to the individual species. It was done in a trice, while the poor empiricist would be sweating away for years before reaching his goal.[74] The future of botany depended on one single sanctified method, which was to be followed by all. To work out its laws and guidelines (*leges et canones*) was regarded by Linnaeus as his completely overshadowing lifework. "If the botanical writings before Linnaeus's time are gone through, no more than sixteen rules will be found, and these weak enough," he states with satisfaction.[75] As early as in his *Fundamenta Botanica* he had brought botany under as many rules as there are days in the year. At long last it stood on unshakable foundations.

In this connection none of Linnaeus's works is more important than *Philosophia Botanica*, the book that Rousseau and Goethe loved. It appeared in 1751, the ripe fruit of twenty years of hard thinking, an introduction to the inventories in which he gathered his descriptions of all the plant and animal forms in the world: *Species Plantarum* and the definitive edi-

74. *Classes Plantarum* (Leyden, 1738), "Praefatio."
75. *Vita*, 136.

tion of the *Systema Naturae*. In the *Philosophia Botanica* Linnaeus has set down his "philosophy," the theoretical basis for his reformation of botany. Nowhere else can one become better acquainted with his conceptual world. Everything is aimed at systematization: describing, classifying, naming. Linnaeus gives an account of morphology, the terms that should be used in describing the parts of plants; he formulates laws about how to construct genera and higher systematic categories, and what principles should be used to differentiate species; and he gives directions for nomenclature in Latin. Even if the species are the smallest, indivisible units, the genus becomes for Linnaeus the real building block of the botanical system, and the ability to correctly gather species to form genera is considered the mark of the true botanist. Here Linnaeus is intractable—creating incorrect genera of plants is "supreme heresy"; only genera based upon the organs of sexual reproduction can be approved. He makes certain mathematical calculations. Purely theoretically, there are 5,776 different ways of combining and varying the parts of flowers; consequently, there may be the same number of genera of plants in nature, never more.[76] In the same way the genera are brought together into higher groups—orders and classes—by means of the essential parts of fertilization (stamens and pistils). From start to finish the method of true systematization was based on fertilization. Down to the finest details Linnaeus prescribes how this was to be accomplished. "If the flowers are alike but the fruits dissimilar . . . the genera should be grouped together." As an example he gives an ideal description of a plant genus. Rules and maxims abound when he enters the field of nomenclature. Naming, "the second basis of botany," becomes for Linnaeus an entire science of its own, obeying immutable laws. Genus names, Linnaeus decrees, which consist of one Greek and one Latin word cannot be accepted. Several other types of Latin genus or species names are "incorrect," "false," and so on. The shorter, the simpler. Linnaeus's practical flair triumphs in these pages—a species diagnosis in Latin (*differentia specifica*) must under no circumstances exceed twelve words. Linnaeus acts in *Philosophia Botanica* literally as a legislator; in paragraph after paragraph he sets down his rules and demands that they be followed by botanists all over the world. All this he performs with his wonderful customary clarity, briefly and aphoristically. *Philosophia Botanica* is at once a code of laws and a catechism, and taken as a whole, a magnificent feat of intellect. Botany emerges as the play of abstractions, with terms and concepts whose eternal validity has been fixed by Linnaeus. With their help, he himself described, classified, and named all plants known at that time—a good botanist was one who could employ the system of concepts correctly, in the manner prescribed by the master.

76. *Philosophia Botanica*, 116 f., 123, 228.

We are beginning to feel at home in the Linnaean world. It was not his own; he had inherited it from preceding generations. Linnaeus was, in point of fact, a scholastic. Logic and definitions of concepts were his tools; his aim, using a fixed point of departure, a dogma if you like, was to order the world of plants into classes, orders, genera, and species. He worked in the same spirit as the learned doctors of the Middle Ages; in both cases Aristotelian logic provided the indispensable basis.

This point of view is by no means new. It occurred among Linnaeus's contemporaries, in circles where it was not possible to accept his pretensions as dictator of botany. When the English Linnaean James Edward Smith was in Paris some years after the decease of the master, he encountered the unconventional botanist Michel Adanson, who was one of the most implacable of the Swede's adversaries. Adanson "accused Linnaeus of being a scholastic"; Smith smiled at such talk, but we should avoid doing likewise.[77] As an ardent supporter of a natural system of plants, Adanson saw in Linnaeus's works the triumph of logic over empirical reality. Much later, the theme was developed by the great German plant physiologist Julius Sachs, in his well-known *Geschichte der Botanik* (1875). Sachs maintains that all of Linnaeus's fundamental ideas may be traced back to his predecessors—Caesalpinus and others. Like them, he was an Aristotelian, but more one-sided—the highest and only worthy aim of botany was that of knowing the names of all species of plants. Sachs sees in Linnaeus a logical genius, who in a brilliant way solved the purely formal task of ordering and classifying nature—but that was all; of scientific method in a modern sense he knew nothing; above all, he did not understand how to test a working hypothesis according to the requirements of inductive research. Linnaeus's writings, Sachs stresses, abound in *a priori* reasoning, deductions, and circular arguments; like all true scholastics, he started with concepts and twisted and turned empirical data until they fit into the preconceived pattern of thought.[78]

One can understand why Sachs's assessment did not arouse any enthusiasm in Linnaean circles in Sweden. It did not fit the Romantic picture of Linnaeus as the humble interpreter of nature, and was, therefore, either consciously ignored or summarily dismissed, and, generally speaking, so it has continued to this day. Sachs appeared as the impious detractor of the Linnaean cult; the only one who seems to have read him with any understanding was, not surprisingly, Bengt Lidforss, always prepared to have a cut at patriotic eloquence.[79] It will not be disputed that Sachs carried things too far. Linnaeus was both richer and more complex than Sachs was will-

77. J. P. Nicolas, in *Adanson* (The Hunt Monograph Series, 1, Pittsburg, Pennsylvania, 1963), 83.

78. J. Sachs, *Geschichte der Botanik* (München, 1875), 84 ff.

79. Cf. *Ur Bengt Lidforss' litterära kvarlåtenskap* (Stockholm, 1917), 56 ff.

ing to admit; the ecological writings have dropped out of the picture, as well as the provincial journeys. Still, any unprejudiced interpretation of Linnaeus's scientific work must reasonably take its point of departure in Sachs's acute analysis, which research has neglected for too long and has thus cut itself off from any chance of understanding Linnaeus's position in the history of ideas.

The scholastic trait in Linnaeus is already apparent in the sexual gospel which formed the core of his botanical system. Behind it lay, it is true, the young student's enthusiasm over the mystery of sexual reproduction and the incomparable discovery of the nuptials of the flowers; but it was general philosophical considerations that led him to base classification on the organs of sexual reproduction. God has determined, Linnaeus says in *Genera Plantarum*, that plants should be distinguished *a fructificatione*, through fructification (i.e., fertilization, fruiting), and in other connections he pinpoints the divine intention more precisely. This is carried out in the spirit of scholasticism. The "essence" of the plants, what makes them plants, is identical with, "consists of," sexual reproduction. All other parts—leaves, stalk, roots—were external adjuncts and had nothing to do with the essential nature of plants. Hence they lacked value from the point of view of systematics.[80] Only a classification based on the flower and its parts was acceptable—"orthodox," in Linnaeus's theologically inspired use of language—and God's will was most perfectly interpreted by the plant system based on the essence of essences, the noblest organs of the flower: stamens and pistils. All this, Linnaeus holds, can be "demonstrated," proved logically. This is, of course, true—provided one were captive to that inherited Aristotelian world of thought which had long since been abandoned by scientists. The dogma that formed the point of departure for Linnaeus's lifework was reached by philosophical deduction, as though he had sat down with an old volume of peripatetic physics. Scholastic to the core was, above all, the fundamental notion in his thought, the quasi-mystical idea of the "essence" of the plant kingdom, a kind of revelation of its "being" in certain organs.

This was the sort of thing that made it impossible for modern scientists on the continent to accept Linnaeus. No part of the plant was inherently, for philosophical reasons, more suited than any other to be the basis of division. Adanson, whom we have just encountered, stressed this in his fight against Linnaean systematics.[81] Organizing natural objects, a necessary undertaking, meant following carefully their own directions, without any preconceived ideas. All botanical systems, Adanson felt, which take into consideration only one part or a restricted number of parts of plants, are

80. *Genera Plantarum*, "Ratio operis"; *Systema Naturae*, 1735 ed., "Observationes in regno vegetabili"; *Classes Plantarum*, 440.
81. F. Stafleu, in *Adanson* 1, 130 f., 178.

"arbitrary, hypothetical, and abstract." Method must be independent of our will. Criticism was also directed at Linnaeus's attempts at creating a natural plant system. For those French botanists—Adanson and, above all, Jussieu—who along with Linnaeus laid the foundation for our knowledge of natural groups of plants, it was self-evident that the scientist must be an empiricist through and through, diligently examining all the parts of the plant. Linnaeus certainly acknowledged the same principle. In the natural method "no rule is valid *a priori*," he said—but did not practice what he preached; he based even the natural orders of plants on the sexual organs of reproduction, on the "essential" parts. Here his procedure was freer, more intuitive—what Linnaeus calls *simplex symmetria omnium partium,* the internal relation of the parts to each other, was decisive—but it still meant that Linnaeus was locked into his prejudices.[82]

What has been said up to this point must not mislead us. Linnaeus lived and worked surrounded by his material, thousands of plant and animal forms, and in that sense he remained an empiricist. He had examined them all, in herbaria and in gardens, in display cabinets of naturalia and in illustrated deluxe volumes; it is unlikely that any other scientist has personally examined such a multitude of forms of life. It was an almost incredible achievement; how Linnaeus found the time is incomprehensible. In moments of weariness, when sheets from the herbaria accumulated on his table, he felt as though he did not have the strength to carry on any longer: "Am I to work myself to death, am I never to see or taste the world? What do I gain by it?"[83] And certainly he followed nature as far as it was possible to do so. His botanical system was artificial only in its upper reaches; the species and genera were natural—Linnaeus repeated this insistently; there he did not violate divine creation. *Species Plantarum*, with its innumerable diagnoses of species, marked a triumph for the empirical study of reality. But species and genera were only raw materials, rather like the chaotic jottings in Linnaeus's Swedish travel books. Order was required; the system must be created; and with that Linnaeus reached the fateful dividing line where construction took over. Nature was remolded by art. An enthusiastic Linnaean like Göran Wahlenberg saw in the harmonious integration of the two, nature and art, a sign of Linnaeus's incomparable mastery and the great genius of his botanical system; Nordic nature with its dualism, its hovering between summer and winter, had here found its noblest expression.[84] This is beautifully said, but is slightly beside the point. The overwhelming problem for the natural history of that epoch was whether "art" in this sense was necessary at all. What was the value of classes and orders that existed only on the desk and in display cabinets?

82. *Classes Plantarum*, 487.
83. Linnaeus to Abraham Bäck in 1749, *Bref och skrifvelser* I: 4 (Uppsala, 1910), 86.
84. Wahlenberg (n. 2, above), 87 ff.

Rigorous construction and intractable discipline characterized not only Linnaeus's consciously artificial sexual system. His grouping of the animal kingdom, in *Systema Naturae* and *Fauna Svecica*, is also essentially an artificial product. There is truth in what has been said about the "rigid, artificial side" of Linnaeus's zoological system; what he gained in clarity and logical acuity, he lost in easy naturalness. Here he had no universal key, as in botany, but tried to follow a single principle of division in each class: in mammals the teeth, in birds the bill, in insects the wings. Within this framework, he could arrive at good and natural groups, sometimes intuitively; but far too many accidents occurred. The slime eel (*Myxine*) he transferred from fish to worms; he placed the rhinoceros among rodents. Occasionally, supreme clarity turns into darkest confusion. An instructive example is provided by Linnaeus's treatment of molluscs and corals, elucidated by Nils von Hofsten in a captivating study.[85] The point of departure, developed in the dissertation *Fundamenta Testaceologiae*, is that they should be classified, not according to their shells, but according to the "animal" in the shell. This may sound reasonable, but in practice it gives curious results. Linnaeus obviously knows that the shell of the molluscs and corals (*lithophyta*) has been manufactured by the enclosed "animal," but he still separates shell and "animal" in the system as though he were dealing with two creatures. The common limpet, *Patella*, he duly enters among the testaceans (*Vermes testacea*), but the "animal" in the limpet is a snail, *Limax,* and as such belongs to a different order, the naked molluscs (*Vermes mollusca*). The "animal" in the snail, *Chiton,* Linnaeus considers to be a sea-snail, *Doris*; it, too, is to be found in its proper place in the system. For a modern reader it is hardly possible to grasp Linnaeus's way of thinking. He apparently does not mean that the "animal" in the shell only "resembles" a snail or some such thing; the only reasonable interpretation is that he naively imagines total identification of the two. When the snail produces a shell, it belongs to another order of animals and is, hence, entered in two places in the system. In the name of logical rationality Linnaeus not only becomes incomprehensible; he dismembers nature and reassembles her again after his own heart.

Order, as Linnaeus understood it, had to be victorious. It is dangerous, he says in *Philosophia Botanica*, to follow nature too closely; the "thread of Ariadne"—the system—may be lost. The words are directed at two of his most eminent precursors, the English botanists Morison and Ray; their system lacked logical clarity. On this altar Linnaeus was prepared to sacrifice nature and naturalness. A simple and beautiful scheme was for him an

85. N. von Hofsten, "Linnés djursystem," *SLÅ* (1959), 9 ff., and "A System of 'Double Entries' in the Zoological Classification of Linnaeus," *Zoologiska bidrag från Uppsala* 35 (1963).

end in itself; its symmetry enraptured him. Admittedly, the scheme had grown out of experience, and had to be tested against it. Linnaeus loved maxims, which he repeated in work after work, and one of them ran thus: "In science the principles of truth must be confirmed by observations."[86] But a medieval philosopher held the same view when he used his Aristotelian system of concepts to describe reality. And in the scholastic manner Linnaeus begins with principles; they are, he must have believed, given *ab initio* to human reason; empirical verification is secondary. How do we know that all plants come from seed? Reason (*ratio*) teaches us, then experience.

The form Linnaeus gives to the more philosophical of his works is illuminating. He likes to proceed like a medieval doctor on the rostrum: first the thesis or proposition, then the proof. The thesis is often, in the scholastic manner, a passage from a text, an authority—not Aristotle, but the highest lawgiver of botany, Linnaeus himself. In this connection the botanical catechism of his youth, *Fundamenta Botanica*, plays a decisive part; it becomes the basic text among his works. Its 365 aphorisms gave him his theses, which he then elaborated, glossing them and deepening them, as though it were a question of annotating Aristotle or Holy Writ. *Philosophia Botanica* is formally a mighty commentary on *Fundamenta*, thesis by thesis, and the same is true of limited areas of the earlier *Critica Botanica*, where nomenclature is treated, and of the dissertation on the reproduction of plants, *Sponsalia Plantarum* (1746). In other respects, too, his works bear the mark of scholastic method. Linnaeus argues in syllogisms after the rules of school logic ("All that lives" . . . "the plants live" . . . "consequently" . . .), and he reasons *pro et contra* like a full-fledged hero of the rostrum from previous centuries: we maintain . . . our opponents assert . . . we reply.[87] In *Sponsalia Plantarum* the contrast between sharp-eyed empiricism and tricks of logic is almost brutal. In parts it is like reading an Aristotelian *physica*—but the subject throughout is the nuptials of flowers, the arrangements of the Maker for the propagation of species, a subject about which Linnaeus knew more than any of his contemporaries.

Scholastic logic is, in fact, the basis of all Linnaeus's work in systematics. It could hardly be otherwise. His aim was to order hierarchically the plant and animal kingdoms in accordance with the most rigorous norms of reason. For the achievement of this task, there was no other possible instrument than that basic Aristotelian logic with which Linnaeus had been thoroughly familiar ever since his school years at Växjö. Its categories and distinctions became indispensable for him. This is increasingly attracting

---

86. *Philosophia Botanica*, 101, and *Fundamenta Botanica*, 1741 ed., 35; cf. ibid., 16.
87. Cf. *Critica Botanica* (Leyden, 1737), 78.

the notice of scholars in connection with the growing interest in Linnaean systematics, its aims and methods, among modern botanists and zoologists. Defining Linnaeus's concept of species, investigating his rules for nomenclature and his working methods as a taxonomist, have all been felt to be urgent concerns. As a consequence, the central problems in Linnaeus's reform of natural history have been brought into prominence. The results that have been reached give us further indications as to his place in the history of ideas.

Not least in importance is a perceptive study by the British zoologist A. J. Cain, "Logic and Memory in Linnaeus's System of Taxonomy."[88] What Cain wishes to establish is the logical basis for Linnaeus's systematic thinking, not just with respect to its smallest logical unit, the species concept, but in relation to all his work as an orderer and a classifier of the kingdoms of nature. Linnaeus went to work as an out-and-out, thoroughgoing Aristotelian, his tools being the terms of scholastic logic: "definition," "genus," "differentia" (difference), and "species." Every scientific definition—of a plant, of any object whatsoever—must, according to this conceptual world, be made "per genus et differentiam," by establishing genus and character of species, and this was Linnaeus's procedure. The character of species (*differentia specifica*) meant a more precise definition within the framework of the genus. In a frenzy of logic, he treated in the same manner the botanical authorities cited by him: the name of the author corresponded to the genus, the title of the book to the species (*species, differentia specifica*).[89] But the undertaking had, Cain stresses, certain hazards when it came to plants and animals—empirical natural objects. There it was not possible to know from the beginning what properties should form the basis of the classification ("taxonomy of unanalyzed entities"). It is characteristic that with all his might Linnaeus strove to construct a botanical system as if it *were* possible to know. As a consequence, logical "division" in the Aristotelian sense became omnipotent; and it followed its own strict rules. The same principle for division (*fundamentum divisionis*) must be applied at every step within the system; as we know, Linnaeus observed this—he found the principle for botanical division in sexual reproduction.

It may be instructive to put the crucial question. We can ask ourselves whether Linnaeus, the prince of botanists, made a single new or remarkable discovery. And the answer, already hinted at by Sachs, is, strangely enough, no, he did not. It is true that whoever makes a mental survey of Linnaeus's writings will recall some beautiful observations; Linnaeus

88. A. J. Cain, "Logic and Memory in Linnaeus's System of Taxonomy," *Proceedings of the Linnean Society of London*, 1956–57, 144 ff.

89. *Philosophia Botanica*, 254.

enriched our knowledge of floral biology and the spreading of seeds, the sleep of plants, the budding of leaves, the host plants of insects, the tapeworm, and other things; and he had some magnificent intuitions about balance in nature and the geological age of the earth. But none of this set science on new tracks; it was not a question of any epochal discoveries; several suggestions he made were taken from older literature. Once more we are faced with a paradox. The empirical genius Linnaeus, the all-seeing, made no great "discoveries," because he wanted to solve problems of a completely different character, and these problems were primarily of a logical nature. As a systematist and reformer of botany he ended up, with the other half of his being singularly suited to the task, in a science of concepts where everything depended upon clarity of thought.

Linnaeus was not the first botanist to work in this way, just as there were heroes before Agamemnon. He followed an old tradition within botany. Ever since the emergence of natural history during the late Renaissance, numerous attempts at ordering natural objects had been based on the rules of logic; every well-thought-out classification was an application of them. Linnaeus—always generous in such matters—admitted his dependence on forerunners. Of special interest is the Italian Andreas Caesalpinus, cited time and again by Linnaeus. Not only did Caesalpinus, with his work *De Plantis* (1583), create the first botanical system in the modern sense, but he was also a militant neo-Aristotelian. Anyone with an intimate knowledge of Linnaeus feels curiously at home with Caesalpinus; the same spirit prevails. Plants, says the Italian philosopher, should be arranged "like armies arrayed for battle," otherwise confusion will arise.[90] It will be remembered that the same martial touch turns up in Linnaeus, who quoted the passage in the later editions of *Systema Naturae*. Caesalpinus made the most rigorous demands for logical order. Like a good Aristotelian, he feels that all science consists in bringing together what is like and separating what is dissimilar; this takes place in groups—genera and species—according to distinguishing marks that express the nature of the object; he himself sought to apply it within botany. And here appears that finalistic point of departure in the choice of the principle of division. Caesalpinus took it from Aristotle himself. The "purpose" of plants is reproduction; the seed must, therefore, form the basis of the botanical system.[91] As we know, Linnaeus endorsed this in the main; the system must be designed in accordance with the highest objective of the plant, its "essential" organs. In private tutorials given in his old age on the natural plant orders, Linnaeus reproduced and

90. Caesalpinus, *De Plantis* (Florence, 1583), dedication; *Systema Naturae*, ed. XIII, vol. I, 13.
91. Caesalpinus, dedic., 11, 26 f.

commented on this passage in Caesalpinus: "as an Aristotelian," Linnaeus says, he always conducted his argument *ex fine ultimo,* searching for the ultimate purpose.[92]

The basic logical structure is also patent in those botanical systems which prevailed when Linnaeus was a young student. His relationship to his immediate forerunners, particularly Ray and Tournefort, has, strange to say, not yet been properly elucidated, but his debt to them is indisputable. To John Ray it was a matter of course to work with the terms of scholastic logic,[93] and the clearness of thought in Joseph Pitton de Tournefort's classic *Institutiones Rei Herbariae* (1700) left nothing to be desired. From Tournefort, Linnaeus learned that the constitution of natural, clearly defined genera was the quintessence of botanical art. No one could stress more emphatically than the great French botanist the importance of a well-ordered hierarchy after the pattern class–genus–species, where the species were defined by flower and fruit, the classes by the corolla.[94] But perhaps Linnaeus was able to gather inspiration also closer to hand. An unsolved, probably insoluble problem has thus been hinted at. During his years as a student at Uppsala, Linnaeus was not alone in his ambitious dream of a reformation of natural history. He had a comrade in Petrus Artedi, a tall and serious boy from the north of Sweden. We know from Linnaeus's autobiographical notes that the two students competed side by side in all amity and in their chambers uplifted each other with new discoveries. Little is known about Artedi, but when on a dark autumn night in 1735 he fell into a canal in Amsterdam and drowned, Linnaeus performed the last office of friendship and saw to the printing of the manuscript on fish, *Ichthyologia,* which Artedi had left behind. In this book Artedi appears as a Linnaean through and through, uncompromisingly logical in the setting up of a system for fish, with exacting demands for definitions and an expressive Latin nomenclature. Artedi's original manuscript appears to have been lost, but under no circumstances can Linnaeus have remodeled it before printing to such an extent that the work lost its original character. Artedi's *Ichthyologia* was his own child. Perhaps we must, therefore, reconsider what we have learned about the young Linnaeus's path to mastery: the intensive exchange of thought with Artedi cannot be left out of the picture.[95] What Linnaeus took from Artedi, and vice versa, cannot now be unraveled, but we must keep open the possibility that Artedi, who was the

---

92. *Praelectiones in Ordines Naturales Plantarum,* ed. P. D. Giseke (Hamburg, 1792), 8.

93. Cf. Cain, 156.

94. J. Pitton de Tournefort, *Institutiones Rei Herbariae* I (Paris, 1700), 63 ff.

95. Cf. E. Lönnberg, "Linné och Artedi," *SLÅ* (1919), 35 ff.

elder by a couple of years, played an important part in the birth of Linnaean systematics.

This is not to deny Linnaeus's originality. What he took from his predecessors, starting with Caesalpinus, he sharpened and refined; with his need for organized knowledge, he was a systematist, a genius, about whose originality there can be no mistake. The smallest fragment from his workshop—a table, a species diagnosis—bears his own stamp. Linnaeus permeated with his indomitable vitality a science which may seem more arid than any other, and this is surely the source of the influence he has exerted on his contemporaries and on posterity.

But he was no revolutionary, opening new vistas for the science of botany. Linnaeus himself, however, was of a different opinion. He alone had transformed botany—"reformed an entire science and created a new epoch"[96]—and that view has been adopted, at least in his native country. But there is no reason to accept Linnaeus's word. He was a natural historian in the old-fashioned sense of the word, an inheritor and a consummator. He solved the great and inescapable task with such mastery within the framework of the conservative intellectual tradition of Europe. With Linnaeus an era in the history of botany reaches its culmination and conclusion: it is the end of scholastic botany. He gave science a new face—but no new soul. As a scientist Linnaeus somehow seems a stranger to his own times, antiquated and primitive; and his enormous influence, based on the lucidity and vigor that flowed from his works, most probably delayed the development of modern biology, and not just in the Nordic countries.

The Anachronistic Linnaeus

But Linnaeus was anachronistic in other respects as well. The more closely he is studied, the more extraordinary he seems. At some moments it may appear as though, with his sober intelligence and his clear eyes, he belonged entirely to the Age of Enlightenment; at other times he reverts to simple superstition and bizarre fancies. Fables and old folklore were often given a solemn scientific blessing by Linnaeus. He could display astonishing uncertainty as soon as he left the sheets of his herbaria and the systematic categories.

It must be admitted that he showed no hesitation when he came to Hamburg as a young man and beheld the seven-headed hydra in the house of the mayor, Mr. Andersson; he immediately exposed it as a brazen forgery. The monster contravened the basic rules of natural history, and in such

96. *Vita*, 146.

cases Linnaeus was always on his guard. Under the heading "absurdities," *Paradoxa*, he compiled in the first edition of the *Systema Naturae* a short list of such zoological monsters; in addition to the hydra we encounter frogs transformed into fish, the unicorn, the Phoenix, and others of the same kind. As a supporter of the Enlightenment and an adversary of folk-myths, Linnaeus appeared in the Proceedings of the Academy of Sciences, showing that lemmings do not pour wholesale from the clouds. Water could not change spontaneously into blood; such things were caused by water mites. No miracle could disrupt the laws of nature. On this basis Linnaeus denied the transformation of oats into rye. He dedicated a separate dissertation to supposed divine interventions in the insect world. The deathwatch beetle did not forebode disaster; miracles disappear "when the natural cause has been discovered."[97]

But nature was inexhaustible—Linnaeus knew this better than anyone else—and it was easy to make a mistake, even within its boundaries. The fact that Linnaeus often did make mistakes is naturally no cause for surprise. The reverse would have been more remarkable; he was not infallible, even in his own eyes. It is the nature of his failures that is interesting, the light it throws upon his singularity. Did swallows sleep at the bottom of lakes over the winter? It is well known that as long as he lived Linnaeus was convinced that they did; during the autumn the swallows gathered in large groups among the reeds and dived down into the water, where they rested under the sheet of ice until spring came and they thawed out. This was old folklore, taken over by Linnaeus without closer consideration. It never entered his head to test it by experiment—that is, by dipping a swallow under water and seeing whether it could live there. The case of the fury of hell, *Furia infernalis*, was no better. Here Linnaeus created single-handed a mythical animal, as fictitious as the Phoenix or the unicorn, which at least had support in literature. *Furia*, or "the shot," avowed Linnaeus—who believed that he himself had had a brush with the animal—was a wingless little creature that fell from the air and pierced the skin of human beings and cattle; shortly thereafter they died or fell seriously ill.[98] Linnaeus and his disciples hunted furies, especially in Lapland, which was believed to be their Eldorado, and where a specimen had once fallen on the plate of a vicar. The Academy of Sciences, on the authority of Linnaeus, offered a gold medal to anyone who sent in a preserved *Furia*, and even toward the turn of the century this imaginary beast was a current topic in Swedish learned circles.

97. Lindroth, *Vetenskapsakademiens historia*, vol. I (Stockholm, 1967), 570; *Miracula Insectorum* (1752), in *Amoen.* 3, 313 ff.
98. Cf. Lindroth, "Naturvetenskaperna och kulturkampen," *Lychnos* (1957), 187 f., and *Vetenskapsakademiens historia* I, 713 ff.

Linnaeus, then, could be highly credulous in his worst moments. If you rubbed the back of a puppy with aquavit—he assured his students—the animal would become a dwarf.[99] The rattlesnake in the forests of North America bewitched birds and squirrels in the trees with its gaze, so that they fell into its mouth; this, according to Linnaeus, was one of the most remarkable discoveries of contemporary natural history.[100] Certainly he shared such superstitions with others, but heavier demands may properly be made on Linnaeus. There were those who did make such demands, even in Sweden. The admired "Archiater" (Linnaeus's title as a royal physician) was not entirely enlightened, something even a few of his own disciples realized. Although Linnaeus could not be criticized openly, dissenting opinions were expressed, more or less covertly. "How can an animal be proclaimed where there is none," exclaimed the Finnish Linnaean disciple Johan Haartman, with reference to the *Furia*. His colleague in Åbo, Johan Leche, professor of medicine, dedicated an entire dissertation to the winter quarters of swallows, carefully avoiding any mention of Linnaeus's name. Factually speaking, the dissertation is devastating: it is physiologically impossible for an animal that breathes with lungs to live at the bottom of a lake; the belief that swallows hibernate under the ice was an "absurd fable," a manifestation of the epidemic misconceptions circulating among the vulgar.[101]

Elsewhere, too, we note that Linnaeus is not on the level of contemporary science. To read him not infrequently means being taken back several centuries in time. The Bible, Roman authors, and the physics of scholasticism became his authorities—not the budding modern experimental philosophy. A well-known and tolerably well studied example is the obscure doctrine about the elements, which Linnaeus time and again hammered home as one of the fundamentals of science, as in the introductions to *Systema Naturae*. Everything in the universe, Linnaeus held, fell into three categories: "stars" (*Astra*), elements, and naturalia. The elements, which together formed natural objects, or "naturalia," were the Aristotelian four—fire, air, water, and earth—but Linnaeus described them in terms inspired by the cosmic physics of the Roman Stoa.[102] Such theories were hopelessly out of date, as was the whole of this naive interpretation of the world; in parts it is seriously confused. Linnaeus, educated in late-Cartesian Uppsala, naturally knew as well as anyone the main aspects of modern

---

99. *Lachesis Naturalis*, 26.
100. *Oratio de Telluris . . .* , 434.
101. Lindroth, *Vetenskapsakademiens historia* I, 714, and "Naturvetenskaperna och kulturkampen," 188.
102. Cf. E. Malmeström, "Linnés religionsfilosofiska betraktelser," *Kyrkohistorisk Årsskrift* (1925), 23 ff.

science, but he was not interested. He was, at his worst, a homespun thinker, remote from ideas that were self-evident to all of his contemporaries with a scientific education.[103]

There are many such passages in Linnaeus's writings; it is even possible to be captivated by them, as long as one keeps in mind the fact that they were outmoded even when they were written. In his dissertation on the metamorphoses of leaves, *Prolepsis Plantarum*, he says that all life consists of movement, and thus far it is possible to follow him. What are the organs of movement in plants? Linnaeus holds that it is the leaves, which are moved by the wind and "as it were fly in it"; it is hardly possible to reason more archaically.[104] Into the same category of error fall his never-ending parallels between plants and animals. In some way they were inevitable. Plants and animals were the two basic forms of organic life, and it was but a short step to regard them as expressions of a common plan of creation. This had long been done, not least by Aristotelian philosophers. But they had proceeded with caution. Andreas Caesalpinus compared the organization of plants to that of animals; the ancients, he says, spoke of heart, brain, and even uterus in plants. Caesalpinus argues for and against such a view, but he does not reach any definite conclusions and emphasizes the difference in principle between animals and plants.[105] The roots are the mouths of the plants, said others—without meaning very much by it. Even against this background Linnaeus appears primitive; he takes a step backward. Rapid and drastic identifications were to his taste, preferably set up in tabular form. In plants, we read in *Philosophia Botanica*, the stomach is the earth(!), the lymphatic vessels are the roots, the legs are the stalks, the lungs are the leaves, and the heart is the "heat" (*calor*); plants, therefore, were called in olden times "inverted animals," *animalia inversa*.[106] In other connections Linnaeus carried the theme further, becoming ever more fantastic. This is especially the case in the obscure introduction to the animal kingdom in the later editions of *Systema Naturae*, where in short maxims he develops his theory about animal life as a mechanical process. Linnaeus launches into bizarre games of imagination, with apparently serious intention; the reader feels close to Swedenborg, who, about a decade earlier, had exposed the secrets of organic life in his *Oeconomia Regni Animalia*. Linnaeus talks about the cranium of an animal as a "tuber," out of which the "stalk" of the spine grows, providing areas of attachment for the "leaves,"

103. One of the few who has noticed this is Erik Nordenskiöld, "En blick på Linnés naturuppfattning," *SLÅ* (1923), 27.
104. *Prolepsis Plantarum*, in *Amoen*. 6, 328.
105. *De Plantis* I: 1, 1 ff.
106. *Philosophia Botanica*, 93.

or muscles.[107] Not even a contemporary reader would have been particularly edified by these lines.

The conviction that there is a basic identity within the organic world also lies behind Linnaeus's speculation about marrow and bark substances, his curious *medulla-and-cortex* theory. It is not difficult to do justice to it. Linnaeus wanted to give a unified explanation of vital processes, above all of reproduction and heredity, based on anatomical and physiological observations. These were problems which at that time were impossible to solve, and Linnaeus's suggestion—which he regarded as one of his primary contributions to science—is not without a touch of genius. But in its drastic simplification, it is typical of its author. Animals and plants consisted, according to Linnaeus, of two substances, pith (or marrow) and bark (*medulla* and *cortex*), of which pith/marrow was "inner," the bearer of vital and generative powers, while the bark stood for the "outer," primarily the nutritive faculty. Should this theory seem adventurous even at this stage—especially in its application to animals—it is even more so in the conclusions Linnaeus drew from it. The pith/marrow substance, he held, stood for the female in reproduction (the pistil in plants) and hence, in the offspring, for everything connected with the inner "life" and its "powers"; the bark corresponded to the male principle (the stamens) and in the offspring found its expression in the body, or the "outer" qualities. Fructification, consequently, meant a fusion of pith/marrow and bark. This speculation, which Linnaeus developed from the end of the 1740s onward in dissertations and private seminars, became in time the cornerstone of his biological thought, and at the same time it grew increasingly wilder. In the female principle, pith or marrow, he proclaimed to his disciples, resided will, that is to say, the ability to expand and contract; proof of this was provided by the lowest of all creatures, the one-celled amoeba (*Volvox Chaos dicta*), which was "pure marrow" and, hence, could assume all conceivable shapes.[108]

It is almost impossible to argue against reasoning of this kind; it cannot be disproved. Linnaeus's speculations on marrow and bark are not his own; they, too, lead back to a more archaic world of ideas. In the much admired Caesalpinus he could read that the seeds of plants were produced from their "marrow" (*medulla*), in which resided the life-giving warmth; here lay the basic notion.[109] But Linnaeus added to it unrestrainedly; it is his way of working, of carrying out scientific research, that is interesting, not the theory in itself. Having once formulated it, he succeeded with the help of

107. *Systema Naturae*, ed. XIII, 1, 15. Cf. Nordenskiöld, 23 f.
108. *Praelectiones*, 14.
109. *De Plantis*, 11.

drastic simplifications and misinterpreted observations in making it ever more self-evident; he "proved" it.

It may be worthwhile to follow him part of the way. For Linnaeus believed that he had acquired experimental evidence for his doctrine about marrow and bark, and in this connection there is reason to inquire about his relationship to scientific experiment in general. His use of the term itself, *experimentum,* must not mislead. Its meaning was far from clear; already in classical Latin "experiment" could mean both "experiment"—testing something—and "experience," and the latter meaning became in time the more common in scientific and medical texts. Proving something by experiment merely meant referring to accurate observations. "Experiment" became the same as "experience," and this was the sense in which Linnaeus normally used the word. When he called his famous lectures on diet a "collegium experimentale,"[110] he simply meant that it was based on findings, "observations," and in the same way he talked of his experimental theology (*theologia experimentalis*) in the notes on *Nemesis;* they were based on gossip and anecdotes, an empirical material intended to illustrate a general law.[111] It may be questioned whether Linnaeus ever really made clear to himself what was actually meant by the term "experiment" in a stricter sense. In one of his autobiographies there is a revealing statement on just the subject of the lectures on diet—he had founded a teaching on diet based on experiment, "on findings and examples, just as modern doctors treat their science and have made it *experimentalem."* Linnaeus could not, or did not want to, differentiate between the honest assembling of facts, and a science which, like the new experimental physics, put carefully defined questions to nature and answered them with the help of experimental arrangements especially constructed for the purpose. Linnaeus, in all innocence, believed himself to be a pioneer of modern scientific methods. The truth of the matter was that because of the whole nature of his biological thinking he stood outside the experimental research of his time.

This verdict must perhaps be qualified somewhat. Within a limited area Linnaeus really did engage in experiments of his own, conducting properly thought-out tests and awaiting their results. This was so in the case of plant hybrids, and thus of the marrow-and-bark theory. Linnaeus's research into hybrids, which had consequences for his botanical system, is definitely interesting, but not easy to judge. For better or worse, it offers a miscellany of attractive ideas and mistakes. Linnaeus was undeniably something of a pioneer when in 1757/58 in the botanical gardens of Uppsala he produced the first artificial fertile plant hybrid (*Tragopogon pratensis x T. porrifolius*)

---

110. Linnaeus to Bäck 20 Nov. 1764, *Bref och skrifvelser* I:5, 129; *Vita,* 173.
111. *Vita,* 164.

a couple of years before Koelreuter in Germany presented his pioneering studies in fertilization and hybridization in the plant world. It is in such connections that Linnaeus comes closest to modern experimental research. In several minor writings, particularly *De Sexu Plantarum* (*On the Sex of Plants*, 1760), which was submitted to the Imperial Academy at St. Petersburg, he gave an account of methods and results and pointed toward further tasks. Behind the artificial *Tragopogon* hybrid lay his own experimental studies and those of others on the reproductive mechanisms of plants. In this work, which was awarded a prize by the Russians, Linnaeus recounts how he manipulated the flowers of *Mirabilis, Cannabis,* and other species; he cut off the stamens, bound paper round the pistils, and so on, in order to confirm the basic principle of botany—that pollination—pollen on the stigma of the pistil—was necessary if the seeds were to ripen.[112] In the case of hybrids, nature had most certainly given him a helping hand. The crossing of the two species of *Tragopogon* had originally occurred spontaneously in the garden, but Linnaeus immediately took advantage of the occasion and produced the hybrid again in carefully controlled conditions.[113]

In other cases he was less fortunate. Linnaeus saw plant hybrids where there were none. Ever since the middle of the 1740s, when he began to brood about them, hybrids had brought about in him a profound disquiet, almost a landslide in his botanical world of thought, and he hunted for them everywhere. In the dissertation *Plantae Hybridae* Linnaeus described a series of forms which for some reason he believed to be crossings, often between species of different genera.[114] Here curious combinations appear: *Veronica* × *Verbena, Saponaria* × *Gentiana, Aquilegia* × *Fumaria*. Linnaeus misinterpreted his material, jumping to conclusions in his eagerness to penetrate the secret of the formation of species. For the hybrids manifestly demonstrated that new species of plants could be formed; they destroyed his belief in the constancy of species. The animal kingdom also provided him with examples, not only those long known, like the mule and the hinny, but even more incredible kinds. On the authority of the great Réaumur, Linnaeus wished it to be received as plausible that a chicken covered with hair had been hatched after crossing a rabbit and a hen; when it suited him he swallowed a story as fantastic as the hydra in Hamburg.[115] Always prepared to simplify and extend the consequences, Linnaeus arrived in due course at his theory, in itself noteworthy and stimulating, that

112. *De Sexu Plantarum* (1760), in *Amoen.* 10, 113 ff.
113. *Generatio Ambigena* (1759), in *Amoen.* 6, 12.
114. *Plantae Hybridae* (1751), in *Amoen.* 3, 34 ff.
115. Ibid., 61. Cf. R. Mortier, "Note sur un passage du Rêve d'Alembert: Réaumur et le problème de l'hybridisation," *Revue d'histoire des sciences* (1960), 309 ff.

the hosts of different plants had arisen through cross-pollination between a limited number of original forms. All species within a genus issued from the same mother-plant, which had received pollen from other plant genera. Linnaeus realized that the problem could be solved by experiment. Artificial pollination ought to be carried out between species of different genera, and he himself very much wished to dedicate the rest of his life to this task.[116]

At the same time Linnaeus saw in hybrids an illustration of his marrow-and-bark theory. If the species within the genus could be traced back to a common maternal ancestor, they must all have the same "inner" nature, the same marrow substance—"the number of species," Linnaeus says in his dissertation *Generatio Ambigena*, "that are to be called related are those that have been produced by the same marrow substance or mother."[117] This was, or could become, after more profound research, a hard and fast rule in botany. Hybrids gave him visible proof that the marrow-and-bark theory was correct. Linnaeus went through case after case and invariably believed that he found confirmation of his basic proposition: the outer characteristics (the bark) come from the father, the "internal" or life (the marrow), from the mother. As far as plant hybrids were concerned, the proposition surely had some kind of meaning, and could be verified in principle in any case: the organs of sexual reproduction belonged to the marrow and, therefore, resembled those of the species of the mother, while leaves and other outer attributes were reminiscent of the father. But within the animal kingdom the characteristics could not be distributed in this way. The mule (horse ♂ × ass ♀) looked like a horse outwardly, while the hinny (ass ♂ × horse ♀) resembled an ass; the "inner," which came from the mother-marrow, was in these cases an ungraspable something, a hidden specific "nature," almost like the substantial form of the Aristotelians.[118] The marrow-and-bark theory gave Linnaeus the satisfaction of having formulated a fundamental law of biology, but in fact it explained nothing. It was a construction from his writing desk, and only afterward did he go out and test it in living nature, where at worst it led him astray.

Linnaeus was in a hurry to find connections and create theories; drastic simplification was, so to speak, his hallmark. There was a gap in him, a sort of no-man's-land between logical thought and empirical reality; they did not penetrate and fertilize each other. Uncovering the secrets of nature step by step, guided by working hypotheses and experiments, did not come easily to him; his impulsive imagination raced off ahead, and in a trice he was ready with his conclusions.

116. *De Sexu Plantarum*, 129; *Fundamenta Fructificationis* (1762), in *Amoen.* 6, 297.
117. *Generatio Ambigena*, 12.
118. Ibid., 12 f.

This is particularly evident in his medical writings. They are more numerous than is commonly realized, and of widely varying quality. Even his own contemporaries and immediate posterity felt slightly ill at ease when faced with Linnaeus's medical authorship. It contained many curiosities. In a commemorative speech on Linnaeus, held by the famous anatomist Vicq d'Azyr in 1779 at the French Société Royale de Médecine, the most important medical works were subjected to severe criticism.[119] Linnaeus's *Materia Medica* was "hardly worthy of its author"; *Clavis Medicinae* should be regarded with forbearance. The Frenchman's attack was rejected by agitated Swedish disciples; the young doctor Sven Hedin began his career as a fighting Linnaean apostle by extolling his master's pioneering contributions to medicine. But in the main the criticism was valid: Linnaeus's weaknesses are magnified in his medical work; occasionally his mistakes are most unfortunate.

Perhaps this was inevitable. Medical science in the eighteenth century was still in its infancy, groping in the dark in such matters as the mysteries of the human body and the nature of disease. The medical literature of the era does not always make edifying reading; it abounds in fantastic hypotheses, as though empirical testing and verification of results did not exist. The spirit of mathematics had achieved its triumphs within physics and other exact sciences; the problems of organic life were far more complex, not least in the case of the human body in sickness and in health. True, certain basic sciences had made some progress—particularly pathological anatomy and parts of physiology, where Morgagni and Haller were the great names—but at the sickbed the doctor was about as helpless as ever. The eloquently developed pathological doctrines of the time with their drastic simplifications were of little value, and the immense battery of medicines in the pharmacopoeia was, with a few exceptions, pointless or pernicious. The most extraordinary cures were tried out and wonder-working miracle medicines were proclaimed, even by professors of medicine and established doctors. The most prominent Swedish doctors of the epoch, an Abraham Bäck, a Rosén von Rosenstein, could hardly note better results than had Hippocrates once long ago. It is against this background that Linnaeus's medical writings must be judged. No one can demand that he should have succeeded where others failed; besides, medical science was not his main occupation. But even when we keep this in mind, Linnaeus appears strikingly uninhibited in his medical speculations, and the discoveries he made and eulogized with extravagant self-esteem soon lapsed into oblivion.

119. Vicq d'Azyr, *Suite des éloges lus dans les séances publiques de la Société royale de médecine* (Paris, 1780).

45

Linnaeus's debut in medicine was already on the adventurous side. The obvious and praiseworthy aim was to procure a doctor's degree from Harderwijk with his dissertation on the causes of ague (*De Febrium Intermittentum Causa*, 1735). Linnaeus asserted—the matter "cannot be doubted"—that ague was caused by particles of clay which, when dissolved in drinking water, entered the body and clogged the capillaries. The theory is interesting as an expression of the mechanistic view of pathological processes embraced by Linnaeus and inspired by the admired Santorio. But it was immediately obvious that it was untenable. In the vehement but otherwise not very distinguished disputation which Linnaeus's competitor for the professorial chair, Johan Gottschalk Wallerius, launched at him in 1741, the dissertation was subjected to harsh criticism. It was not true that ague always appeared in areas where clay was to be found; Linnaeus had been too hasty in drawing his conclusions.[120]

He was as quick off the mark where other diseases were concerned. A few scattered observations, and Linnaeus was ready to solve the problem. He was loath to do this in the form of cautious assumptions; the matter was as plain as a pike-staff, and Linnaeus congratulated himself. In one of his autobiographies he made a list of all his discoveries within medicine and physiology: he was the first to have held "as an axiom" that the lung in breathing took electricity from the air and conveyed it to the marrow-substance; and it was he who had revealed the causes of leprosy and ergotism.[121] On ergotism, which was endemic in certain counties in southern Sweden, Linnaeus published a dissertation, *Raphania*, in which he claimed that it was caused by seeds of the common black turnip-radish, *Raphanus*, mixed in the grain.[122] To make this discovery, he explained, "required a complete knowledge of nature." That the turnip-radish was innocent was shown after a few years through simple experiments by a young Swedish doctor, Anders Magnus Wåhlin; Linnaeus had reasoned his way to his explanation. The same was true of leprosy. Here the idea was not Linneaus's own, and in the beginning he expressed himself with praiseworthy caution. His itinerant disciple Anton Martin, who had collected naturalia on the Atlantic coast of Norway and studied leprosy there, believed that it was caused by little worms, *Gordidae*, which entered the body with herring and other food fish. Linnaeus was enchanted by the idea and backed it with further evidence.[123] As we have seen, he was more categorical in the matter of the fury of hell, or "the shot," a figment of the imagination which he raised to the level of the greatest medical certainty. Or consider his attempt

120. J. G. Wallerius, *Decades Binae Thesium Medicarum* (Uppsala, 1741), 4 ff.
121. *Vita*, 163 f.
122. Cf. Lindroth, *Vetenskapsakademiens historia* 1, 713.
123. *Lepra* (1763) in *Amoen.* 7, 94 ff.

to explain epilepsy. The reason falling sickness was so common in the border areas between the counties of Skåne and Småland was that mothers washed the children's heads with cold water; the sharp fluids were thus driven inward and damaged the brain.[124] The underlying pathological doctrine was in its way irreproachable (being more or less common property among doctors at the time), but what is shocking is the lighthearted way of reaching conclusions. Linnaeus was always prepared and had immediate explanations to hand.

Further, there is his theory about live carriers of infection, sometimes regarded as his most farsighted contribution to medical science. Linnaeus had already touched on the subject in his first lectures on medicine at Uppsala, developed it in the well-known disputation *Exanthemata Viva* (1757), and gave some concluding observations ten years later in the dissertation on the invisible world, *Mundus Invisibilis*. The basic thought was in a very general way "correct." Linnaeus held that epidemic diseases, such as the plague, smallpox, dysentery, certain fevers, were caused by microscopically small animals, most closely resembling "insects," or mites; later on he thought of them as organic particles of a less specific character. But the suggestion was not new. The idea of a living *contagium* as the carrier of infections and contagious diseases had been eloquently put forward already by the sixteenth century Italian doctor Fracastoro, and recent discoveries of a previously invisible world under the microscope gave it renewed topicality. Linnaeus's opinion that it was specifically mites (*acarus*) which caused the ravaging endemic diseases was scarcely a step forward, but rather a crude simplification. Perhaps his mind echoed with the songs so often chanted by pious entomologists of old in praise of the mite as the smallest and most perfect of creatures. Certain it is that he was confirmed in his conviction by the illness scabies, which he clearly showed to be caused by the tiny scabies mite. Scabies became for Linnaeus the paradigm, the striking example. He was immediately prepared to find mites at the back of all infectious diseases connected with skin rashes—even dysentery, which was an "internal scabies of the entrails." Similar thoughts had occurred to others before him; Linnaeus himself cites as an authority a German, August Rivinus, who claimed that plague is generated by "very small mites."[125] On weak grounds, entomology was linked with medicine. Linnaeus's proofs are treacherous, consisting mainly of conclusions based on analogy, supplemented by occasional observations. He related a story about his disciple, the unfortunate Daniel Rolander, who had fallen ill with

124. Cf. Lindroth, op cit., 1, 687.
125. *Exanthemata viva* (1757), in *Amoen.* 5, 97. Cf. F. Berg, *Linnés Systema Morborum* (Uppsala Universitets Årsskrift 1957:3), 45 ff.; O. T. Hult, "Om Linné och den osynliga världen," *SLÅ*, 1934 and 1935.

dysentery, and who found in his feces myriads of the same kind of mites that are found in flour; when he examined with a magnifying glass the beaker of juniper-wood he used to quench his thirst during the night, he discovered a white line of densely packed flour-mites.[126]

Linnaeus is most difficult to follow when he grapples with the deeper secrets of life and pathology. The speculation about marrow and bark returns, supplemented by impenetrable oracular dicta. The main document is the little monograph *Clavis Medicinae*, "the key to medicine," with which Linnaeus sought to open the lock of the innermost chamber of medical science. He himself held it to be one of his masterpieces; through his *Clavis* pathology had gained more than from a hundred authors and folio volumes; it was "one of the greatest jewels in medicine."[127] Linnaeus dedicated the book to the foremost authorities in medicine of his time: Albinus, von Haller, van Swieten, Sauvages, and his friend Rosén von Rosenstein; this was his *tour de force*.

It is hardly possible to understand properly Linnaeus's *Clavis Medicinae*. Nor was the reader meant to: it was conceived as a bare outline, to which he gave flesh and blood in his lectures.[128] On the other hand, no explanations could surely give these aphorisms a more reasonable meaning. The point of departure—the body as a kind of "pneumatic-hydraulic machine"—was understandable enough. Linnaeus was a devoted admirer of the iatromechanical school of those times, which interpreted the organic processes in the easily understandable terms of mechanics. But then he took off, becoming ever more singular. Linnaeus, who loved working with extreme opposites, imagined the key of medicine to be double, consisting of an outer and an inner key. The former gave access to diseases of the "bark" (fluids, fibers) and was, therefore, masculine, "fatherly," the latter to diseases of the "marrow" (the nervous system, manifestations of the mind), corresponding to the feminine, the "motherly." In the same way remedies must be divided into two groups: "substances of taste" (*sapida*), which worked on the complaints of the bark, and "substances of smell" (*olida*), which cured diseases of the marrow. Linnaeus considered the formulation of this basic rule of pharmacology to be a pioneering contribution to science—thus, he said, all nature balanced "on contraries," on opposites.[129] But the modern reader, along with Vicq d'Azyr, finds only the wildest arbitrariness. Admittedly, Linnaeus gave examples and based them on observations, but he proved nothing; passing fancies became eternal truths.

In this mysterious *Clavis Medicinae* there is yet another curious element.

126. *Exanthemata viva*, 97.
127. *Vita*, 164.
128. *Clavis Medicinae*; cf. E. Müller in *Hygiea* (1907), 569 ff.
129. *Vita*, 164.

Linnaeus was, he later recounted, the first to see that nature always divided itself in fives, "numero quinario." When he made the discovery, he does not relate: *Clavis Medicinae*, in which it is proclaimed, is from 1766, and within a year he was prepared to work with other series of numbers. With copious citations from Ovid and Virgil he did this in a curious dissertation, *Metamorphosis Humana*, on the ages of man.[130] It is an old man's mournful sermon, delivered by a Linnaeus who sensed the approach of the ultimate metamorphosis, full of tables on the ages of human life. There the reader finds a division based on the number twelve. Just as the day had two times twelve hours and the year twelve months, so the life of man comprised twelve ages, from the foetal stage to doddering old age—oh, how we do change! But Linnaeus here also works with a climacteric scale based on the holy number seven. It is confirmed, he holds, by experience. Every seventh year a decisive change takes place: at the age of seven the milk teeth are lost; at fourteen puberty commences; forty-two is the apex of life; at sixty-three the sexual drive is extinguished; at seventy life comes full circle and you are a child again. It is unclear how these series, which are actually based on ancient ideas, relate to the "quinary," the speculation on the number five in *Clavis Medicinae*. It is, in a way, more dogmatic. The two keys to the art of healing, Linnaeus holds, each possess two five-fingered hands turned away from each other. Following this principle, he divides, in columns as was his habit, the domains of the "outer" and the "inner" keys. Each section (the pathology of diseases of the bark, etc.) is divided up after the pattern of the two hands—five fingers (for example five or two times five different changes of the body fluids) to the left, and five fingers (corresponding to changes in the fibers) to the right. In his lectures on *Clavis* Linnaeus penetrated deeper into the mysteries of the quintuple. His searching gaze discovered groups of five at every turn: there were five senses, five organs of the body, five viscera, and now there were also five elements, since ether had been added to complete the pattern.[131]

Even before this, Linnaeus had taken up curious numerological speculations, though, as far as can be judged, in a more playful spirit. When in the *Fundamenta Botanica* of his youth he summed up botany in 365 rules, or the same number as the days of the year, he surely did not mean very much by it. The speculation in numbers of his later years—in *Metamorphosis Humana* and *Clavis Medicinae*—must, however, be taken seriously. Thus did Linnaeus think primitively; he could even be incomprehensible. Of course, it is not impossible to understand why he was captivated by these thoughts. They met his insistent need for structure and order; the numer-

130. *Metamorphosis Humana* (1767), in *Amoen*. 7, 326 ff.
131. O. E. A. Hjelt, in *Carl von Linnés betydelse såsom naturforskare och läkare*, 164.

ological pattern which he had found was an expression of the divine Order in nature and in human life. Nature was always the same, or—when he wished to explain the scale of twelves in *Metamorphosis Humana*—displayed in all its processes "analogy and uniformity."[132] But this hardly makes the numerical speculations of the aging Linnaeus more reasonable. They belong most immediately to that esoteric tradition which began with the numerical mysticism of the ancient Pythagoreans and burgeoned into new life in the occult and magical wisdom of the Renaissance, which had many representatives as late as the seventeenth century. A hundred years earlier the extraordinary English doctor Thomas Browne had published *The Garden of Cyrus or the Quincuncial Lozenge*, in which he collected learned and complicated evidence to show that everything in nature was ordered in fives, in accordance with "the quincunx." He had, Browne said, often admired "the mystic science of Pythagoras" and the secret magic of numbers.[133]

Here it is not only a modern observer who stands puzzled before Linnaeus. If he is to be compared with any of his Swedish contemporaries, our thoughts turn most immediately to Swedenborg, not to any of his medical or scientific colleagues. Linnaeus's undisciplined speculations about organic life and the keys of medicine stood little chance of commanding attention; nor, as far as we know, was anyone influenced by them. Linnaeus lived and worked as *primus inter pares* in the golden age of Swedish science; he knew all the great ones and was the friend of some: Anders Celsius and Klingenstierna, Wargentin, Cronstedt, Wilcke, Charles De Geer, Rosén von Rosenstein, and the young genius Torbern Bergman. Even so, it appears in certain situations as though he did not belong to their circle. He played according to different rules, and he spoke a different, more archaic tongue. With all his whims, Linnaeus is often muddled, in some curious way unintellectual. He believed in reason as firmly as did any of his contemporaries, but his impatience and his passions broke through, and he gave them free rein. In men like Klingenstierna and Wargentin, or a doctor like Rosenstein, the emotional tone is quite different—critical and testing, skeptical toward too magnificent ideas.

This does not mean that Linnaeus was the last of the old guard; in fact, the future lay with the speculative spirit. With Romanticism it was to become supreme wisdom even within the sciences, and it may appear as though Linnaeus in his more uncritical moments was moving along the same lines of thought. We do not know to what extent the "quinary," the marrow as identical with will, or muscles as "leaves," fascinated the Schell-

---

132. *Metamorphosis Humana* 331.
133. J. Finch, *Sir Thomas Browne* (London, 1950), 185 ff.

ingian *Naturphilosophie* of the early nineteenth century, but they would have had excellent prospects of doing so. Through the Enlightenment there runs an undercurrent of mystical thought which combines with the Hermetic-magic world view of past times and the visions of Romanticism to come; it is of a certain interest to fit Linnaeus roughly into this tradition.

Linnaeus's religious world view was magical, too, or at least primitive. Here it is a question not of his physico-theological wonder at the divine wisdom in nature—that was now common property—but of *Nemesis Divina* and the Old Testament, his thoughts about God, destiny, and happiness in this world. These are imposing and awesome, as always when Linnaeus is inspired by the majestic preaching of the Bible. In the Old Testament character of his piety, he already deviated from that of his own age. The God of creation and revenge was his; legal orthodoxy, with its robust way of interpreting the Bible, lives on with undiminished strength in Linnaeus. During his childhood he had imbibed it in the shadow of his father's pulpit; it is quite another matter that as the years went by he lost faith in its Christian message—punishment meant more than grace. Inevitably, the accent becomes more somber when Linnaeus, with the prophets of Israel and men of God in mind, interprets the circumstances of human existence. Among other documents, there is the curious disputation on old age according to Solomon, *Senium Salomoneum*. Its subject is man as a physical being, the fifty-two-year-old professor's own frail mortal clay. Line by line, Linnaeus comments on the twelfth chapter of Ecclesiastes on the wretchedness of old age. He does so in the form of an undisciplined allegorical exegesis, which, although not original (Linnaeus had taken hints from older theological and medical literature), still makes a bizarre impression as a literary specimen from a faculty of medicine in the middle of the eighteenth century. Aging itself was disease: the sun being darkened refers to the brain, the sun of the microcosm; Solomon's quaking guardians are the old man's trembling arms and hands; the flowering almond-tree is his silver-white hair. When "the golden bowl be broken, or the pitcher be broken at the fountain, or the wheel broken at the cistern," is interpreted to mean that the lacteal vessels are constricted, the bladder cannot hold the urine, and the kidneys no longer function.

But the main text is *Nemesis Divina*. Much has been written on these unique notes, and several scholars, especially Elis Malmeström, have investigated their importance and place in the world of thought of the aging Linnaeus. They are like nothing else; in their mixture of high and low, of simple superstition and chilling fatalism, they make a savage impact. There can be no doubt that they are profoundly anachronistic. With this testimony to the glory of God and the moral order of the world, we find ourselves, both intellectually and emotionally, miles from the lucid world in which Linnaeus's scientific colleagues dwelt. Yeoman Slickert, he relates, loved the widow von Bysen and gave her a manor house. This upset his son-in-law, who fired three bullets through the window one night; they entered Slickert's stomach and led to his death. A few years later, the son-in-law began to suffer from cancer of the stomach, with three holes that grievously killed him.[134] Reasoning cannot be more simplistic; the reader feels as though he has been set back into the medieval world of miracles—but an inverted world, more somber. Three bullets, three cancerous tumors—an eye for an eye, a tooth for a tooth, "by what things a man sinneth, by these he is punished." The Lord our God is a God of retribution, implacable Destiny. Linnaeus shows this by a host of cruel instances from the canonical and apocryphal books of the Old Testament, as well as by those anecdotes from the chronicles of scandal of his own age which make *Nemesis Divina* such entertaining reading. The issue is always happiness or unhappiness; one false step, one low act, and destruction is certain—"after twenty-eight years it had not been forgotten by God." Linnaeus is filled with a sense of the numinous, of the Lord's active presence everywhere, even in trivialities. His beloved disciple Löfling stumbled when about to take leave of him before his departure for Spain; he never returned.[135] True, Linnaeus has some difficulty with those cases, honorably related, where punishment either did not follow or had not been preceded by any obvious moral culpability. But they never make him doubt the principle. Linnaeus fills in what is lacking. He relates an episode about the great Marlborough and the fall of the Tory party: "some sin had been committed before, unknown to me."[136] Or the terrible story of Baron Yxkull, who broke into and plundered the coffin of his ancestor in the Cathedral of Uppsala. The Baron was apparently going on prosperously at the time the note was written, but Linnaeus wags an admonitory finger: posterity will see the consequences; "guess what will happen."[137]

These last examples are instructive. In his own opinion, Linnaeus was certainly conducting scientific research according to all the rules, even in his speculation concerning Nemesis. He had found a general law of human life, an unshakable balance, which expressed the moral side of the same divine order that he encountered in living nature. In principle he had reached it empirically, or could at least claim so. He had made a motley collection of personal histories from which he drew his conclusions; the reader could keep a check on him. Linnaeus heaps up the evidence; he finds

---

134. *Nemesis Divina*, ed. K. Hagberg, 85.
135. Ibid., 107.
136. Ibid., 45 f.
137. Ibid., 95.

it everywhere—even Governor Råfelt, who drank and whose nose turned a reddish blue, was an example of the laws of retribution. Linnaeus manages to twist the most insignificant chance occurrences into proofs of Nemesis; he makes too much of his examples and supplements when necessary. There is something wrong with his method, just as in the case of the fury of hell, or the causes of ague. Linnaeus is imprisoned in his pattern; reality must—once again—adjust itself to the scheme.

Linnaeus's speculations about Nemesis do not make him any less strange to our eyes. Even in his scientific works, among which *Nemesis* must be included, he was extremely personal, and we recognize him in every line. But it is impossible to reduce him to a simple formula; his life's work is characterized by profound complexity. To link up again with Göran Wahlenberg, it is as though Linnaeus as a scientist had two "main sides," as though he were a man with two faces. The one was full of life, with an ample wig above a silk ruff and the Order of the North Star—that is the Linnaeus familiar to us, the cheerful observer, at home in the society of the Swedish Age of Liberty, where he preached the improvement of agriculture and the usefulness of dye plants. The other was more rigid and inaccessible; we glimpse an old-fashioned costume, almost a clergyman's gown. This Linnaeus is a complete stranger to us, a preacher and a scholastic, caught up in dogmas and prejudices.

Linnaeus the Man

But the portrait is not complete—the intimate, human traits remain. Here, too, it is tempting to discern the same duality, to provide two interpretations. During his later years, Linnaeus brooded intensively on happiness and unhappiness in the life of man, those two powers that had governed his own life. Happiness had had the upper hand in the fabulous years of his youth, when he made his way to eminence and glory; then came the hard years, when he discovered that all this was not really worth having. Linnaeus began to lose his footing in life; he became an increasingly isolated human being—this is true even at a more superficial level, in his everyday Swedish milieu. The sources speak plainly on this point, but research has until now hardly been willing to heed them; the romantic Linnaeus legend has barred the way to their acceptance.

Of course, Linnaeus was admired and celebrated as long as he lived, both at home and abroad. He was one of the great men, and innumerable were the tokens of esteem he received. There was hardly a learned society in Europe of which Linnaeus was not a member; kings and princesses paid their respects to him; from England, the eccentric Lord Baltimore sent a gold casket worth a hundred ducats to the admired master. The foreign disciples who sought their way to his rostrum filled him with joyful self-esteem. His Swedish contemporaries were not sparing in their acclamations. Linnaeus was our greatest name in science, our pride and honor; with him Swedish science for the first time attained a worldwide reputation; no one was indifferent to this. Patrons like Hårleman and Tessin supported and encouraged him; the Academy of Sciences in Stockholm never neglected to gladden its most illustrious member with tokens of reverence, and Gustavus III proclaimed his reputation from the throne. Gratefully, Linnaeus noted all this; he needed the homage and enjoyed it. Surely it was not just a tribute to his scientific greatness. That Linnaeus in moments of joy and relaxation radiated a rather devastating charm seems indisputable. Even the fastidious queen, Lovisa Ulrika, was susceptible to it; and the incomparable success of the young Linnaeus during the years in Holland must probably be ascribed to a large extent to his personal attractiveness, his capacity for captivating grizzled authorities and winning them to his purposes. The Linnaeus we meet in his letters and private effusions, especially in the many letters to his friend Abraham Bäck, was the natural Linnaeus of real life—or at least as he could be. In his sunny mood we find Linnaeus irresistible, and it is a reasonable assumption that his friends and acquaintances found him so also. All that was extrovert in him—all that was eyes and ears, the spontaneous eagerness, the drastic sense of humor, the unaffected manners—cannot have failed to produce their effect. Linnaeus found a response and gratitude, even in later years; there was warmth and harmony in his life.

This is true not least of his relations with his disciples. As an academic teacher Linnaeus was incomparable; the traditional view of him here requires no correction. When he lectured, the students thronged to the auditorium at the Gustavianum; he induced large crowds to make their disputations. The young adepts basked in his glory; he loved them and they him. Linnaeus's warmest affection was surely always reserved for his itinerant apostles in foreign countries: Kalm and Hasselquist, Löfling, Forsskål, and others. He struggled and fought for them, found scholarships for them, admonished and gave instructions. He worried with them and mourned bitterly when they passed away; if they returned heaped with treasures he could hardly contain himself for joy. "Take fire-brands and throw them after Professor Kalm, that he may come without delay to Uppsala, for I long for him like a bride for one o'clock at night."[138] Linnaeus's generosity toward his disciples found spontaneous expression. He praised them lavishly, called them his "mates"; his easily aroused enthusi-

138. Linnaeus to Bäck 28 May 1751, *Bref och Skrifvelser* I:4, 149.

asm warmed them and spurred them on. The smallest find of each of them was an "immortal discovery"; he proclaimed them geniuses time and again. The occasionally revived discussion about who was Linnaeus's favorite disciple seems in this perspective fairly pointless. In the exhilaration of the moment he might designate one or the other: Löfling was his best disciple, Hasselquist would "go higher in name" than any other, Solander was the "wittiest" man he had ever had, Fagraeus had the keenest mind of all the medical students of his time.

Such behavior was obviously naive, but disarming. Linnaeus had adopted the maxim "my children are beautiful children." Outsiders perhaps did not always recognize the merits he praised in his disciples. There is a story about the above-mentioned Jonas Theodor Fagraeus, who, enthusiastically commended by Linnaeus, applied for a professorship at the Imperial Academy of Sciences at St. Petersburg; he submitted a specimen of his work, the meagerness of which appalled the learned gentlemen of the Academy.[139] Linnaeus looked after his own; he was like a father among his children, and never does he appear so attractively human as in the middle of his flock of students, during the excursions around Uppsala, or surrounded by more proficient pupils out at Hammarby on a beautiful summer's day.

But there was another side to the matter. Linnaeus was delighted that one of his disciples wished to be "a confessor and apostle of the faith."[140] The words had a jesting ring, but were sincerely meant. Linnaeus among his disciples was also a dictator among his subjects, the ruler of slaves. Woe betide the young Linnaean who did not swear by the writings of the master, who was not orthodox; the adepts must be drilled in the true botanical faith. They were apostles in the most literal sense, and Linnaeus expected them to spread the light from Uppsala out over the world. During their journeys on the Continent for purposes of study they proclaimed the greatness of the master and disputed with his opponents; a true Uppsalian arriving in Paris was likely to fling a Linnaean anathema at Buffon, Adanson, and other heretics. And here we approach the more dubious traits in Linnaeus's character. Outside the admiring circle of his disciples another Linnaeus was known, not as a fatherly friend, but as an easily wounded and egocentric celebrity who could not bear to be contradicted. The prevailing image of Linnaeus as highly esteemed and loved, as the Prince of Flowers held in affection by all, has little foundation in reality; his contemporaries, or a large number of them, saw him with different eyes.

The character traits that offended and disturbed appear plainly to view. Linnaeus was an ingenuously candid man—he could not "dissemble and

139. Cf. Lindroth, *Vetenskapsakademiens historia* I, 201.
140. Linnaeus to Bäck 13 Mar. 1752, *Bref och Skrifvelser* I:4, 174.

play the hypocrite," he himself said—and he has exposed himself, not least in the autobiographies, with a frankness that makes him almost physically present. First and foremost there is his inordinate self-esteem. This was, it might be said, a necessary prerequisite for the enormous lifework he carried out. Even as a young student Linnaeus felt a power within himself; he was born with a sense of mission. In his early twenties he found it quite natural that the botanists of the world obeyed him; his little *Fundamenta Botanica* would live "in the palace of the princes of botany."[141] Certainly he could be spontaneously gay and disarming in such connections, even late in life. By Jove, he would let people know; "the foreigners will be stunned by it."[142] Linnaeus strove body and soul for the honor, the triumph of being foremost among botanists. His ambition, one of his foreign disciples stated, "was boundless."[143] In one way, too, this ambition was anachronistic, being reminiscent of the humanists of the Renaissance and their passionate cult of an immortal name as a certain hallmark of greatness. Linnaeus himself has, in a rather unexpected context, developed the theme. This is in *Critica Botanica*, the work on botanical nomenclature written in his youth. Why should only heroes and kings win immortality? Did not justice demand that botanists should enjoy the same honor? Who wanted to work without reward? Therefore, the naming of plants after celebrated botanists was a laudable enterprise; their names would live as long as the world remained verdant. They, too, Linnaeus stresses, were heroes in the real sense of the word. Dangers and hardships were their lot; he reminds the reader of his own adventures during the journey to Lapland, and of the Dane Simon Paulli, who broke his leg while gathering plants among the rocks![144]

As the years went by, Linnaeus discovered full well that all such things— glory, honor, titles—were sheer vanity, but for his own part he never could abstain from them. In his old age he enumerated all his distinctions, noted them down one by one, and saw his own glory reflected in them. Up to a point this may, of course, be considered the amiable foible of a great man; yet there is something insecure in Linnaeus's self-esteem. It continually required fresh nourishment. To witness him appearing publicly on his own behalf, praising his scientific eminence, is unpleasant, sometimes frightening. An instance of this is the hastily concocted pamphlet *Orbis Eruditi Judicium*, in which Linnaeus attempted to strengthen his position in the face of the competition for the professorship in 1741. Such works were not unknown during the boastful Swedish seventeenth century, as Linnaeus surely knew. The genre had the advantage that the writer did not himself

141. Preface to the planned *Fundamenta Botanica*, ed. E. Ährling, I. 95.
142. *Bref och Skrifvelser* I:2, 161.
143. Said by Fabricius; cf. E. Malmeström, "Linnés sjävkänsla," *SLÅ* (1927), 90.
144. *Critica Botanica*, 81 ff.

have to provide the encomia. Linnaeus reproduced the sincerely meant praise which he had received in reviews and intimate letters from foreign scientists, Boerhaave, von Haller, and others—he was *botanicorum princeps*, prince of the botanists, a new Charles XII subjugating the botanical world. When Linnaeus wrote the history of botany, or dictated it to his disciples, the goal was glorification of himself. He dedicated two dissertations to the subject. With the *Systema Naturae* began a new epoch in botany, "the era of reformation"; consequently, the dissertation *Reformatio Botanices*, although formally in the name of the respondent, is through and through a monument to Linnaeus himself.[145] And there are his reviews of his own works in Salvius's *Lärda Tidningar.* Such self-reviews were not considered unseemly at the time, but surely no one but Linnaeus would have taken it upon himself to speak of his own "masterpieces" and to congratulate himself.[146]

The peak of Linnaeus's glorification of his own contributions was reached in his autobiographical notes. These were to provide material for his biographers and were, therefore, intended for the public in the final instance. A certain egocentricity was inherent in the genre; but even so, Linnaeus's effusions come as a shock; one almost hesitates to take him at his word. Some of these passages have been briefly glimpsed above. Enraptured and enthusiastic, Linnaeus evaluated his published works. They are without blemish or defect. The prefaces to *Systema Naturae* cannot be sufficiently read and admired; for anyone else the *Hortus Cliffortianus* would have required ten years of labor; merely to review *Philosophia Botanica* would demand a separate book; *Fauna Svecica* was a masterpiece "which did not yield place to any of his other books."[147] It may possibly be held that Linnaeus was correct in his facts—he had reason to be contented when he looked back on his life; but it is certain that such self-glorification has not many counterparts in the history of science. One single parallel offers itself, and that is the great medical mystic and revolutionary of the Renaissance, Paracelsus. He was the king of medicine—behind me, behind me, he exclaimed, behind me you of Paris, you of Montpellier, you of Cologne, you of Vienna; Galen and Avicenna were not worthy to tie his shoelaces. We know that Linnaeus could be wrought to the same pitch of exaltation. This occurs in that curious passage in the longest autobiography, already referred to, where he sums up his triumphs on earth.[148] "No one ... no one ... no one ...": no one had been a greater botanist or

---

145. *Incrementa Botanices* (1753), in *Amoen.* 3, 387 ff.; *Reformatio Botanices* (1762), in *Amoen.* 6, 305 ff.
146. Cf. Malmeström, "Linnés självkänsla," 88.
147. *Vita*, 135 ff.
148. *Vita*, 145 ff.

zoologist, no one had written a larger number of works, no one had become more renowned throughout the world. In cadences recalling the Old Testament, Linnaeus invokes the Lord God, who has let him shoot up and grow to such glory, kept his house from fire, exterminated his enemies, and given him "titles of honor, star, shield, name in the learned world." We may be moved by this outburst. It is magnificent, but at the same time desolate. By such means Linnaeus sought in his darker moments to muffle the clamor of his anguish and disgust.

He wanted to be the one and only. His was the kingdom. What Linnaeus had to offer the world was not a collection of scientific discoveries, but rather a doctrine of salvation to which all must submit. Its contents were the sexual system and the dogmas of the *Philosophia Botanica*. Linnaeus appears in this connection as the founder of a religion, a Church Militant with devotees, martyrs, and apostles. There was, as we have seen, one "true" doctrine in botany, and one heretical. From his study in Uppsala Linnaeus followed the spread of the true doctrine over Europe. Letters and reports poured in. It would probably be easy enough, wrote Löfling, one of his disciples, from Spain, "to bring in a new religion here on your principles."[149] Sudden, well-nigh miraculous conversions occurred. Manetti the Italian, says Linnaeus, "who has written against Linnaeus, repents it"; the true light had appeared to a sinner.[150]

But it needed only the slightest touch for Linnaeus to be wounded in his self-esteem. No one had a more sensitive disposition. An unexpected consignment of plants from Surinam and he shouted for joy; an unfriendly glance from an important patron and he could not sleep "for weeks." As soon as he met with opposition he gave up and complained bitterly; he would sulk like a child. He had labored and toiled more than anyone else, but hate and envy were his reward. Linnaeus threatened to write not a single line more, he would lay down his pen forever—"I will sail into port," he wrote Bäck, "and no one shall ever hear a word from me."[151] Such things were passing moods, but they were painful enough and could be aroused by the most trifling causes. Linnaeus suspected enemy plots. When a prohibition was issued against printing Swedish books abroad, he believed that it was directed only against himself; when Merckell the printer advertised a popular history of animals, he was convinced that it was a piece of plagiarism based on his lectures.[152] From earlier years there is the curious story, often commented on, about his colleague Nils Rosén, against whom Linnaeus in his autobiography directs violent accusations. Its factual basis will

149. S. Rydén, *Pehr Löfling* (Stockholm, 1965), 93.
150. *Vita*, 126.
151. Linnaeus to Bäck, 1749, *Bref och Skrifvelser* I:4, 106.
152. Cf. Lindroth, *Vetenskapsakademiens historia* I, 573.

probably never be accessible; we have only Linnaeus's impassioned testimony; what he relates is, in any case, incompatible with everything we know about Rosén's character.

Linnaeus reacted in the same way—egocentrically and suspiciously—in larger connections, on the stage of Europe. Those who did not accept him persecuted him; it is as though he could not imagine any but unworthy motives. Linnaeus concludes the preamble to the botanical *magnum opus* of his life, *Species Plantarum*, with an address to his enemies. He had, he assures them, never taken any notice of them, never returned their arrows. Patiently he had borne their "impudent revilements, accusations, jesting, fanfares of war"; such things had been the lot of great men throughout the ages. It was a matter of indifference to him whether his antagonists were applauded by the great mob; such things did not touch him; it was sufficient consolation that he had been lauded by the greatest botanists of his time.[153] Linnaeus lived, it might be conceded, according to this program. As is well known, he had taken a sacred vow never to answer his foreign adversaries, and he kept it. While they raged, he put his faith in the justice of his cause; he was magnanimous, and he did not take revenge. But the happiness of a pure conscience was not vouchsafed him. In the New Year of 1751, in his famous letter of complaint to Abraham Bäck, he summed up his own situation. Others lived happy, they did their duty and let the world take its course, loved by all; he himself had for all his toil received only sorrow and shame; in the future he wanted to do as little as possible, eat, sleep, and be happy.[154]

Linnaeus, who liked maxims, had an adage for such moods too. It was a standard Epicurean phrase that he had learned from his beloved Roman authors. Best to live innocently and out of sight, *qui bene latuit, bene vixit*— "who lives hidden, lives well." The world should not be challenged with pretentious airs, nor the mighty, nor God. Bow down, and the storm will not reach you! Thus, Linnaeus could in moments of weariness and resignation reject all he had otherwise striven for. He swung between violent self-assertion and brooding despair; he had the temperament of a hysteric, a need to dramatize himself and all that happened to him. When, in the autobiographies, he looked back upon his life, it became a series of resplendent triumphs, dangers, and ambushes. In vivid colors he depicted the poverty of his youth and the tribulations of his journey to Lapland; time after time he was in mortal danger; a slab of rock came close to crushing him; in Norway a Lapp shot at him. As a prince in disguise, he had in his youth unveiled his glory to grizzled scholars—Stobaeus, Olof Celsius,

---

153. *Species Plantarum* I (1753), Lectori.
154. Linnaeus to Bäck 2 Jan. 1751, *Bref och Skrifvelser* I:4, 133.

Boerhaave, Dillenius. His life had been a gamble for happiness and unhappiness; sensitive as the needle on a compass, he registered the signs.

All this made him difficult in human society. Linnaeus had to be treated with the utmost caution; everybody in Sweden knew that. It was a notorious fact that it was not permissible to criticize what he had written. A well-known parson in Lapland, Pehr Högström, had several critical remarks to make on Linnaeus's Lapland discoveries, but stated them only in letters to Wargentin; in print, he felt, such things could not be said.[155] The story about Torbern Bergman is illuminating. In 1763, Linnaeus had taken part in a competition announced by the Academy of Sciences concerning worms on fruit trees. All seemed cut and dried; Linnaeus appeared using a transparent pseudonym (C. N. Nelin, i.e., an anagram for C. N. [ilsson] Linné). The gentlemen of the Academy had only to pick out his answer and give it the award. But the gold medal went to someone else, the young genius Torbern Bergman; wounded to the core, the world-famous professor revealed his identity by losing his temper with the young assistant professor.[156] It was not permissible to compete with Linnaeus. Another person to experience this was his former disciple Peter Jonas Bergius, a professor and well-established doctor in Stockholm. He was the only one of the Linnaeans to break away from the paternal home, to the indignation of the master. Even Bergius's appointment as Professor of Natural History made Linnaeus complain bitterly. He reacted in a typical manner: one sky, he wrote to Bäck, "cannot contain two suns"; he now wanted to withdraw into some quiet nook. At that time relations between them had been chilly for several years. Bergius devoted himself more and more purposefully to botany, writing about the flora of the Cape Colony, and in Linnaeus's view, he seized plant collections that ought really to have gone to Uppsala.[157]

Linnaeus, for his part, could never understand that others were repelled by his impetuosity. He was equally surprised each time he discovered that he was not loved. The *Linnaea*—wrote Linnaeus in *Critica Botanica* about the flower that bore his name—is "a plant in Lapland, low, insignificant, forgotten, flowering for a short time; it is named after Linnaeus, who resembles it."[158] Surely none of his contemporaries would have been prepared to endorse these lines. This is true not least of his professorial colleagues at Uppsala. Naturally, pure academic envy played its part; they saw with mixed feelings how Linnaeus filled his lecture hall to bursting-point ("no one has had more auditors at our Academy"). Sometimes, when Linnaeus's behavior became too provocative, the irritation found free vent.

155. Pehr Högström to P. W. Wargentin, ms. in the Academy of Sciences, Stockholm.
156. Cf. Lindroth, *Vetenskapsakademiens historia* I, 574.
157. Ibid., 604.
158. *Critica Botanica*, 80.

In the summer of 1748, Linnaeus received a letter from his influential friend and patron Carl Hårleman. We know that it agitated him violently—it "almost killed" him; for two months he lay sleepless. Hårleman had received complaints from Uppsala about Linnaeus's botanical excursions. They created too great a commotion; Linnaeus, Hårleman felt, ought to stop using special tunics, French horns, and such gaudiness. Botany did not need to be supported with "so much ostentation and such clamor"; suppose Klingenstierna or Strömer followed his example and put uniform and armor on their students in order to distinguish them from the multitude.[159]

It may be superfluous to amass further evidence; everybody knew Linnaeus's quirks. We must remember that these traits belong to the picture of Linnaeus; he cannot be imagined without them. That was the way he was, a clamoring, egocentric, and unpolished genius, who was incapable of estimating the influence he had on others. His Swedish contemporaries were surprised and shocked. Here lies the core of the matter; Linnaeus's personal position in the learned and bourgeois Sweden of the Age of Freedom was different than what has commonly been supposed. There is a statement by Pehr Wilhelm Wargentin which illuminates the matter with a flash of insight. Everybody values Linnaeus, he wrote, "but hardly anyone loves him, not even here."[160] This frank verdict was expressed in a letter to Albrecht von Haller, who was Linnaeus's enemy; Wargentin knew that it would be well received. But its truth is indisputable. Wargentin, the secretary of the Academy of Sciences, knew better than anyone the moods and opinions in Swedish learned circles; he was integrity itself and probably stood closer to Linnaeus personally than did anyone else with the exception of Abraham Bäck. Other knowledgeable persons had an equally undistorted view of Linnaeus. He was, thought Charles De Geer the entomologist, "blinded by his own opinions" and seldom liked what others wrote.[161]

A few went further, among them Torbern Bergman, who, with Linnaeus, was the most brilliant Swedish scientist of the century. The episode over the prize competition of the Academy of Sciences made a profound impression on him; after that he despised Linnaeus and in intimate letters told of his shameless plottings. Lecturing on Cronstedt's mineralogy and having a large audience, sighed Bergman, was *lèse majesté* in Uppsala.[162]

---

159. Carl Hårleman to Linnaeus 28 July 1748, *Bref och Skrifvelser* I:7, 138. Cf. R. Sernander, "Hårleman och Linnaei Herbationes Upsalienses," *SLÅ* (1926), 78 ff.
160. Wargentin to Albrecht von Haller 13 Nov. 1764, in N. V. E. Nordenmark, *Pehr Wilhelm Wargentin* (Stockholm, 1939), 64.
161. Lindroth, *Vetenskapsakademiens historia* I, 575.
162. Torbern Bergman to Bengt Bergius 21 Apr. 1769, Bergianska brevsamlingen in The Academy of Sciences Library.

With certain reservations, it is possible to discern an anti-Linnaean group during Linnaeus's later years, with its center in the Academy. The above-mentioned Peter Jonas Bergius belonged to it; even earlier he had in Linnaeus's opinion distinguished himself by going about "everywhere disparaging" his master.[163] In the autumn of 1777, at some time before his father's decease, the junior Linnaeus gave a glimpse of the situation in a letter to Abraham Bäck. Bergius and Torbern Bergman are here depicted as the detractors of the name of Linnaeus, doing everything to belittle his father's reputation.[164]

Linnaeus could always console himself with his ever-increasing international fame. But this was not enough. The situation was strange. At home, in his native country, Linnaeus was not really loved; he was too close to hand. As long as he moved in the environment he himself had created, among disciples and cabinets of naturalia, he was happy and at peace; there everything complied with his will. But the world outside became more inhospitable as the years went by, and Linnaeus's loneliness increased. Bäck and Wargentin, he said, were his only loyal friends in the world; they had never failed him.[165] Others did not care for him; he was surrounded by enemies. Thus did Linnaeus regard his position in dark moments; he was tormented by his isolation and became bitter. His desolate philosophy of life, the cries of vanity and Nemesis surely had their real root here. What was the use of a great name in the world? "We go about here," he wrote in his inimitable way, "puffing like turkeys"; we are worried and tormented, but what did it amount to? Transience and vanity—aging and death were the only certain things, and a God, Who in the greatest confusion governed all according to His own inscrutable Will.[166]

Thus that weariness of life which cast its gloom over Linnaeus's later years had, as far as can be judged, a more trivial basis than is commonly imagined. This does not lessen the tragedy. His personal life was as full of contradictions and tensions as were his works. What Linnaeus was he always was to the extreme. Deep down in his being lay a violent obstinacy; he pursued his prejudices with a passionate and guileless eagerness that makes him one of the most difficult figures to deal with in European scientific history.

163. Lindroth, *Vetenskapsakademiens historia* I, 605.
164. Linnaeus junior to Bäck in 1777, *SLÅ* (1956/57), 141.
165. Linnaeus to Wargentin 1 Jan. 1769, *Bref och Skrifvelser* I:2, 312.
166. Linnaeus to Bäck 3 Mar. 1767, ibid., I:5, 149 f.

Portrait of Linnaeus as a young man. This is the "bridegroom" portrait painted by J. H. Scheffel in 1739. The portrait is kept at Hammarby, Linnaeus's summer house outside Uppsala. (Courtesy of Hunt Institute, Carnegie-Mellon University, Pittsburgh, PA)

Portrait of Linnaeus, three years before his death, painted by Alexander Roslin in 1775 (courtesy of the Royal Academy of Sciences, Stockholm).

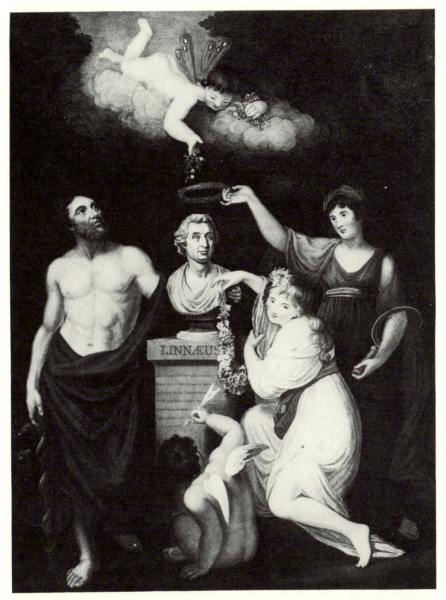

A romanticized view of Linnaeus: Aesculapius, Flora, Ceres, and Cupid paying honor to the bust of Linnaeus. From R. J. Thornton, *Temple of Flora*, Volume II, 1807. (See p. 2.)

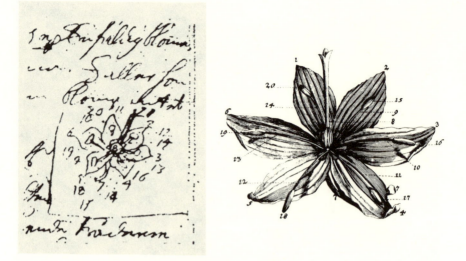

Linnaeus's early drawing of a flower, showing the influence of
C. B. Valentini's *Tournefortius Contractus*. (See p. 63.)

Hortus Upsaliensis, the botanical garden at the University of Uppsala, where Linnaeus
worked and taught. He and his family lived in the professor's residence, the house at
the right. The garden is still arranged according to Linnaeus's plan. From Linnaeus's
dissertation, *Hortus Upsaliensis*, 1745. (See p. 55.)

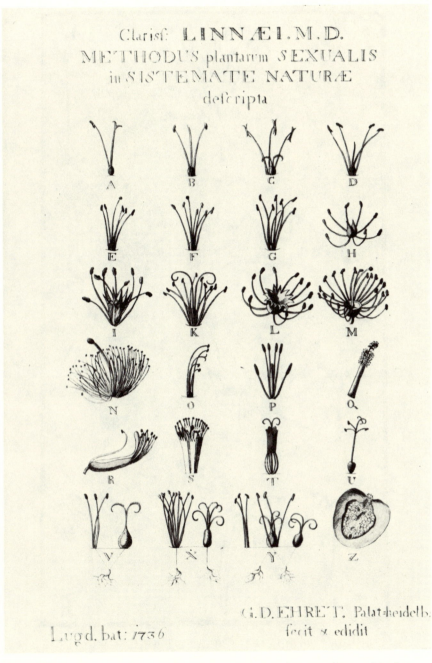

Georg D. Ehret's famous illustration of Linnaeus's sexual system, first used in the Leiden, 1736 edition of *Species Plantarum* and used in a different form, in the first and second editions of *Genera Plantarum*. (See p. 76.)

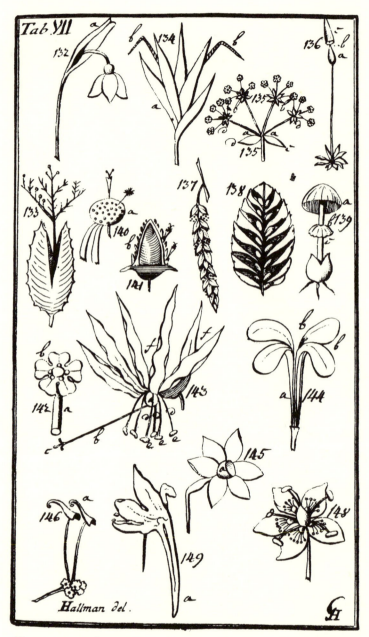

Flower types and parts. From *Philosophia botanica*, 1751. (See p. 82.)

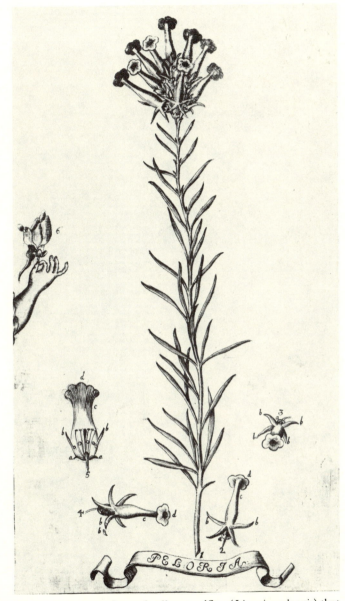

Peloria, the strange form of yellow toadflax (*Linaria vulgaris*) that inspired Linnaeus's speculations about the role of hybrids in species formation. From his dissertation, *De peloria*, 1744. (See p. 94.)

Adam in Paradise before the Fall, from J. J. Scheuchzer's magnificent illustrated Bible, *Kupfer-Bibel* (1731), a work Linnaeus knew well. (See p. 111.)

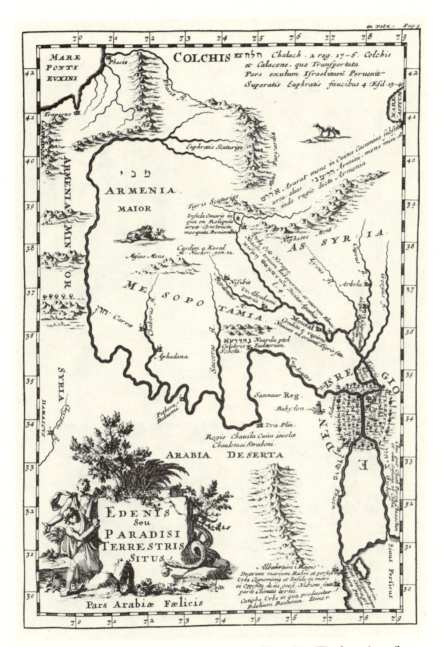

One of the many maps showing the geography of Paradise. The four rivers flow into *paradisus terrestris*, where the tiny figures of Adam and Eve are shown rejoicing. The Garden of Eden is depicted as an island (*Eden Insula*) immediately north of Paradise. Linnaeus also thought Eden was an island, but placed it in the southern hemisphere. From Samuel Bochart, *Geographia Sacra*, third edition, Leiden, 1692. (See p. 115.)

Linnaeus and Artedi both accepted the authenticity of this mermaid, which was reported to have been found near Brazil. The illustration, from Thomas Bartholin's *Historiarum anatomicarum centuria secunda* (1664), shows the bones of the rib and "hand" of the *sirene* as well as the mermaid swimming. (See p. 178.)

The original for Linnaeus's illustration of the troglodyte, here called "ourang-outang." From Jacob Bondt, *Historia Naturalis Indiae Orientalis*, 1658. (See p. 191.)

The *Anthropomorpha* in the dissertation by Linnaeus of the same title. From left to right (and from more human-like to less): the troglodyte, the tailed man, the satyr, and the pygmy. From Linnaeus-Hoppius, *Anthropomorpha*, 1760; also in his *Amoenitates academicae*, volume 6. (See p. 183.)

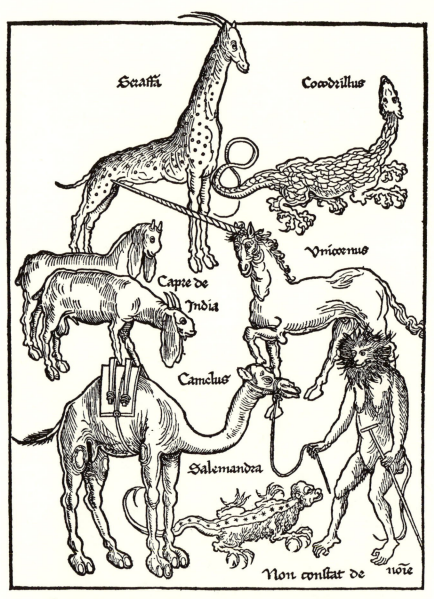

In the lower right corner of this woodcut of "animals . . . depicted truly as we saw them in the Holy Land," Bernhard von Breydenbach shows the original of Linnaeus's tailed man, an animal whose name Bernhard says he does not know. From Hugh W. Davies, *Bernhard von Breydenbach and His Journey to the Holy Land, 1483–4*, 1911, plate 42. (See p. 191.)

GUNNAR ERIKSSON

Linnaeus the Botanist

Just as Linnaeus was about to leave the Gymnasium, his botanical horizons were decisively and, it appears, suddenly broadened. He himself has spoken of the private tutorial he received from Johan Rothman, the lecturer in physics. This tutorial consisted for the most part of an exposition of the physiological theories of Boerhaave: "Finally Doctor Rothman showed the youth that all his work in botany would be nothing, unless he could tell the plants by their flowers, as one Tournefort had taught, whereupon Carl had to copy *Classes plantarum* from Valentini's *Historia Plantarum*, as the young man's only idea was to learn to place every single plant in its class according to the system of Tournefort."[1] Carl had suddenly been brought face to face with modern systematics. Whereas he had previously devoted all his attention to the individual plants and their names and virtues, he now became conscious of the relationship between them and their groups and classes. He discovered that an awareness of this grouping enhanced his knowledge of the individual plant, for anyone who wishes to examine an unknown plant first establishes the major order to which it belongs, and then notes the increasingly detailed specific features.

Linnaeus's extant manuscripts happen to include a sheet of notes made under Rothman's guidance.[2] They make fascinating reading, and deal with an extremely important stage in the development of Linnaeus as a botanist—possibly more important than Linnaeus himself later realized. Here

1. E. Malmeström and A. Hj. Uggla, *Vita Caroli Linnaei* (Stockholm, 1957), 93.
2. In the Linnean Society of London collections of Linnaeus's manuscripts. First observed by S. Savage in *Proceedings of the Linnean Society* (1936), 16.

we recognize, in a childish and clumsy hand, the type figures of flowers of the various classes which Tournefort reproduced in his *Institutiones*, and which were subsequently reproduced by Christopher Valentini in his attractive little compendium, *Tournefortius Contractus*, which is undoubtedly the book which Linnaeus refers to as *Historia Plantarum*. We also see how Rothman demonstrated to Linnaeus how to examine a plant according to Tournefort's system. When one finds an unknown plant, Rothman explains, the first thing is to see if the flower bears petals or not. If there are petals, one then examines whether the flower is single or double and notes whether it is formed like a bell, or has some other shape. If the flower is bell-shaped, "then the plant belongs to the first class, that is, to those plants which bear a monopetalous, bell-shaped flower." The particular genus within the class is best determined with the aid of the fruit, its position and relationship to the pistil, and other peculiarities. The last step is "to consult botanists, both *mortales* and *divos*." The scientific revolution had not yet occurred which would allow a single work to claim that it included all known plants.

Rothman's teachings kindled a new enthusiasm in the young man's heart, of that we may be sure; this led him to procure for himself a printed outline of Tournefort's botanical classification system soon after his arrival in the university town of Lund in the autumn of 1727. The book that was available on the subject was the *Hodegus Botanicus* of Martin Daniel Johrenius, which Linnaeus acquired on September 25 of that year.[3] That Rothman had given his pupil an extremely important stimulus is beyond doubt. On the other hand, it is clear that Linnaeus would have come to know botanical taxonomy in the course of his diligent youthful studies, even without Rothman. But this was not in fact the full extent of Rothman's contribution. As has been no more than hinted at in later Linnaean literature, Rothman not only gave his pupil instruction on Tournefort as interpreted by Valentini; he also introduced him to the modern theory that flowers were the sexual organs of plants. This theory was by no means generally accepted or even very widely known. He supplied a short commentary on Sébastien Vaillant's *Sermo de Structura Florum*, which had been published on the initiative of Boerhaave in 1717, and in which the essentials of the new theory were set forth. Linnaeus makes no mention of this in any of his many autobiographical outlines, but we learn of it from the page of the notebook previously mentioned, on which Linnaeus had committed to paper Rothman's description of the Tournefortian classification system.

---

3. His own copy of *Hodegus* with the acquisition date is in Uppsala University Library.

Rothman began his short survey by demonstrating the plant and its various parts, a necessary preparation if the pupil were to grasp the way the system of Tournefort is built up. When Rothman deals with the inner parts, the stamens and the pistils, he brings together the traditional theory of their function, namely preparing nutrition and excreting waste products (a theory of which Tournefort was an adherent), and the ideas which Vaillant had taken from Camerarius. The nutritive juices, he says, go from the flower stalk into the pericarp, "that which Vaillant calls the ovary," and the nutriment eventually reaches "the surrounding filaments," in other words the stamens, the anthers of which he calls *vasa spermatica,* following Vaillant. Rothman also relates that Vaillant knows those plants which have only "*testes* and *vasa spermatica* as *mares,* those with pistils only as *feminae,* and those which have all these parts as hermaphrodites." What gave Rothman the idea of inserting all this information from Vaillant at this point is not known. In the work upon which we assume him to have based most of his instruction, the *Tournefortius Contractus* of Valentini mentioned above, the author's father, Michael Bernhard Valentini, includes in his preface some explanatory remarks on the subject of a figure—also found in Linnaeus's notes—which depicts a flower with its parts numbered. However, he speaks only of the passage of the nutritive juices and says nothing of the sexual theory, despite the fact that he had probably been closer to Camerarius than any other writer on botany. Be that as it may, we must attach tremendous importance to Rothman's synopsis. Just as Linnaeus was acquiring his first knowledge of modern systematic botany, the basic outline of the sexual theory was revealed to him at the same time, and from the same source. Even if Linnaeus did not remember exactly what Rothman had taught him, we may suppose that henceforth there would always be for him a subconscious link between the two matters—classification and the sexuality of plants.

The road that led Linnaeus to his first major achievements in the reform of botany may also be discerned from other documents. From the very start of his student days in Lund from 1727, in Uppsala from 1728 on, he appears to have set about the task of widening his reading in botany with an almost superhuman enthusiasm. Abstracts, commentaries, and shorter paragraphs, together with tabular arrangements of plant classification systems then in use, fill several thick volumes of those of his papers which have survived, and even so we must assume that a certain amount of evidence of his industry has been lost over a period of more than two centuries. The examination of this mass of manuscripts, which naturally also sheds light on the progress of his studies in medicine and other branches of natural history, and the dating and marshalling of the papers in relation to his later scientific output, are among the most pressing and immediate tasks of

Linnaean research. Here it is not possible to do more than make a few forays into the piles of material not yet dealt with, linking the results of these with what we otherwise know of his development as a botanist.

Linnaeus's conviction of the *sexual function* of the stamens and pistils was first clearly and definitively expressed in the neat little manuscript *Praeludia Sponsaliorum Plantarum*, which he presented to his patron, Olof Celsius, on New Year's Day, 1730. But this does not mean that the idea of a *classification system* based on the sexuality of plants was a matter of course. In fact, it is possible to observe the way in which the young Linnaeus, in spite of Rothman's teaching, long kept the question of the sexuality of plants and that of their classification clearly distinct. Only when they again converged was his first major scientific achievement, the sexual system, a reality. Admittedly, Rothman had drawn a connection between the two matters, but Linnaeus seems not to have searched consciously for a key. In order to gain a clear picture of his development into an independent system-atist, we must, therefore, begin by looking at how he acquired his insight into the sexuality of plants, and then follow the way in which this inspired his studies of classification.

Not only Rothman, but also Professor Kilian Stobaeus at Lund University, a good naturalist, guided Linnaeus's thoughts on the question of the sexual relationships of plants, albeit less directly. Among his early notes at Lund, Linnaeus has jotted some almost aphoristic sentences, the origin of which he himself ascribes to Stobaeus: "Sequuntur nonnulla D[omin]i Stobaei verba."[4] Among other pronouncements, one notices a number of propositions in which Stobaeus compares plants and animals. He points out that the two groups of organisms resemble each other in many respects and that plant life is really not unlike animal life: the life of plants has an end, as does that of animals—trees grow old and finally cease to bear fruit. Like animals, they also have diseases—cancer, for example. And by way of illustration, Stobaeus mentions a blight which had spread among trees in Germany a few years earlier and which "worked more harm than ever the axe did." Our source does not state that Stobaeus compared the sexuality of animals and trees (the term *steriles* in respect to old trees cannot be inter-preted so narrowly), but these reflections may have led Linnaeus's thoughts in this direction. Excellent support for such a theory is lent by the fact that Linnaeus uses the ideas of Stobaeus—without mentioning their origi-nator—in *Praeludia*, where he draws a parallel between the lives of plants and of animals and includes almost verbatim the notes which he made on Stobaeus's lectures.[5]

There are two published works which may conceivably have had a deci-

4. Linn. Soc. London: "Linnaeus, Manuscripta medica, III."
5. The great similarity between the notes from Rothman's lectures and the text of *Praeludia* (published by K. Svenska Vetenskapsakademien in *Linné, Skrifter 4*, Stockholm,

sive influence on Linnaeus when he embraced the sexual theory. He refers in *Praeludia* to two authors: Vaillant and Morilandus. He himself states—what is contrary to the facts that we possess—that he became acquainted with Vaillant from a commentary in *Acta Eruditorum*, which he read in the autumn of 1729, and which he considered vital to his new system. By Morilandus, Linnaeus means Samuel Morland, who had a work reviewed in the 1705 edition of *Acta Eruditorum* (Linnaeus quotes both title and page). This work was an essay entitled "Some New Observations upon the Parts and Use of the Flower in Plants," and was published in *Philosophical Transactions* in the same year. If these actually were the only authorities upon whom Linnaeus based his position, then his first work on the flower bears witness to highly developed and original powers of observation. Morland, adducing Grew, takes sexuality for granted and discusses the more particular question of whether it is the pollen itself or some vapor or exhalation emanating from it which is the actual fertilizing agent. He concludes that the former is the case, whereas Vaillant takes the opposite view. Morland does not, therefore, expend any energy on proving that stamens and pistils are sexual organs, which for Linnaeus is the fundamental question. Nor does Vaillant produce all the reasons which Linnaeus later puts forward. Indeed, he learned more, perhaps, paradoxical though it may seem, from a quite different direction, for before he brought out *Praeludia* he studied the arguments against Vaillant that were expounded by the very capable opponent of the sexual theory, the Italian Julius Pontedera. In his voluminous work *Anthologia sive de Floris Natura*, which appeared in 1720, Pontedera had given a detailed summary of contemporary knowledge and of his own observations of the flowers of plants and their various organs and functions. He consistently opposed the sexual theory, but his exhaustive discussion and excellent illustrations could have

---

1907) may be seen by comparing the following sentences:

"Manuscripta medica, III":

Vita vegetabilis är så rigtigt som animalis, har determinatum vitae tempus, gambla träd giör mindre nytta, alt för gamle steriles. Fiat apoplectio.

Hafva morbos analogos morbis nostri corporis, ut cancer. Ett åhr gik en päst på träden i Tyskland, som mehr skadat än någonsin öxan.

Praeludia:

Af desse och otalige flera skiähl kunne de lättel. sluta att dett vita vegetabilis war nästen så ricktigt som animalis, och fast än de icke hafwa någon kiäntsla kan därför ingen neka dem lif. Ho will näka en Apoplectio lif, fast han mist alla sensus.

... huru de hade sina vissa Siukdomar icke annors än wij, såsom Cancrum, Perniones, Lumbricos, Acaros, Tabem, Pestem, etc. I Tyskland gick för en tijd sedan en Pest på träden, som giorde större skada på skogarne, än någonsin yxan hafwer giort.

had an effect on many readers quite opposite to that intended, convincing them rather that the functions of the stamens and pistils were most likely to be of a sexual nature. Linnaeus answers Pontedera in *Praeludia*. Only one case is involved: the Italian's observation that a female mulberry tree *(Morus Foemina)* had borne fruit although there were no male trees within a distance of three hundred miles. Linnaeus easily finds a flaw in the reasoning. Pontedera has not shown that these mulberries contained germinative, viable seeds. A good deal of Pontedera's argument collapses on similar grounds, and his work then becomes no more than an unusually clear and detailed statement of the fascinating problem, useful even to those who oppose his opinions.

The inspiration which he derived from his mentors and from the literature does not detract from the part played by Linnaeus's own observations of nature in his acceptance and utilization of the sexual theory. One imagines that his studies of diclinous plants must have been of particular importance in this connection. It was generally known that there was a kind of flower that did not bear fruit, but merely withered after releasing an abundance of pollen. The phenomenon was described in the literature, and Linnaeus must himself have noticed it in the Swedish countryside, where hazel, alder, birch, pine, spruce, and many common herbaceous plants have this feature. A number of notes on his own copy of Johrenius's *Hodegus Botanicus* show that his attention had been drawn to the occurrence. In the case of the hop, he quotes Ray: "Lupulus mas fructu caret, foemina flore," a comment which is based rudimentarily on sexual differences—the male flowers alone are called flowers, while the fruit is presumed to appear without any flowers at all. This is, in fact, an ancient belief, and Linnaeus seems also to have thought about the hazel on similar lines: "These reddish fringes *(cirri)* which burst forth from the buds of the hazel in February are not flowers, but the styles of the little fruit *(stili in tenella embryone)*, whereas the catkins *(juli)* are true flowers." It can be seen here that the concept of a flower is a rather evasive one; the red stigmas of the female flower are not considered worthy of the designation "flower," which is granted only to the more striking and splendid male catkins. Linnaeus does not refer to "males" or "females" at all here, and may not have thought of any difference in sex between these organs. As is shown by the quotation from Ray, the male and female organs had to appear on different individual members of the species before traditional botany could speak of a sexual difference. For them to be found on different parts of the same individual was not enough.

Other notes by Linnaeus in *Hodegus* indicate a higher degree of awareness, but, as in earlier literature, the concepts "male" and "female" continue to be used in connection with dioecious but not with monoecious plants. In *(Silene) Otites,* Linnaeus observes, flowers of two kinds are found—here both kinds are, in fact, given the name flowers—one having larger petals attached to the stamens, and the other having smaller ones attached to the pistils, which are on the embryo. Of the species of *Salix* he states quite plainly that the two kinds of flowers are called *mares* and *foeminae,* and he describes the former as per se steriles, no fruit resulting from their inflorescence. So it is perhaps possible to trace the development in Linnaeus's own reflections and observations on the subject of diclinous plants. This development has proceeded even further in some retrospective notes in his papers for 1728, and especially for 1729.[6] "In the month of May," he writes, "I observed that *Flores amentacei s stamina* on our *Pinus* [pine] have always been separate *a fructu* of the same tree. So that there have never been any cones on those which have *stamina* and vice versa." Only in one case had he later discovered an exception. And he found the two kinds of flower to be equally distinct in the case of the juniper, where bushes with stamen flowers never bore berries. "Pollen is shed from the *flores amentaceius s staminibus,*" he notes, establishing that his observations "are entirely contrary to Tournefort's institu[iones]." One sees here how Linnaeus's thinking on this biological phenomenon is becoming increasingly independent and that he is setting his own observations against those of the great authority of the period. When he wrote this, the sexual theory was not far off. It is not surprising that in *Praeludia* he attaches considerable importance to his studies of diclinous flowers.

Praeludia was quickly followed by a new and very similar manuscript, which was submitted to the Society of Science in Uppsala in the spring of 1730: *Exercitatio Botanico-Physica de Nuptiis et Sexu Plantarum.*[7] A brief look at the contents of the two tracts reveals Linnaeus's sexual theory in its first full-fledged form. In its essentials it hardly differs from the formulation which he was to give it much later, notably in the dissertation *Sponsalia Plantarum* (1746) and the prize treatise for the Petersburg Academy *Sexus Plantarum* (1760).

After his celebrated poetic opening on the loveliness of springtime and its amorous joys, Linnaeus turns his attention to the ancients and their views on the sexuality of plants. By *mares* and *feminae* among flowers, they meant plants with hard or with pliable stalks, or other anthropomorphically "masculine" and "feminine" characteristics. He includes as belonging to that tradition the recently defended Uppsala dissertation of Georg Wallin the Younger on the marriage of plants. In his "Gamos fyton" of 1729, Wallin had used what were in themselves very well balanced arguments to

6. Linn. Soc. London: "Manuscripta medica, I."
7. Edited in a dissertation by A. Afzelius, *Symbolae ad Historiam Sueciae,* I:1 (praeses E. G. Geijer, Uppsala, 1828).

refute the traditional opinions on the sexuality of plants, but he had not appreciated that what was said about the date-palm, in particular, had a much better foundation than the many examples in which the attribution of sexuality was based on superficial and external characteristics alone. Linnaeus argues his own dissenting point of view, first by indicating the analogy which in many cases exists between plants and animals: both suffer from diseases, both are dependent upon nutriment and upon the seasons, and both convey their nutriment through a system of veins and vessels. Linnaeus finds it natural to extend the analogy to their sexual circumstances. As animals procreate sexually, it is likely that plants do also. However, he ascribes this reasoning not to himself but to "the newer *Botanici*" collectively, among whom he names Vaillant as foremost.

The next step is to show that these sexual organs consist of the stamens and pistils of the flower. By considering one part of the flower after another, and excluding all those which could not possibly fulfill this function, Linnaeus arrives at his goal. He maintains that the relationship between the stamens and pistils may take one of three forms: they may be united in the same flower, as is most usually the case; they may be separated but found on the same individual plant; or they may be found on separate individuals. In detailed tables, taken in part from Tournefort, he gives examples of these arrangements. He draws a parallel between the ovaries, ova, and testicles of the animals and the organs of the plant. How fertilization takes place is, he considers, a bigger problem, on the subject of which he contents himself with a few negative observations. The pollen of the male flowers must play a less exclusive role than that envisaged by Morland and others. Morland had imagined that as far as plants were concerned, every part of the incipient plant had its genesis in the pollen and that the role of the ovules was only that of passively receiving and providing nourishment. In the terminology of the age, Morland was an animalculist. But the question of *how* fertilization happens cannot obscure the fact that it *does* happen.

Linnaeus amasses seven items of empirical evidence for his sexual theory: that there exist flowers whose long pistils bend down when they bloom to receive the pollen and then straighten up again; that rain is harmful to the setting of fruit if it falls when cereals are shedding pollen or when fruit trees are in bloom, so that the pollen is beaten to the ground instead of finding the pistils; that plants with their sexual organs located apart generally have the male flowers above the female flowers so that the pollen can easily fall onto the latter; that catkin-bearing trees bloom before the leaves come out, enabling the pollen to reach its target unimpeded; that the stamens and the styles and stigmas of the pistils come out simultaneously (the many exceptions had apparently escaped his notice) because their functions have to be coordinated; that the ancients had pointed out that in the nutmeg and in the palm the males had long been regarded as absolutely essential to the fertility of the female trees. Finally—and unusually—Linnaeus refers to an experiment, one which had previously been quoted by Camerarius: if the anthers are removed from a hermaphrodite flower, it may sometimes bear seed notwithstanding, but these seeds will not prove germinative. In a utilitarian spirit, Linnaeus rounds off his presentation with some hints on horticultural matters, pointing out the usefulness of helping to fertilize flowers by dusting the pistils with pollen.

Linnaeus later gave the autumn of 1729 as the date of his conceiving of the sexual system. In the summer of 1730 he applied the new classification for the first time in a version of *Hortus Uplandicus*, the handwritten guide to the botanical garden of Uppsala, which was produced in several editions during that and the following summer.[8] What he himself relates of the origin of the sexual system is extremely interesting, and contains, if we dare to rely on the account, much important information. After describing in an autobiographical fragment how Vaillant had finally given him an understanding of the sexuality of plants, he mentions in the same breath that his student friend Petrus Artedi "left botany" at this time, but retained the umbellate plants "because he intended to use them to devise a new method, whereupon Linnaeus also became of a mind to create a new method covering all plants."[9] Linnaeus thus appears to assign a key role to Artedi. It was Artedi who first had the idea of independently constructing a new system— admittedly one dealing only with a limited group of plants and not based on the sexual principle—and this gave Linnaeus the idea of embarking upon the same course. To what extent did one touch upon the field of the other in their discussions that autumn? How much of his inspiration did Linnaeus really draw from Artedi? We can hardly hope to find a definite answer to this question, however important it may be to throw some light upon it. At the beginning of the year (1729) Artedi had written a catalog of the plants of his home parish, Nordmaling, in which he had arranged the plants according to an adapted version of the system of Tournefort. There he had shown himself to be aware of the importance of systematics, particularly in bringing some semblance of order to the works of nature, and in making it possible to discover the names of unknown species. Being able to discuss Tournefort with this intelligent and methodically-minded friend must obviously have been very stimulating.

The new system which Artedi devised for umbellate plants is known to us, since Linnaeus published it in the first edition of *Systema Naturae* in

8. Edited by E. Åhrling, *Linné, Ungdomsskrifter* I (Stockholm, 1877), and by Th. M. Fries in *Uppsala Universitets Årsskrift* (Uppsala, 1899), Program 1.

9. *Vita Caroli Linnaei*, 98. For the influence of Artedi, cf. Lindroth's essay in this volume.

1735. The system groups the umbellifers according to the occurrence of separate involucels or common involucres. This division has not yet taken shape in the catalog of the Nordmaling plants, where the genera are generally distinguished with the aid of their various fruits. The first traces of the new classification of umbellifers appear in Linnaeus's manuscript *Hortus Uplandicus II*, dated 29 July 1730, the title page of which promises a new division of the group. This differs somewhat from that presented in *Systema Naturae*, but not more than is consistent with the fact that it must be regarded as being as much Artedi's arrangement as Linnaeus's. Thus we may indeed consider it fairly probable that Linnaeus and Artedi discussed systematics in 1729, while we *know* quite definitely that they did so in the summer of 1730. It is perhaps worthy of note that *Hortus I* from spring of the same year does not follow the Artedian division. It is also interesting that in *Hortus II* Linnaeus introduces his umbellate classification with a general description of this group of plants, including stamens and pistils as important distinguishing characteristics. But he also gives the same date, 29 July 1730, to *Hortus III*, in which his own sexual system is presented for the first time. The sources thus give us our first knowledge of the new classificatory systems of both Artedi and Linnaeus at exactly the same time.

Artedi was certainly not the only guide to Linnaeus's new understanding. Plant systems had already been published, which in many ways anticipated that of Linnaeus, being based upon the number, position, and relationship of certain parts of the plant. Tournefort's system took considerable account of such factors, and the same applies to the arrangements of Cesalpino, Ray, and Rivinus, to name only a few of the more important. Linnaeus naturally read the works of a great many of his predecessors. Among his notes, presumably from his period at Lund, 1727–1728, we find that he has recorded in tabular form two of the most important contemporary systems, those of Tournefort and Rivinus (after Heucher), and also included a number of systematic tables of different groups of animals. In various of his other early papers we find him trying out these systems one after another, with the result that he became very familiar with them before bringing out his own.

The great authority Tournefort has, in fact, two large groups that Linnaeus could transfer to his sexual system intact. The sixth section of the fifteenth class thus includes herbs "flore apetalo, quarum aliae in eodem genere floribus, aliae vero fructibus plerumque donantur," that is, herbs belonging to the class *Dioecia*; the similarity is even more marked in the eighteenth class, the second section of which includes trees and bushes "flore apetalo, in eodem planta a fructu separata," which is the *Monoecia* of Linnaeus. The same groups occur in two other places in Tournefort's system. What is more significant, perhaps, is that both Camerarius and

Vaillant commented on the variety of the arrangements of stamens and pistils in different plants. Although neither of them appears to have proposed a system based on their observations, in effect they provided a number of useful hints for drawing up such a system. In Vaillant, initially the authority most closely followed by Linnaeus, we find the following observations: the filaments are single as in grasses, sedges, crucifers, umbellifers, etc., or ramified, as in *Ricinus, Laurus,* etc. They are separate from each other in these plants but coalesce in most mallows, cucurbits, legumes, etc. The filaments are attached at different points in different cases. It is also pointed out that the placement of the ovaries differs in relation to the petals and other organs. Sometimes the stamens and pistils are separate, either on the same plant or on different ones, and sometimes they are combined. Vaillant also discusses the *number* of stamens in a systematic connection, although only in one particular context. He considers that in order to distinguish gamopetalous from choripetalous flowers it is worth noting that in the former the number of stamens never exceeds that of the lobes of the petals, whereas in the latter the stamens are usually more numerous than the petals. He also gives many examples of the various numerical relationships in different flowers and uses these as a part of the basis for his groupings. At the end of his *Sermo,* he draws up three new genera, *Arialastrum, Sherardia,* and *Boerhaavia,* including in the generic characters *hermaphroditus,* scarcely a sweeping step, but nevertheless an unambiguous introduction of the sexual theory into classification.

Linnaeus was able to read something of all this in the commentary on Vaillant's work in *Acta Eruditorum,* although nothing was mentioned of the connection between petals and stamens in gamopetalous and choripetalous flowers, nor of Vaillant's generic characters. Several months elapsed between Linnaeus's seeing the review in *Acta Eruditorum* and the summer of 1730, and it is not impossible that during this period he obtained more detailed literary information on the sexuality of plants. He must already have known of Pontedera, for example, when he wrote *Praeludia,* presented on New Year's Day, since he directed a vigorous polemic against him. The variations in the appearance and position of stamens are brought out very clearly by Pontedera's figures. A figure in *Praeludia* depicting different types of flowers does not, admittedly, appear to be directly inspired by Pontedera's plates, even if a certain affinity with his Tabula XII may be discerned. But on the other hand, Pontedera's illustrations show such a clear kinship with those of Tournefort (in *Institutiones,* Part 2) that we may assume that from this familiar source Linnaeus drew the inspiration for his illustrations, which could so easily lead to the idea of the utility of the sexual organs for classification purposes. Tournefort's Tabula V, for example, shows a series of different types of pistil, with the differing numbers of stigmas on the different types—a basis for Linnaeus's division into orders—clearly visible. Had Linnaeus seen the work of Camerarius he would have acquired approximately the same information as he did from Vaillant. It appears that Camerarius gave Vaillant a number of the ideas included in his *Sermo*, although no direct mention of this is made by Vaillant.

The fact that Linnaeus may have drawn inspiration from his reading of these authors in developing his sexual system does not, of course, detract from his own contribution. Nobody had had the idea of using stamens and pistils consistently to create a comprehensive system, although it was an idea that seemed obvious—once somebody had thought of it!

As far as we can now see, it is remarkable how late all the documents giving reliable clues to the history of the development of the sexual system have to be dated. The first presentation of the system is dated 29 July 1730, also the date of the first known version of the umbellate system of Artedi, which Linnaeus reports influenced his own classificatory thinking. These facts are certain, but everything else quickly boils down to speculation. One document which is shown by the rudimentary shaping of the idea to be of earlier origin—how much earlier it is difficult to determine—is a little list of the number of stamens in different groups of plants. We find it in Linnaeus's copy, mentioned previously, of Johrenius's *Hodegus*, where he has written:

Cruciformes	6 stam sed 2 minor
Ringentes Labiatae pers[onatae]	4 apices, tuba 2 fido q[uorum?] 1 longior
Papilionacei	9 stamina in tubam quat:
Caryophyllei	10 stamina
Pentapetali certi	10 stamina
Umbellati	5 stamina, tuba bifida
Liliacei	6 stamina?

Here we have evidence of his system in the making which is clearly of an early date, a testing of the extent to which the number and relation of the stamens correspond to several long-established plant groupings.

The year 1730 is given by Linnaeus himself as the date of a significant document which illustrates both the growth of his sexual system and the more general trend of his thinking on the question of classification. This is the first corrected draft of *Fundamenta Botanica*, subtitled *quibus nova et naturalis plantar[um] Methodus Superstruitur, exhibita per regulas ultra Centum aeternae veritatis non e libris, sed ab ipsius Naturae thesauro haustas; in quarum explicatione Methodi omnes hactenus principales, experimentis infallibilibus, observationibusque immensis plane Novis de-*

struuntur. There is also the legend and date: "Doctis in arte scribo, indoctos docebo, Upsal. 1730."[10] This enables us to put the first definite date of the sexual system back just a little earlier. The manuscript refers to *Hortus Uplandicus,* in which the new system was to be published, as being still unwritten. It also promises *"Nuptias Plantarum"* to come, before *Hortus,* but, Linnaeus continues, "as I have a few more observations to make, I shall have to wait until the summer has passed," which makes the most probable dating the early summer of that year. It is also clear that Artedi's system was at hand when Linnaeus wrote this. He describes his friend as deeply devoted to natural history and declares that he has much for which to be grateful to him, "praeprimis divisionem Arctaedianarum," a family name which Linnaeus in his enthusiasm writes instead of "Umbelliferarum."

The preface to the *Fundamenta* manuscript bubbles with reforming zeal, with the desire to topple the old authorities and to look at nature with an unprejudiced eye. His doubts do not go as far as those of Descartes, but there is much of the Cartesian spirit in his words: "For when I first examined nature myself and saw her striving against the opinions of the savants, I laid aside all preconceptions, became a *scepticus,* and questioned all, and only then were my eyes opened; only then did I see the truth." Linneaus has a warrior's conviction that he will encounter stiff opposition, both from those who have written on botany and are not willing to alter views they have once adopted, and from those who are in the process of turning out works that put forward a different point of view and who will thus be compelled to adjust to the new theses, with all that this means in the way of extra toil and trouble. But Linnaeus hopes that a few will accept his system and that it will in time come to "dwell in the palace *Botanices principium,* and indeed ofttimes be their counsellor and friend." These few will preferably include "those who have the greatest *vota,*" and Linnaeus states that he knows who these are, and that among them is an Englishman, by which he presumably means J. J. Dillenius, professor of botany at Oxford. The difficulties in interpreting the unedited manuscripts make it impossible to date anything more than the actual preface as early as the first half of the summer of 1730 without further exhaustive research. The title page informs us that Linnaeus now had "more than a hundred" rules of botany prepared. On May 3, 1731, when commencing his lectures at the Botanical Garden, he declared that he had managed to compile more than 150 *regulas universales,* which suggests that work had not progressed as rapidly as he had at first anticipated. So *Hortus III* remains the only document dealing

10. This manuscript may be regarded as the first preliminary version of *Fundamenta Botanica* and is printed in *Ungdomsskrifter* I, 92 ff.

with the first statement of his classification which we can date with certainty.

The system in *Hortus III* is built up in fundamentally the same form as that finally set forth in *Systema Naturae* in 1735. The number of stamens and their relation to each other thus forms the basis of the major divisions of the vegetable kingdom into classes, and the number of pistils distinguishes the different orders within the classes. But the differences in detail are relatively substantial. A number of species are, as T. M. Fries has pointed out, assigned to the wrong groups, and a number of classes are still missing. There are twenty-one classes. Heptandria and Gynandria are not yet included, and the three Adelphia classes are grouped as one, the class Polydynamia. Certain of the names were later changed also. It is interesting that the classes are, in turn, grouped into larger units on the basis of important similarities or differences in their sexuality. Linnaeus begins by differentiating between "public" and "clandestine" marriages, that is, between phanerogams and cryptogams. The phanerogams are subdivided into "one or two beds," the first category being grouped according to the "indifferentism" (equality in size), "subordination" (coalescence of the stamens), and the second according to their "legitimate" or "illegitimate" nuptial relationship (monoecious or dioecious).

The year 1731 signals the penultimate stage in the development of Linnaeus's sexual taxonomy. A new version of *Hortus* was almost completed during that spring, together with another improved variation on this theme, entitled *Adonis Uplandicus*. Both show certain differences in the details of the system when compared with *Hortus III*, and there is also a development from the one to the other, which indicates what is confirmed by other reports, namely, that Linnaeus was now working on his taxonomy very intensively. The number of classes in *Adonis* is twenty-three (except in an introductory table), whereas by *Hortus IV* they have reached the final total of twenty-four. One of the most important items in Linnaeus's main reform program has thus found its final shape. Much of what remained was commentary—at times leading a long way away from the original matter— on this exceptionally cogent system.

The various versions of *Fundamenta Botanica* that are known, right back to the first fragment of 1730, may be regarded as forming a part of this commentary. At the same time, these fragments indicate that Linnaeus, consciously or unconsciously, was working on a broad front on the program for a "fundamentalis plantarum notitia," which had once been outlined by his patron, Olaus Rudbeck, Jr.[11] This was a program for the development

11. Olaus Rudbeck, Jr., professor of medicine (including botany) in Uppsala during the long period 1691–1740, had in his doctoral dissertation *De Fundamentali Plantarum Notitia Rite Acquirenda* (Utrecht, 1690, reprinted in Augsburg, 1691) briefly fore-

of standards, not only of classification in the narrower sense, but also of nomenclature and description with its definitions and its terminological procedure. Whether Rudbeck actively encouraged and supported him in all this—whether, in fact, he gave his protégé suggestions and inspiration—is shrouded in uncertainty. But it is tempting to see a historical continuity when the leading representatives of the Rudbeckian and the Linnaean epoch of Swedish natural history lived for a considerable period of transition under the same roof.

After the short years of rapid development in the early 1730s, Linnaeus appears, with the publication of the results of his early studies, as a mature and, in most respects, fully formed man of science. Most of what he now proclaimed to the world, he continued to believe until the final years of his life. It is time to examine this lifework.

The Main Taxonomic Works

In 1735, as is well known, Linnaeus's student years ended. He went on his journey to Holland, received his doctorate at Groningen, and established himself in Holland for the next three years. Before that time he had published almost nothing. But he had written a great deal, and as a matter of fact, most of the scientific principles to which he adhered during the rest of his life were laid down in his many manuscripts. These were published during his years in Holland, together with the new works he created during his stay as garden director under Georg Cliffort at Hartekamp. His output was really astonishing. In 1735 he published the first edition of *Systema Naturae*, in 1736 the *Fundamenta Botanica* and *Bibliotheca Botanica*, in 1737 *Hortus Cliffortianus, Genera Plantarum, Flora Lapponica,* and *Critica Botanica,* in 1738 *Classes Plantarum.* Back in Sweden, first as a physician in Stockholm, and from 1741 on as professor of medicine at Uppsala, he could to a considerable degree strengthen his scientific fame by reediting his works from the years in Holland.

The cardinal points of Linnaeus's thought and work during his first period as an independent botanist are concisely summarized in the first edition of his *Systema Naturae* (1735). This remarkable systematic table in folio size puts the vegetable kingdom, with its twenty-four classes and its orders and genera, in its place among the works of nature. The genera are represented by selected examples but are not listed in full. In the brief but integral *Observationes in regnum vegetabile* which accompanies the tables, he sets forth his opinions on the purpose and methods of botany, at the same

---

shadowed much of the progress of taxonomic and descriptive botany that was brought out by Linnaeus. During the student years in Uppsala Linnaeus lived in Rudbeck's home and became his close friend.

time presenting his systematics in more detail and giving some explanatory notes. From these we learn the questions that most occupied Linnaeus's mind. To some of them he gives his final answer here—to the matter of the sexuality of plants and the sexual system, for example, which had engaged him so intensively ever since his student days. Others are only mentioned in passing, to be developed in detail in his later work. Yet others are problems to which Linnaeus never managed to find a satisfactory solution.

First, Linnaeus shows that all flowers have parts, either visible or concealed, whose purpose is fructification (i.e., fruiting, or sexual reproduction), whereas other organs may often be absent. With this he has laid the foundation for his argument that plants have sexuality, and that the starting point for their classification ought to be fructification. He develops the first of these propositions in observations eight to eleven, in which he refers to many authorities: Camerarius, Vaillant, Grew, Ray, Morland, Blair, Jussieu, Bradley, and Royen. The second, in which he was far more alone, is advanced in the fourth aphorism. Since fruiting occurs so consistently, nature herself has confirmed that it ought to be made the basis for classification. Linnaeus shows that the foremost botanists from Cesalpino onward have realized this. Extending this argument, he concludes that the system ought to be based on the most essential of the sexual organs of reproduction which, if the sexual theory is accepted, are fairly obviously the stamens and the pistils. The fruit itself may, of course, be regarded as equally essential, but in the seventh aphorism Linnaeus explains how literally he considers that nature's own order should be followed, and on the strength of this he gives precedence to the organs of the flower. The flowers, he says, precede the fruit in time, and for this reason their essential parts should be considered first.

Even before presenting this detailed argument, Linnaeus sets out what might almost be called the quintessence of his own scientific philosophy. The fundamentals of botany, he asserts, consist in the systematic classification and naming of plants, both by genus and by species. The observation has been made, quite justly, that by attaching such weight to this dictum, Linnaeus decreed the form that botany was to take for a century or more.[12] At the close of the seventeenth century, plant anatomy and physiology had come to the fore, and it seemed possible that the problems posed by these branches of the science might dominate botany, questions about the general nature of the plant, its growth and survival, its observance of chemical and physical laws, and its dependence on external environment, climate, and soil. Linnaeus did not dismiss such matters; indeed he held an opinion on

12. Cf. J. Sachs, *Geschichte der Botanik* (München, 1875), 108 ff; A. J. Cain, "Logic and Memory," *Proceedings of the Linnean Society* (1958), 1–2, and Lindroth's essay in this volume.

most of them, but he regarded them as being of secondary importance to his efforts to master the names of all forms of plants and to obtain a comprehensive view of their place in the whole. The plant was described, therefore, for the sake of the systematic overview. Those organs were to be described which would serve in the definitions to point out the *differentia specifica*; they were not accorded any intrinsic value as objects of study. An overall view and a system demand clarity and order, uniformity and verbal economy. Here Linnaeus displayed his organizational genius. But complexities and detailed studies were often uncongenial to him, and he left such problems unsolved.

Linnaeus, therefore, puts the description of organs at the service of taxonomy. In aphorism five of *Observationes* Linnaeus classifies the organs of fructification in a way that admirably serves the purposes of systematic description. The spirit of this classification is best captured by reproducing it in tabular form:

I. *Flos.*
    1. *Calyx* of 6 types: *perianthium, involucrum, amentum, spatha, gluma, calyptra*
    2. *Corolla* of 2 types: *Petalum, Nectarium*
    3. *Stamina* of 2 types: *Filamentum, Anthera*
    4. *Pistilla* of 2 types: *stylus, stigma*

II. *Fructus*
    5. *Pericarpium* of 9 types: *capsula, conceptaculum, siliqua, legumen, nux, drupa, pomum, bacca, strobilus*
    6. *Semina* of 3 types: *seminulum, corona, floccus*
    7. *Receptaculum* of 3 types: *floris, fructus, fructificationis*

Linnaeus does not give a precise indication in these brief observations about how he visualizes the *generic and specific concepts.* As we have seen, he designated as the basis of botany just that field of generic and specific classification and nomenclature in which he was, in fact, to do his greatest work. These views were developed in the writings of his years in Holland.

While formulating the sexual system, Linnaeus had touched briefly on a problem which he was never to solve. It was one where his need for clarity and order met its antithesis in the complexity and ambiguity of nature. Is there a system that really reflects nature? And, if so, can it be tracked down and given written expression? Initially, he appears to be convinced that nature's own secret organization of the vegetable kindgom has been revealed with the demonstration of the significance and variety of the sexual organs. An echo of this conviction may still be discerned in several of the theses of *Systema Naturae*, but, in fact, he had already realized that the natural system still had not been fathomed in its entirety. As yet, he says in aphorism twelve, no system has been designed which is natural. Nor does he claim to have achieved this himself—but he promises that he may perhaps produce the fragments of a truly natural system at a later date, and this is indeed what he did. He also has a definite theory about why all attempts have failed; a natural system cannot be constructed until all the plants that belong to the system are fully known *(notissima)*. Until then we must be content with artificial systems, which in the present situation are absolutely necessary. In the nineteenth aphorism he puts forward the thesis that the members of natural plant groups correspond in their medicinal and similar properties, an idea which had long been current, and he indicates some of the places in his system where he considers that the natural affinity is reflected. The grasses, for example, are contained in Triandria digynia; Stellatae Rajus (*Galium* and other closely related genera) in Tetrandria monogynia, the Boraginaceae in Pentandria monogynia, the tobacco plants in Pentandria monopetala, bacciferae, the umbellifers in Pentandria digynia. He also regards the groups of bacciferae, drupiferae, and pomiferae of Icosandria as natural (Rosaceae and members of the genus *Citrus*), as he does Polyandria (Ranunculaceae), Didynamia gymnospermia (labiates), Tetradynamia (Cruciferae), Diadelphia (legumes), Monadelphia (Malvaceae), Syngenesia (Compositae) and Gynandria (orchids). There is *one* category in the system which he regards as entirely natural—the genus—which he says was "thus created in the very beginning." Botanists before Linnaeus had, of course, succeeded quite well in establishing the concept of genus, thanks not least to the efforts of Tournefort, whereas the species occupied a very imprecise position as a category, and was to be raised to the status of the fundamental taxonomic unit of biology only as a result of the work of Linnaeus himself. Linnaeus says no more of the problems of the natural system at this point, but he was to return to them again and again, in tones of increasing resignation.

Questions of nomenclature are closely linked with problems of classification. At the same time it is nomenclature which often conflicts most strongly with the idea of a natural system of classification. In giving names, Linnaeus's formalistic ingenuity and sense of order are seen to their full extent, undeterred by the complexity and ambiguity of his experience and his material. Although he had certainly not yet reached his final position on these matters, he speaks in aphorisms fifteen and sixteen as the full-fledged nomenclator. He has replaced incorrectly formed and confusing generic names with the best of the synonyms offered by the ancients or, "in a few cases," with names he has devised himself. He has some serious words for those who aggravate the difficulties by changing the most widely accepted names (although he himself was later to receive much criticism for all his innovations among generic names). However, he looks forward with expectation to the day when "a new and more precise generation" will clear away all the absurdities which are to be found, particularly among specific names.

These observations in *Systema Naturae* offer an excellent point of departure for a scrutiny of Linnaeus's scientific opinions. They yield the essence of his achievement and the most important principles of the work which made his fame. A very large part of what he accomplished later in life shows itself, as we have seen, to be a development of the themes which he sounded here. It is hardly possible to keep to a chronological framework in portraying the botanical ideas of Linnaeus. He remains true to the same basic view on a large number of points throughout his life, and indeed some of the impact of his theories is due to this consistency. It seems natural, therefore, to introduce a survey of Linnaeus as a botanical thinker by analyzing the main ideas of *Systema Naturae* point by point and examining the way in which they are elaborated upon, first in other works from the Holland years, and then in the variegated literary production of the years of his professorship.

As far as the sexuality of plants and its application for purposes of taxonomy is concerned, *Systema Naturae* (1735) represents something of a final position. Plant sexuality was taken up again later, notably in the dissertation *Sponsalia Plantarum* (1746), but this adds little to what we already know of Linnaeus's views. Nor was the arrangement according to the sexual system altered to any significant extent once Linnaeus had recognized its limitations as a mirror of the natural order. In the major surveys that were to come, Linnaeus applied the same system consistently, and its lucidity and ease of use, particularly in the examination of specimens, have given it a leading place in the floras into modern times.

Genera Plantarum, published early in 1737, is the shining example from the Holland years of the capacity of the Linnaean system to bring order to a large body of material and make it easy to grasp. Using diagnoses of a uniform pattern throughout, the plant kingdom is laid out in all its known diversity, genus by genus, in its ranks and classes. The definitions are unambiguous; everything is clear, definite, and extremely concise. The 384 pages deal with 935 genera, of which 686 have been examined from living material. The work is based not only on Linnaeus's own studies in the field, but also on an examination of virtually all the earlier works of importance giving information relevant to the determination and definition of the groups that really deserved the name of genera on the criteria applied.

Linnaeus was not yet in a position to make a survey of all the species in the vegetable kingdom. But in more limited fields he gave evidence of his lucid style in dealing with taxa of this rank also; he made an authoritative investigation of the species concept and allotted to it an independent position separate from varieties and other less significant groupings. *Flora Lapponica* was probably the work of this type which made the greatest impression on contemporary botanists; the magnificent *Hortus Cliffortianus* evinces the same qualities. Not until 1753 did he publish his *Species Plantarum*, of which a second edition followed in 1762, applying his authoritative method and his all-embracing sense of order to all the plant material then available in the world.

Principles of Plant Description

In describing the various taxonomic categories, Linnaeus achieved lucidity by specifying which organs and parts of organs were to be used in the description, and which characteristics of those organs were to receive the closest attention. The organs of the flower which he considered relevant to a description of the genera or higher groups were enumerated in *Systema Naturae*, and he reproduced the same tabular arrangement with little modification in *Fundamenta Botanica* (1736) and in the interesting introduction to *Genera Plantarum* (1737). In the latter work he refers to a total of twenty-six organs or types of organs as "vegetable letters." These are used for the purpose of generic description in conjunction with four "sound and constant mechanical principles" or attributes: *number, form, position,* and *relative size.*[13] On this well-defined basis Linnaeus undertakes the gargantuan task of describing all known and accepted genera. In *Fundamenta* the rules are worked out in greater detail and have attained a considerable degree of complexity, inevitably so in view of the profusion of forms encountered among plants. The celebrated *Philosophia Botanica* of 1751 is no more than a version of *Fundamenta* with additional commentary, and it follows the wording and layout of the aphorisms of the earlier work quite faithfully. Even the simple basic plan is easily discerned. We can check the ways in which the principles are applied in practice on virtually any genus picked at random from *Genera Plantarum—Ajuga,* for example. Its calyx is described as a perianth (letter), monosepalous (number), short (proportion), *semiquinquefidum* (number, form), of almost equal length (proportion), and remaining after flowering time (the only characteristic that falls outside the framework). The corolla is gamopetalous (number), open, a tube (form), and so on. The filaments (letter) of the stamens are four in number, "awl-like, curved" in shape, two of them shorter, hardly longer

---

13. Those four mechanical principles could further be applied to each part of the whole plant and thus lay the foundation for species determination. *Fundamenta*, paragraph 327.

than the upper lip (proportion), and in the same position as the stamens, and so on.

Fundamenta also outlines those other parts of the plant that Linnaeus regards as essential to the description. Here he makes a major distinction between *planta* and *fructificatio,* that is the plant's vegetative organs and its sexual organs of reproduction. The plant is said to have four main vegetative organs: root, stem, leaf, and supporting parts *(fulcra),* which is not unlike the old scholastic division used throughout the seventeenth century in botanical dissertations. These main organs are subdivided neatly and simply into different types: the root into three *(bulbosa, tubulosa, fibrosa),* and the stem also into three *(caulis, culmus, scapus).* The leaves may be simple or compound, each with a considerable but not confusing number of different configurations, degrees of smoothness, and positions. The supporting parts are divided into six types: *bractea, cirrhus* (tendril), *mucro* (point), *aculeus* (thorns), *petiolus* (leafstalk), and *pedunculus* (flowerstalk). In his description of the organs of sexual reproduction, Linnaeus advances the theory that there is one set of circumstances which represents a norm, a "most natural" condition for the four aspects number, form, position, and proportion.[14] As far as number is concerned, the most natural condition is for this to be the same for all of the main organs, so that the calyx has the same number of segments as the corolla, and that this is the same as the number of stamens. In a similar way the pistils correspond to the fruit in the number of chambers, or the number of rows of seeds. The most natural form of the flower is as follows: a half-open calyx containing a funnel-shaped corolla ("a corolla which is gradually spread out"), that closes at night and that contains upright, gradually shriveling stamens and pistils; its fruit grows when most of these organs have fallen off and it is filled with seeds. The proportional norm is for the calyx to be smaller than the corolla, and at the same time for the stamens and pistils to be equal to each other in length; but if the pistil is longer, the flower leans, the fruit thickens, and the seeds are small. The normal condition with regard to position is for the calyx to encompass the receptacle, which is alternately attached to the corolla; internally, the corolla is matched alternately by the filaments, on the tips of which are situated the anthers; the center of the receptacle is occupied by the ovary, on the tip of which is the style, which in turn bears the stigma. After stigma and style have withered away, the ovary fills out into a fruit, which is supported by the calyx and contains seeds attached to the receptacle of the fruit. The receptacle of the flower is either under, around, or on top of the ovary. Linnaeus states that even those plants which deviate from the usual pattern are subject to definite laws and may be

14. Ibid., paragraph 92 ff.

described using the same organs, considered from substantially the same aspects.

Why did Linnaeus choose the particular organs which he did, and why did he consider them—the reproductive organs in particular—from just those four aspects, *numerus, figura, proportio,* and *situs?* And what are the criteria which led him to select the particular "normal types" which he describes? Even if the answers to some of these questions appear obvious, other groupings and characteristics and other normal types are quite conceivable. It is not easy to be altogether certain of his line of reasoning. It seems clear that Linnaeus took the view that nature herself had attached greatest importance to those particular organs, characteristics, and types which he had chosen to discuss. In this way he adopts a line of thought which is not uncommon in the history of ideas, namely, the belief that nature conforms to an underlying pattern, an "archetype," which may have certain variations, but which is never wholly abandoned. In its original form this way of thinking is platonic speculation; but when expressed as vaguely and unconsciously as it is by Linnaeus, it may be regarded as having a much more general content, being, in fact, related to the conviction of modern science that nature obeys a limited number of laws, which have universal validity.

Linnaeus's conviction that nature can be described in simple formulae appears in a similar way in another important chapter of his reform work, namely the description of genera and species. Such descriptions, together with definitions of varying length and comprehensiveness, are to Linnaeus a part of what botany is all about. The basis of botany, he says in *Fundamenta* and later again in *Philosophia,* is disposition and naming, *dispositio* and *denominatio.* The primary division, that of genera and higher groups, is based, as we have seen, on the reproductive organs. For this we need a *definition* of the genus, and this definition is what Linnaeus also refers to as the generic *character.* The character specified by the botanist may be of one of three kinds, which Linnaeus calls *factitius, essentialis,* and *naturalis.* The two named first take note of the characteristic or characteristics that immediately distinguish a particular genus from all others. In the case of *character factitius* this means a comparison with other genera within an artificial order, whereas *character essentialis* denotes a similar comparison within a natural order. Where one has a choice, Linnaeus remarks, one should, of course, strive to discover the essential character. But what is even more important is to attempt to work out the *character naturalis,* that is, all the material distinctive features of the genus according to the rules for the "letters" and the "mechanical principles." Of course, if all the plant genera on earth were known, a *character essentialis* for each of them would be sufficient to permit recognition. But as long as our knowledge remains partial, as long as it is possible that new species and new distinguishing features may be discovered, then it is necessary to draw up natural characters as comprehensively as we can. This is what Linnaeus has attempted to supply in *Genera Plantarum.*

The species, like the genus, may be furnished with its *character naturalis,* which means its detailed description *(descriptio).* This entails taking note of the important species-distinguishing features of all parts of the plant with regard to number, form, proportions, and position. In indicating the natural character, we ought, according to Linnaeus, to observe a definite sequence in our description. He chooses *ordo nascendi* from root to stem, leafstalk, leaf, flowerstalk, and flowers.

A shorter method which Linnaeus recommended and employed to indicate the specific character was, however, to state the *differentia specifica,* which need only contain a few identifying features distinguishing a given species from all the others in the same genus, a sort of equivalent of the *character essentialis* of the genera and the larger groupings. Indicating the *differentia specifica* in this way was what Linnaeus originally meant when he spoke of *naming* a species, the second fundamental purpose of botany. Whereas the generic name would be single and must, therefore, have a fixed import by indicating the *character essentialis* or *naturalis* of the genus, the specific epithet should encompass the essential character of the species. A complete specific name, including the generic name, thus gave a true definition of the species in the best Aristotelian manner, for it gave *genus proximum* and *differentia specifica* as scholastic logic required. For Linnaeus, therefore, naming a species was synonymous with defining it and was a form of description, so interwoven are description and nomenclature for the master of terminological precision. The whole rationale illustrates his unshakable conviction that his species are those of nature and that his terms and his names are faithful translations of nature's language.

The Fixity of Species

Linnaeus stands out as the foremost creator of the modern concept of the species. The greatness of his achievement here, notwithstanding the importance of his precursor Ray, lies in the fact that it was Linnaeus who demarcated the lower boundary of the concept. Occasional forms and varieties of different kinds are distinguished; what is to be called a species must have a greater degree of constancy, more definite characteristics. Before Linnaeus, this demarcation was scarcely made. Casper Bauhin sets down all the members of his genera without further differentiation, red-flowered, white-flowered, and double-flowering forms being enumerated side by side with the main species, without being specially marked. The genus was, it would appear, the fundamental unit, the lowest essential quantity in the taxonomic series. Tournefort had done a great deal to stabilize the generic concept, but in his great *Institutiones* he listed undifferentiated species and varieties under the various genera in the same way as Bauhin.

The resemblance between Linnaeus's notion of the limits of the species and that of John Ray is, of course, striking. In a number of his writings, most notably in the huge *Historia Plantarum* (1686), Ray clearly defined such distinguishing features as merely denote chance variations within the framework of the species.[15] Just as Linnaeus does, he maintained that the number of species now existing is the same as that formed at the time of creation. Linnaeus must undoubtedly have been strongly influenced by Ray's concept of species. One can only observe that the world of botany paid more attention when it was laid down by Linnaeus than when it was introduced by his great predecessor.

It is noticeable that Linnaeus's writings during his Holland years deal with the species with considerably less certainty than the genus, with the exception of the clear-cut demarcation downward. This is explained partly by the fact that the species concept quite simply *is* a more intractable one, but also by the rational way in which Linnaeus planned his work. He devoted himself first and foremost to the broader surveys and must certainly have regarded it as more urgent to bring some order to the genera than to the innumerable species. The contrast between the precise definitions of the genus and the definitions of the species is most conspicuous. In the case of the genus the most important statement in the definition is marked by that typical dictatorial formalism which brought such clarity to the Linnaean system: "We admit as many genera as there are different groups of natural species of which the fructification has the same structure" (*Fundamenta Botanica* 159). The corresponding sentence establishing the species concept reads: "We count as many species as there were different forms created" (*F. B.* 157). In other words, whereas the genus may be determined by the particular structure of the plant and its reproductive organs, we have to go back to the day of creation in order to decide which forms constitute species. The definition is in practice unusable. By the time of writing *Genera Plantarum* Linnaeus has put his ideas into a somewhat more manageable form. Here he extends the proposition with the corollary that the species is all those forms of *structures* which occur in nature and whose appearance is not due to the nature of the habitat or other chance factors. This formulation is then confirmed in *Philosophia Botanica*. But even with this he does not give any clear indication of how the "essence" of the species is to be determined.

15. For Ray's concept of species, cf. C. E. Raven, *John Ray, Naturalist* (Cambridge, 1942), 189 ff.

As far as the varieties are concerned, we can detect a shift between two interpretations, the one narrower but less serviceable, the other vaguer but more widely used. According to the former, each individual plant originating from the seed is, strictly speaking, a variety. There is hardly any other way of reading the sentence: "There are as many varieties *(variationes)* as there are plants produced by the seed of the same species" (*F. B.* and *Ph. B.* 158). But this telling observation is not applied to his more practical concept of variety, where only the more striking departures from the normal specific character are taken up. He divides such varieties into two groups, the natural and the monstrous. The natural varieties are based on sexual differences; the male individual is thus one variety of a diclinous species, and the female individual is the other. The monstrous varieties arise when the flowers have multiplied, or are filled (i.e., have only petals), or are proliferous (i.e., a new flower grows out of the pistil), or when the actual plant luxuriates, or fasciates, or is transformed in shape, proportion, or the position of the various organs. The variations may also involve temperature, taste, scent, and time. The very expression "monstrous" shows that Linnaeus felt that this whole group of deviations was at odds with nature, and in particular with the "nature" of the species. He also emphasizes repeatedly that the great creator of varieties is man, who with his arts—and thus against nature—intervenes and changes the appearance of plant forms. Thus the variety is seen as a very unimportant taxonomic unit by comparison with the species. That any genetic differentiation might be at the bottom of the emergence of the monstrous variety appears never to have occurred to Linnaeus, despite the way in which he framed the narrower, never-to-be-used, natural varietal concept. The principal function of the varietal concept is a kind of negative one; it is a reasonable way of keeping down the number of species by ensuring that excessively diffuse forms do not come to be regarded as independent species. It protects the species concept by enabling a species to include a number of more occasionally appearing divergent types. By referring to a form as a variety instead of elevating it to the status of a new species, we can cope with multiplicity, taking account of it without being overwhelmed by it. We often find that Linnaeus accepts much more extensive species than those of modern taxonomy.

The question of the multiform "problematic" genera, such as *Rosa, Rubus,* and *Salix,* is one which is closely connected with the problem of variety. How did Linnaeus uphold his views on the species in these cases? We may glean some information on this matter from his early descriptive works, *Flora Lapponica* and *Hortus Cliffortianus.* The former work in particular may be considered of interest, since it deals with many species with which he had become familiar in the course of several years' work in the field. He has a little to say about *Rosa* and names only two Swedish species without further comment (one of them from Rudbeck without having seen a specimen himself). *Rubus* could hardly cause much trouble in a work where the blackberry did not need to be dealt with, so Linnaeus's observations on *Salix* are all the more interesting. He devotes most space to the problems that are encountered when we attempt to understand the descriptions of the older botanists and to draw up a correct taxonomy. But he does not round off these remarks by acknowledging that the different species of *Salix* can often be very difficult to identify with certainty; instead, he solves the problem by proposing entirely new names and drawing up his own table. His youthful self-assurance is scarcely anywhere more evident than in his masterly treatment of this difficult genus. Only at one point does he reveal a slight hesitancy. In describing a species which he calls *Salix foliis serratis glabris ovato-lanceolatis acuminatus* he has to make a comparison with the *Salix foliis serratis glabris lanceolatis acuminatis appendiculatis* which grows farther south in Sweden. He finds that they differ in three respects: unlike the southern version, the Lapland one has no stipels, is a shrub rather than a tree, and has a red stem rather than a white one. But, Linnaeus adds, "I doubt greatly whether this is sufficient to establish it as a species." Otherwise, he is unwilling to see any great difficulty even in so complicated a case as that presented by this genus. At this time he was still working much harder on the larger groupings, but in fact he retained this restrictiveness with regard to the use of the species concept throughout his life. Those who are at all familiar with the commoner Swedish flora will easily find examples of this in the two editions of his *Flora Suecica* (1745, 1755).

Higher Categories and Natural System: The Hybridization Theory

With the question of the "naturalness" or otherwise of forms, we have come to one of the most interesting questions in Linnaean taxonomy, but at the same time one of the most difficult to pronounce upon with certainty: that of the natural systematic units and their relation to the artificial ones. To a modern botanist, a natural system usually means a system based on the grouping of plant forms by kinship. A natural systematic unit is a grouping consisting of closely related forms. Kinship is understood in a narrow sense, with a genetic content. Most biologists from Darwin onward assume a theory of descent. They regard large groups of forms now living—perhaps all of them—as having a common origin, as being branches of the same family tree. It may still be a troublesome problem to determine the criteria of closer or more distant kinship in the individual case; nevertheless, the concept of kinship has in theory a precise meaning. The writings of Linnaeus from his years in Holland do not yet give any trace of this genetic view of kinship other than with regard to the individuals within the boundaries of the separate species. "We count as many species as there were forms created in the beginning," is a pronouncement which establishes unequivocally that when at this time Linnaeus talks about natural taxonomy and natural groups he does not mean that the taxonomy will in the majority of instances clarify the genetic relationship, or that groupings other than those of individuals that exist within the same species will reflect genetic affinity. What, then, is the exact content of the term "natural" as he uses it?

We realize that the species is the easiest natural unit to handle because of its exceptional position. God created each species separately in the beginning and caused it to produce all its offspring from seed. All individuals of one and the same species which now exist can trace their origin to a single parent individual, or, if the plant is dioecious, to a single male and a single female individual. The genetic connection makes the species a natural unit. But Linnaeus states that the genus, too, is natural. The genus cannot derive in its entirety (if it includes more than one species) from a single or from only two individuals; nor, even less, can the larger categories which Linnaeus also wishes to call natural—for example, many of the classes of the sexual system—do so.

For the purpose of determining the relationship between two different individuals (membership of a common species), species (membership in a common genus), orders, or classes, systematics relies on the *similarity* between them. Linnaeus has, of course, to do the same. Admittedly, he did have a "more profound" criterion of natural kinship within the species in the assumption of a common origin on the day of creation, but in practice he could not verify this situation more than to a very slight degree. Naturally, the sowing of seed demonstrated that in the generations observed the seed always produced individuals that resembled the parents in all material respects. Such a test was possibly regarded as more significant by Linnaeus than it would be by a modern taxonomist, assuming that he agreed initially with the theologians in accepting that the earth was created in about the year 4000 B.C., a date which would hardly leave room for the idea that there might have been changes from the original forms. But not even this criterion could be applied to the broader categories, and there was no genealogical relationship in these cases. Here the criterion of resemblance was everything. But at the same time it was a resemblance with certain qualifications. Although they belonged to the same genus and were thus similar to *a certain degree,* the species within the genus did, after all, differ from each other. Which particular residual similarity was it which in that case led Linnaeus to include them in the same natural genus? We have already touched upon the answer: all the species within the same genus are similar in their fruiting.

In *Genera Plantarum*, which is where he dealt in greatest detail with the natural affinity of the genera, he advances a more generalized argument before establishing this axiom.[16] The species, he says, have a community of structure and form, which must coincide exactly in the different individuals if these are to be regarded as belonging to the same species. The number of genera, moreover, was equal to the number of sets of *common attributes* among the species created in the beginning, or more precisely, *attributa communia proxima,* an expression borrowed from the realm of logic and indicating criteria of membership of the next category upward. The definition does not appear to say very much, but Linnaeus seems to have taken God's creation of the species in categories united by many common attributes as an indicator of the "naturalness" of the genera, just as he regarded the species as natural by virtue of the fact that they had been provided with their distinctive characteristics on the day of creation. The conclusion is, in fact, formulated very succinctly: "Hinc omnia Genera et Species naturalia sunt." Linnaeus is himself clearly aware that the expression *attributa communia proxima* has to be given a more clearly defined content. Horses and pigs have the same sort of integument on their toes, but this does not lead us to consider them members of the same genus; nor can roe-deer, elk, and reindeer be regarded as belonging to different genera, even though their horns are of different forms. It is difficult to establish the boundaries of the genera *a priori,* says Linnaeus. It has to be done by attentive and patient observation. But observation on the basis of what principle?

A priori deductions are adequate for an artificial grouping. But in order to group in the same way that God grouped, one must resort to meticulous observation of nature. This appears to be the difference, for Linnaeus, between artificial and natural as far as investigative method is concerned. He appears also to mean that it was empirical observation that led to the practical criterion of the natural genera. Conrad Gesner and Cesalpino had been the very first to make the discovery that nature in her infinite wisdom had seen fit to distinguish her genera by their fruiting process.[17] But even this step—the realization that the similarity which indicates a relationship is to be sought in the fruiting—is not enough to bring us to the natural genera. There are, after all, a variety of parts to the fruiting which might have been considered, thus leading to an arbitrary number of groupings and

16. Cf. W. T. Stearn's excellent preface in his edition of *Genera Plantarum* (Weinheim, 1960).

17. Linnaeus refers to Gesner's posthumous letters and to his plant illustrations edited by J. Camerarius. Probably the letters meant are those in *Epistolae Medicinales,* ed. C. Wolf (Tiguri, 1577), see pp. 66ᵛ and 113ʳ. The illustrations are to be found in Camerarius's edition of *Matthioli de Plantis Epitome Utilissima* (Francofurti ad Moenum, 1586), which is furnished with Gesner's illustrations often showing the fruits.

90

divisions. Invoking Boerhaave, Linnaeus asserts that no criteria can be chosen beforehand which can be applied in a strictly logical fashion, first to the division into classes, and then to the orders, genera, and species. The inductive method which has to be applied instead starts from the bottom, from the lowest systematic units, those given in an observable form in nature. But an inductive method does not lead us to select certain organs of sexual reproduction in order to compare just *their* particular similarity. *All the parts must*, in fact, be considered. Then we arrive, Linnaeus tells us, at the twenty-six "letters of nature's alphabet" of which he had spoken and which we considered earlier. With these letters, he believes, God himself wrote in the great book of nature. Whether the four "mechanical principles"—number, form, position, and relative size—were arrived at inductively is not clear from Linnaeus's exposition. He acknowledges that one may also take account of other circumstances and other kinds of characteristics. That he does not do so himself is because the four principles themselves give a more than adequate basis.

The problem of the extent to which genera were natural clearly led to some conflict in Linnaeus's mind. The ideal form of scientific description was for him one that was logical, distinct, and precise in every respect. But when it was a question of keeping as close as possible to God's creative activity in the realm of nature, logic still came off second best. Here painstaking observation came to represent another aspect of his investigative method, sometimes opening upon an enigmatic abyss. For it seems that not even the twenty-six letters and the four mechanical principles were always enough to clarify the generic relationship of a group of species. Alongside the definable characteristics that were obtained from them, Linnaeus had also to take into account what he describes in *Fundamenta* as *facies,* to which he gives the following strangely elusive definition: "Facies est similitudo quaedam vegetabilium affinium et congenerum nunc in hac nunc in alia, nunc in plerisque vegetabilium partibus manifesta" ("*Facies* is a certain similarity in related plants and plants of the same genus, which is manifested sometimes in one part, sometimes in another and sometimes in several parts of the plant").[18] The importance which he, nevertheless, attaches to it becomes apparent when in the same work he advises the botanist to let himself be guided by it in investigating the secrets of nature, in order to avoid the formation of artificial genera, which otherwise can easily happen. This striking line of reasoning ties up with his discussion of the risk of creating too many genera. This may arise if characteristics of the reproductive system which appear peculiar to a certain genus should turn out to be lacking in a particular member (which is, therefore, taken out to

18. *Fundamenta*, paragraph 163.

form its own genus) or if a similar characteristic should turn up in a closely related genus. The implication of this must be that it is always difficult to find the really distinguishing or unifying characteristics, for which reason this *facies,* this overall impression of the plant as a whole, acquires an important function. This is consistent with the fact that one of the aphorisms states that the natural character is extremely difficult to define, but that once it has been established it forms the firm foundation for all subsequent taxonomy (within the genus). These departures from the precise and the clearly defined may have alarmed Linnaeus himself. Later he suddenly gives a warning against placing too much faith in *facies!*

These problems apply not only to Linnaeus's natural genera but also to his natural orders and classes. The only difference here is that finding the right criteria is even more difficult, he says. The common characteristics must, of course, be fewer in number, but what are they? For once Linnaeus is not absolutely positive. In *Classes Plantarum* he hesitantly draws up a number of orders which he regards as natural. But they do not cover the entire vegetable kingdom, and he does not venture to say anything of a natural link between whole classes. One important reason for his reluctance to pronounce upon the structure of the natural system as a whole is that he is aware that many plants have still to be discovered. He points this out in several places. Until we know the vegetable kingdom in its entirety we cannot really unravel all the relationships within it. It is in *Classes Plantarum* that he dwells longest on this problem.[19]

The creation of a *methodus naturalis* is the most important task in botany, he states. But the difficulties are great. There are fewer plants than one would imagine which can, in fact, be assigned to their correct orders. He says that he himself has been working on the problem for a long time, and he promises to go on working on it for as long as he lives. But the one who manages to place those plants which have still not been cleared up will, Linnaeus predicts, be called a great Apollo by all. Linnaeus cannot yet provide a key to his natural system, and this is an extremely serious limitation to what he has achieved. Such a key will be a practical possibility only when all the orders are known. When this position is reached, it will not be such a difficult matter to see how all the natural classes are composed. Until then, he will refrain from grouping other than in orders. On this more general level, too, he regards observation of nature as more important than *a priori* rules about the characters that are to apply. The whole plant must be considered—perhaps it is his *facies* which he still has in mind when he says that the right characteristics are only to be found in the simple symmetry of all the organs of the plant. But he does give one intimation of a

19. Ibid., 485–486.

practicable way of making progress: if we wish to design a key to the natural orders, we should note that no single characteristic of the plant is of as great a value as that based on position and, in particular, the position of *punctum vegetans* in the seed, from which growth takes place in opposing directions. Here he touched upon a characteristic which came to play a significant part in the important eighteenth-century French literature dealing with the natural system. He himself refers to his influential predecessor Cesalpino.

It was only to be expected that the wider questions of taxonomy which we have been discussing would remind Linnaeus strongly of a number of classical problems. Is there a definite sequence to the various orders and classes? Do they form coherent series and perhaps a continuum from a lower to a higher degree of perfection? This is what Aristotle had believed. Linnaeus is notably reticent about these matters. He says quite simply, by way of introduction to the sixty-five natural orders which he has drawn up, that he has not placed them one after another according to any natural law *(nulla lege naturali)*. He has merely wished to point out which genera belong to the same order. Maybe his ideas on the subject of the meaning of natural kinship were already running along the lines developed in his later work, which, as we shall see, in effect ruled out the possibility of any sequence of orders on such a natural basis.

In the later editions of the works from the years in Holland, which Linnaeus brought out during the rest of his long and active life, as in the later more important writings, he allows his theories on the concepts of genus and species to stand undisturbed. The species are no better defined in *Philosophia Botanica* in 1751 than they are in its predecessor *Fundamenta*. Admittedly, there is much more attention paid here to the actual characters, but this concerns their form more than anything else. The clearest statement of what constitutes a species is still contained in the proposition that there are as many species as there are different structures or forms. The absolutely central and essential *Species Plantarum*, the first edition of which appeared in 1753 and the second in 1762, is perhaps the work above all others where a thorough account of the species concept might be expected. It has, however, a very brief foreword, which does not even mention the basic question of definition at all. Our picture of Linnaeus's generic concept is not really much clearer. In *Philosophia Botanica* he maintained that the genera are to be defined on the basis of the reproductive organs; natural species with common arrangements of these organs together form a genus. But this is not the final word on the way Linnaeus's views on these concepts developed in the course of his unceasing work on the detailed description of innumerable genera and species. As J. Ramsbottom has pointed out, where Linnaeus's concept of species is concerned a distinction has to be made between the strict stance he adopted in his definitive works, *Philosophia Botanica* in particular, and the more fluently formulated opinions which he permitted himself to advance in the more detailed accounts and which are also to be inferred from passing observations in his descriptive works.[20] The rigid concept of species served his purpose, which was to protect botany from the chaos which threatened continually if firm principles were not insisted upon. His more flexible attitude is an attempt to adapt the science to the inexorable problems that it was called upon to answer.

The difficulty of distinguishing between species and varieties was no doubt one of the reasons for Linnaeus's less exact view of the nature of the species. Whereas he found that the genera could normally be delimited very easily, the species often formed a continuum that was tricky to deal with. Therefore, it gradually occurred to him to wonder whether all the species really had existed at the moment of creation and remained constant within the limits of relatively insignificant variations determined by type of soil and climatic conditions. In the essay *Oratio de Telluris Habitabilis Incremento* (1743) he does indeed appear to retain still the basic static theory from the relatively recent Holland works. Here he demonstrates that every species was represented in the beginning by a single pair (or, in the case of hermaphrodites, by a single individual) and that there was room for all of them in paradise on an equatorial island which has at its various altitudes from sea level to the mountain peaks all types of climate and soil. But the main idea of his essay is not that of establishing the stability of the species concept, but rather that of making the words of the Bible more credible to a modern student of nature. He wants to show that it is quite possible to conceive of a single individual's being the starting point of, for example, all the specimens now in existence of a common species of plant, and that it, therefore, becomes possible to narrow down the site of creation to a very restricted locality.

By the following year, 1744, which was, in fact, the year when the essay first appeared in print, we find that he was already casting doubt on the absolute fixity of species, although without implying any glaring contradiction of the point of view advanced in *De Telluris*. He set out his new ideas in his well-known dissertation *Peloria*. A student had shown him a plant, apparently a progeny of the species *Linaria vulgaris*, which differed strikingly from any specimen he had previously seen: instead of the usual asymmetrical flowers it had perfectly regular ones. It was this plant—far too aberrant to be dismissed as a variety in the Linnaean sense, indeed far too

20. J. Ramsbottom, "Linnaeus and the Species Concept," *Proceedings of the Linnean Society* (1937–1938).

94

aberrant even to be included in the genus *Linaria*—which Linnaeus endowed with the name *Peloria* and thus established it as a genus of its own. This empirically demonstrable case of specific alteration must have played a large part in causing him to doubt the fixity of species.

The example was, however, a most extreme one. In possessing five identical and regularly placed stamens, *Peloria* belonged not only to a new genus, but even to a class different from that of its parent species. So Linnaeus could assert justifiably, not without consternation, that if *Peloria* proved to have constant progeny, a large part of established botanical theory would be overturned. It would be impossible to base the genera on the reproductive organs, and the most natural classes would be demolished. Perhaps *Peloria* was really too monstrous and exceptional a case to lead Linnaeus to truly new thinking on the species concept. Nevertheless, in the same dissertation he advanced the theory that the plant in question may be a *hybrid* between *Linaria* and some quite differently constituted plant. If the *Peloria* is a hybrid and has germinative seeds, then, Linnaeus believes, an entirely new state of affairs would suggest itself, with far-reaching implications for the problem of the species.

Linnaeus's dissertation attracted attention abroad, and his cautious hypothesis of the hybrid was taken up by one of his correspondents, Johann Georg Gmelin, who, in a letter of May 17, 1745, gave an account of his observations of the *Delphinium,* among other genera, which gave strength to the view that new forms may arise through hybridization. In the first volume of *Amoenitates Academicae* (1749), in which the *Peloria* paper is reprinted, Linnaeus quoted Gmelin and added a few reflections of his own—all most circumspectly worded and presented first and foremost as a state of affairs deserving further investigation. Shortly afterward Linnaeus was ready to put forward a much more fully worked out and radical hypothesis, which presents the concepts of species and genus in an entirely new light. He takes up the problem of hybrids in a number of dissertations during the 1750s. In *Plantae Hybridae* (1751) he drew up a list of plants which may be assumed to have two different species as parents and asked whether truly new species can arise in this manner. Here he puts forward, albeit rather hesitantly, a proposition about the varieties which is most startling. Varieties, he now explains, do not (ever?) arise as a consequence of the soil's differing from that in which the parent plant grew. A change in soil composition does not change a cultivated peony or double narcissus into a wild one. He does not consider that this means that parent and progeny are to be regarded as separate species, but at the same time he has apparently accepted the idea of *permanent* varieties, which are, therefore, in certain respects credited with the same essential characteristics as the species. In *Somnus Plantarum* (1755), he states that such permanent varieties may have originated as a result of hybridization—they arise, therefore, from genetic circumstances, not from the nature of the soil. He still prefers to speak in this case of varieties, although it is evident that the idea of considering fertile hybrids of this sort as species has occurred to him. His words also imply that he can now conceive of one of the parent species (the father) as belonging either to the same genus or, remarkable though it may seem, to another genus. In 1759 he develops these ideas further in *Generatio Ambigena*. Linnaeus now begins to depict the genus as held together by a genetic relationship. It is possible, he considers, that someday a genus will be found to be made up of the species which have arisen in the medulla substance of a common mother species. He says more or less the same thing in the following year in *Theses Medicae*. Plants with the same form of reproductive organs (i.e., of the same genus) but with differing external structures (i.e., of different species) are presumably descendants of the same plant. The differentiation may have taken place either at the creation or subsequently, although he is unwilling to say with certainty which. But by showing himself aware of the nature of the question, and by being able to suggest that new species have been formed over the ages, he has taken a significant step toward a new and much more dynamic view of the species.

If we are to understand fully Linnaeus's reasoning on the subject of hybridization, we must recall his theory of the origin of the sexual organs from different parts of the plant. His views on these matters were a development of the singular views of Cesalpino on the medulla and cortex substances. Anatomists such as Malpighi and Grew had adopted the opinions of Cesalpino and regarded the different parts of the organs of reproduction as outgrowths of the different layers of the stem. Grew, for example, analyzes the parts of the apple as developing from the outer cortex (the peel of the apple), the inner cortex (the flesh), the ligneous parts (the core), and the medulla (the pip).[21] In Linnaeus's version, linked to his theory of sexual reproduction and presented in a series of dissertations during the 1740s and later, the plant was built up of two distinct anatomic structures: the cortex and the medulla. The stamens of the flower were extensions of the cortex, and the pistils were extensions of the medulla, so the sexual differentiation itself was a special case of the cortex-medulla contrast. When Linnaeus spoke of the metamorphosis of plants (as, for example, in the dissertation *Metamorphosis Plantarum* in 1755), he was referring first and foremost to the emergence of the two substances as different organs of the developing individual plant. The flower was for him a formation of transformed embryonic buds for the next six years. Thus the bracts were an advance formation of the buds which "properly" belonged to the next year, the

---

21. N. Grew, *Anatomy of Vegetables* (London, 1672), 151 f.

sepals were buds for the third year, the petals for the fourth, and the stamens for the fifth year ahead.[22] All of these formations belonged to the cortex substance, whereas the embryonic buds of the sixth year, the pistil, consisted of medulla. The male cortex was responsible for the supply of nourishment and for the external appearance of the plant, and the female medulla for its inner life; indeed Linnaeus goes so far here that he is inclined to attribute a sort of will, an inclination to form, to the medulla. This is as near as he ever came to a vitalistic point of view. Both male and female individuals contribute to the formation of the progeny, which inherits something essential from each parent. In this respect Linnaeus may be described both as ovist and as animalculist. He applies his theory to the study of hybrids. A genus is composed of species with the same medulla substance, the same mother, whereas the different species owe their differences to different cortex substances. They have originally been fertilized with different pollen.

In the same year, 1759, that he wrote *Generatio Ambigena,* he extended the logical conclusions of his new ideas in a more radical direction in *Disquisitio de Sexu Plantarum,* a prize essay that he submitted to the Petersburg Academy. In this work he enumerated several species which had to be considered the result of hybridization. In most cases these were hybrids of representatives of different genera. He recorded them consistently under the genus which he regarded as containing the maternal species, the medulla of which built up the ovary. *Veronica spuria* was thus a hybrid of *Veronica maritima* and *Verbena officinalis*; *Delphinium hybridum,* of *Delphinium elatum* and *Aconitum napellus*; *Hieracium Taraxaci,* of *Hieracium alpinum* and *Leontodon Taraxacum.* He noted all the various forms of *Geranium* of Cape Province and found that they too confirmed the hybrid origin of many species.

Linnaeus went ahead rapidly with these new ideas, which obviously carried him along irresistibly. In *Fundamenta Fructificationis* (1762) he produced a counterpart of the theory of creation which he had developed in his essay twenty years earlier on the origins of the earth. The Creator, Linnaeus now believed, created in the beginning only one species in each natural order; in other words, a very small number of species. These original species had the ability to fertilize each other, and this they immediately did. In this way one species arose for every genus; all the genera were thus virtually primordial, even if they were genetically derived by means of a first hybridization. Over the ages the primordial species within the genus has crossed with species from other genera; the manifold species which have come down to us, and which are often difficult to distinguish, have emerged

22. These ideas are fully exposed in Linnaeus's *Prolepsis Plantarum* (1760).

gradually. The earlier theory that permanent varieties might also be hybrids is also completed: they arose as a result of hybridization between species from the *same* genus. For Linnaeus this fantastic theory of derivation was hardly a fanciful hypothesis any longer. It is repeated in the sixth edition of the extremely important *Genera Plantarum* in 1764.

As has been pointed out by Ramsbottom, who has brought out this important line in Linnaeus's thought most admirably, the ideas of the 1760s are also reflected in Linnaeus's treatment of individual species. In the second edition of *Species Plantarum*, which came out in 1762–1763, we find that Linnaeus employs terms such as *filia* and *soror* much more often than previously, even if they were not entirely new. It is reasonable to assume also that the relatively neutral expression *affinis* has now acquired a more genetic content. Although it was based on pure, untested speculation, Linnaeus's theory provided a logically satisfying solution to one of the most troublesome problems of early taxonomy—that of the origin and interpretation of these relationships.

There is in aphorism seventy-seven in *Philosophia Botanica* a well-known comment on the natural system which lacks a counterpart in *Fundamenta:* "All the *taxa* show relationships on all sides, like the countries on a map of the world." At this time he had not yet disclosed very much of his theory of the hybrids, but it was evidently well advanced, and he had come farther privately than he was willing to reveal outwardly. The proposition becomes plain in the context of the fully developed hybridization theory. If the parents of a species belong to different orders, and if a great many different genera and orders have supplied parent species to the members of each and every one of the individual genera, the relationships and affinities within the plant kingdom must be very intricate and run in every possible direction. The larger genera, in particular, will show a multitude of boundaries. It becomes quite meaningless to talk about linear relationships. Aristotle's conception of a *scala naturae* in which all organisms had their place, and which formed a gradually rising progression up to *Homo sapiens,* has scarcely anything in common with Linnaeus's way of looking at matters, even though Linnaeus himself in his more rhetorical moments employed the same image. In the later debate about the appearance of the natural system, especially in the early eighteenth century, it was just this degree of perfection which came to be regarded as an important criterion of where in a large or small class a work of nature should be placed. On the other hand, the idea of degrees of perfection played an extremely subordinate role in the work of Linnaeus in this area.

In his consideration of the question of system Linnaeus clearly attaches great weight to the old statement "Natura non facit saltus." In *Philosophia Botanica,* under *Methodi Naturalis Fragmenta,* the aphorism seventy-seven previously referred to, he goes so far as to repeat it twice. It appears as one of the small number of introductory aphorisms and then it forms the close of the paragraph. Linnaeus apportions most of the blame for the shortcomings of his natural system to the fact that we do not yet know all the plants in the world, because there are no leaps in nature, whereas there are gaps in his arrangement. The very hybridization theory upon which he was working led easily, of course, to a notion of smooth transitions and complete continuity everywhere. The only necessary presupposition is that hybridization has proceeded far enough and in all conceivable directions. The same thoughts are expressed in the private lectures of his later years. Many of these were published after Linnaeus's death by Paul Dietrich Giseke, a German who received private instruction from Linnaeus in 1771. In addition to his own notes, Giseke also made use of a manuscript by Johann Christian Fabricius, which dates from 1764 and contains a fuller introduction to the most important part of the readings, an exposition of each order in turn in accordance with the natural method. In Fabricius's version, the system is natural if a genus which has been placed between two other genera really has a connection with the preceding and the following genus, forming a sort of "chain." The same reasoning may be applied to the orders. This causes problems, however, because there are missing links in our knowledge of the world's flora. Linnaeus picks an illuminating example. In his opinion there are affinities between *Fumaria, Impatiens,* and *Utricularia,* which form a natural group. Another equally natural group is made up of the genera *Papaver, Argemone, Chelidonium,* and *Bocconia.* But the first group seems also to be related to the last-named genera of the second. Truly intermediate genera are lacking, however, and for this reason the affinity is not absolutely certain. So do the groups constitute one order or two? Linnaeus's view is that only when it is known whether the intermediate group does or does not exist will it be possible to answer this question.

Here Linnaeus also discusses a major division of the plant kingdom which was to attain increasing importance during the late eighteenth and early nineteenth centuries, and which remains of relevance even in modern taxonomy. The ancients, he says, were aware that the grasses and the lilies were very like each other, but they could not find a common character which distinguished them from other plants. Finally they began to look at the seed leaves, and this led to the division between monocotyledons and dicotyledons. As he had shown earlier in his work in Holland, Linnaeus himself is skeptical about the basis of this division. All the grasses are regarded as monocotyledons, whereas they ought, in fact, to be called acotyledons, because they have no seed leaves at all. Linnaeus reasons in this way because he considers that genuine seed leaves are composed of the seed's own "intrinsic substance," which has forced its way up above the soil, and that this differs from the substance in the stalk and in the normal leaves, which comes from *corculus* (the "germ" of the seed). The "seed leaves" of the grasses also come from *corculus*. In this we find a variation on the old, and, in the case of Linnaeus, cherished idea of the two main substances of the plant, the medulla and the cortex layer. On the other hand, he considers that certain cacti, which are not regarded as monocotyledons, are in fact members of the category. There are also polycotyledons, such as *Pinus, Abies,* and almost all other conifers. He cannot, therefore, see that a division by cotyledons offers a royal road to the natural method, although he recognizes the value of this character in many cases.

His arguments show clearly that he never possessed the key as long as he lived. In a letter to his pupil Fagraeus, which must without doubt have been written during his last years, we see how he continues persistently to grope for it.[23] He has, he recalls, done a great deal of work on his *ordines naturales* and managed to "bring 3, 4, 5, and 6 together here and there, taking over where the one before leaves off, like orders in a class." If he could just complete these series, then the real key might well be easier to discover, but he admits that it was all too late that he began to believe "that the natural key may lie in a certain organ of fructification." Jealously guarding his new project, as always, he goes on: "I cannot say which [part] I mean until next summer, when I shall be able to see whether I have guessed correctly by examining all the orders to see if it holds good." He believes that this may make it possible to divide all the orders (with the exception of acotyledons and monocotyledons) into two parts, which may facilitate the later work. As far as we know, this was as far as he progressed, and the problem was inherited by later generations of botanists.

Nomenclature

The reforms initiated by Linnaeus in the field of nomenclature are the complete antithesis of his hesitant explorations in search of a natural system. Where the giving of names was concerned, he was able to follow to a large extent his liking for *a priori* reasoning and for drawing up rules to govern the entire system with an unrelenting consistency. Only such consistency could give any purpose to this reform. I shall not give a detailed account of his rules for nomenclature. Nothing can compete with his own account in the major work *Critica Botanica*, a marvel of pithy literary economy. There is, however, every reason to pause to examine some of the fundamental points. Linnaeus lays down that the name of the plant should have two parts. The first indicates the genus to which the plant belongs, and

23. The letter is known, thanks to a copy made by Linnaeus, Jr., found in the manuscripts of the Linnean Society of London: "De ordine Naturali Fagraei observatio. Min Fars svar."

the second is a short but factually descriptive specific epithet, which includes the *differentia specifica,* the essential character. He emphasizes that all the species belonging to the same genus should have the same generic name and, therefore, that every genus (and similarly every species) should always be known by one and the same name. His own great taxonomic survey, using names given in accordance with these principles, naturally stands out as the model to which the whole world of botany should adhere. His rules of nomenclature would surely have had great difficulty in winning international acceptance had they not been put forward at the same time that the enormous lists of names appeared in *Genera Plantarum, Systema Naturae, Hortus Cliffortianus,* and so on.

Linnaeus gives detailed instructions for the more aesthetic and educational aspect of naming which not even he himself, let alone anyone else, could quite follow in practice. For this reason substantial passages in *Critica Botanica* are, strangely enough, among the least influential parts of Linnaeus's work. The examples that were given in the systematic works undoubtedly had a greater practical effect.

It need hardly be emphasized how sorely a standardization of naming was needed. Errors of nomenclature meant that one botanist could not understand what another was talking about. Nor is there any doubt that Linnaeus was the right man to carry out this standardization. It was his clear determination of the concepts of species and genus that paved the way for clarity in naming. Linnaeus's success as a nomenclator is a direct consequence of his ability to bring order and lucidity to botanical classification.

As we have seen, the specific element in Linnaeus's nomenclature always consisted of the *differentia specifica* of the species, true to the principles in *Critica.* The *differentia* was a logically composed definitive element containing the attributes that distinguished the species thus named from all other species in the genus. This meant that the *nomen specificum* described above became something more than merely a name; it became a reflection of the essential nature of the species and threw a direct light on its relationship with other species. Linnaeus considered that the characterizing specific name need not contain more than twelve words, which enabled him to keep nomenclature manageable, despite the great demands made upon it. It is clear, however, that this function of distinguishing the species would constitute an obstacle to the hope of being able to retain the same name for a species for all time, which was naturally something that all botanists longed for, then as now. For if a new species was discovered which was distinguished from some of the other species in the same genus by characteristics that it shared with another species of the genus previously known and described, then clearly the name of this earlier species must immediately be modified if it was to continue to contain the true *differentia specifica.* Only later was Linnaeus to overcome this problem by abandoning the logically applied *nomen specificum* in favor of an unambiguous, but at the same time much less informative, *nomen triviale.*

The distinction between naming and describing was clearly not a sharp one in the case of the species. But Linnaeus was not content just to give *differentia specifica,* the content of the *nomen specificum.* He required that species, like genera, should be furnished with a *descriptio,* a more exhaustive description, which in the case of the species must include considerably more organs than just those of sexual reproduction, since the latter were in important respects virtually the same throughout the genus. In *Critica,* therefore, he makes a distinction between *descriptio* and *differentia. Differentia* is what distinguishes the different plants within the same genus, while *descriptio* is what marks a species out from all other plants, regardless of genus. He recognizes that the *descriptio* "is often obscure and almost incomprehensible" for us, whereas the *differentia* is simple and straightforward. And for this reason we seldom find real descriptions in *Hortus Cliffortianus* and *Flora Lapponica,* although the *nomina specifica* containing the *differentia* are always given. It is an interesting if almost paradoxical consequence of Linnaeus's decided views on the specific epithet as a *differentia specifica* that species in monotypic genera are named only with the single word of the generic name. Since there are no other species in the genus, there is no *differentia specifica* to be given. On the other hand, a *descriptio* is obviously possible in such cases.

One of the enduring contributions to the progress of botany attributed to Linnaeus is, of course, the binomial nomenclature he later introduced. This gives virtually every species a name of only two words, the generic name and the specific epithet. Linnaeus himself, however, regarded this reform almost as a side issue. The first work in which binary nomenclature is consistently employed is, as is well known, *Pan Suecicus* (1749); the system is fully implemented in *Species Plantarum* in 1753, two years after its principles are set forth in *Philosophia Botanica.*[24] Its introduction does not at all mean that Linnaeus was abandoning his earlier principles for the correct naming of species. His rules for the *nomen specificum* in *Philosophia* are those which he formulated in *Critica.* The *nomen specificum* should always contain the *differentia specifica* of the species and be as brief and concise as possible while still clearly representing the species concerned. It should, therefore, also be possible to alter it. The real name of the species should thus depict the essence of the species. What Linnaeus did

24. There is a rich literature about the binomial nomenclature of Linnaeus. Among works in English are to be mentioned W. T. Stearn in his introduction to *Species Plantarum* (London, 1957), J. L. Heller in *Huntia* (1964), and James L. Larson, *Reason and Experience* (Berkeley, Calif., 1971).

now was to introduce an abbreviated designation alongside the proper specific name. The designation could consist of any word at all, a *nomen triviale,* the specific epithet of the binomial system. Linnaeus may not have realized himself just how extremely practical this trivial name was to be. It was a label which could be attached to an accepted species once and for all, and which never need be changed, no matter how many new species within the genus came to light. His lack of certainty about the importance of his reform is shown by the fact that to begin with he indicated that the trivial names might be applied more or less at random and could be altered if necessary. But by the second edition of *Species Plantarum* (1763), he had realized the significance of his innovation, and he states that every alteration of the trivial name does more harm than good.

Plant Biology

However fundamental and dominant the part played by taxonomy and nomenclature in Linnaeus's scientific achievement, he is remembered today, in Sweden at least, almost as much for other things, even when we are assessing him as a botanist. In the many dissertations which he presided over, suggested, and in many cases more or less dictated, we find a Linnaeus very different from the taxonomist. He brought these dissertations together in a number of volumes under the title *Amoenitates Academicae,* which brings lighter moments suitably to mind, and for long stretches they have a carefree charm. They are entertaining, and they are products of that *curiositas naturalis* which Linnaeus applauded and which pursued not only the utilitarian but also the pleasurable. He often remarks upon biological phenomena which did not attract general attention until many generations later and which have in many cases become the subject of quite independent branches of science in modern times. On all of these occasions Linnaeus is given the opportunity to demonstrate his acute powers of observation, his scientific imagination, and his facility for finding new and surprising sides to apparently trivial and everyday occurrences. "Omnia mirari, etiam tritissima" was a Linnaean motto to which these academic pamphlets live up admirably.

With what joy must his pupils, both those who accompanied him on his botanical excursions and those who were already practicing their craft in the field, have studied his demonstration of the floral clock, in the paper *Horologium Florae,* in which he shows how different plants open and close their flowers at set times of the day, adhering always to a precisely defined rhythm. And no less novel must have been the related thesis on the sleep of the plants and the resting positions that characterize many species during their biologically more inactive periods of the day. His method of studying seasonal changes was also new to some extent, even though this was obviously one of the much-trodden paths of natural history. Over the course of one year, 1755, he made a detailed study of the timing of a series of different floral occurrences, such as blooming, fruit setting, withering, and related them to other natural happenings—the climate, the behavior of animals, agricultural activity. He outlined a division of the year which was based, not upon the inflexible columns of figures in the calendar, but upon the natural rhythm, differing in date from year to year, but regular in its sequence and temporal consistency. He obtained twelve natural months by this method, and called them wintertime, thaw, sowing time, leafing, flowering time, ripening fruit, haymaking, harvest time, fruit season, leaves falling, slush and ice. Similar observations crop up at many places in his works, particularly in his provincial journeys, where they provide pleasant interludes between the lengthy reports on the rural economy. At the same time that they give notable evidence of his powers of scientific regeneration, they also constitute an essential part of his literary greatness, for the freshness, the novel and unusual impressions upon the senses—of which he is so artistically capable—derive their inspiration from his unique observational ability.

A fundamental biological phenomenon—which was, moreover, of a very special interest to Linnaeus—was, of course, the sexuality of plants and their fertilization. Although he had made up his mind about this at a very early date, there was extensive scope for detailed observations because of the infinite variety of nature with regard to the fertilization process. Linnaeus was happy to spend a while on this subject whenever he found it necessary to defend the basic theory of the sexuality of plants against the recurring objections of other botanists, even though these were always disposed of quickly enough. The foundations of his argument remained those which we examined in his earlier works. But new elements were added to this framework, consisting mainly of observations of various arrangements for promoting pollination, which are typical of this facet of Linnaeus's botanical research. In a number of contexts he pointed out the way in which the stamens, in *Saxifraga tridactylites, Parnassia,* and *Scleranthus,* for example, leaned inward toward the stigma to facilitate pollination, and in *Dianthus* he noted how it is the pistil which leans to reach the vicinity of the pollen.[25] He drew no clear distinction between cross-pollination and self-pollination. Evidently he found self-pollination to be the rule, but at the same time he was very conscious of the part played by the wind in carrying the pollen to the pistils. There were at any rate a large number of

25. Cf. C. A. M. Lindman, "Linné som botanist," *Carl von Linnés betydelse som naturforskare och läkare* (Uppsala, 1907), 106 ff.

cases among both monoecious and dioecious plants where it was natural to consider cross-pollination. He studied the spreading of pollen by wind in both trees and rye, and he undertook a great many experiments in his garden, carrying pollen himself from one plant to another whose stamens had been removed. But his belief in self-pollination was so firm that he never really realized the enormous importance of the insects to the fertilization of a great many of our most common flowers. Christian Konrad Sprengel was the first to do this in his *Das entdeckte Geheimniss der Natur* (1793), a work which was long overlooked.

For a long while, in fact, Linnaeus shared the widespread misconception that the nectar of the plants constituted the nourishment for the fruit, and that the insects, bees in particular, therefore damaged the flowers. To begin with, he had the same idea about their pollen-gathering, which seemed to mean that the fertilization process was destroyed by being deprived of the participation of one sex. Gradually he came to see that the bees were useful rather than harmful, in that their energetic movements inside the flower spread the pollen around; but he never made very much of this and appears not to have become aware of the full significance of what he had himself said. Only in one extremely specialized case had he really understood the importance of pollination by insects. This was the case of the fig, whose enclosed reproductive organs would be unable to communicate with the world outside but for a particular species of hymenopteron, which pushes its way through a hole in the isolating walls.

As far as the actual process of fertilization is concerned, once the pollen has adhered to the stigma, Linnaeus progressed a surprisingly long way. He understood that something, "an elastic substance," was carried through the style to the seed-germs, and that this process was the vital one. He was able to support his opinion with at least one remarkable observation, involving *Amaryllis formosissima*. The stigma of this flower secretes a drop of clear fluid every forenoon and sucks it in again a few hours later. When he sprinkled pollen over this drop it became cloudy and turned yellow, and some time later he was able to observe dark streaks in the pistils going from the stigma to the ovules. The grains of pollen were still on the stigma, but they had changed in form, in such a way that it could be concluded that they had lost a part of their contents. Morland's theory that the pollen grains themselves find their way to the ovules had thus been empirically refuted or at least substantially modified in an actual case.

Perhaps the most noteworthy of all these observations are Linnaeus's discussions of the way in which plants are adapted to their environment, both in their dependence upon a particular soil, certain climatic conditions, and other organisms in the immediate vicinity of each individual, and in their geographical adaptation to different regions and latitudes of the globe.

It is true that Linnaeus never prepared a comprehensive survey of this complex series of questions, which is now handled by such major sciences as ecology, plant sociology, and plant geography. The enormous zest for systematization which was the mainspring of his work on taxonomy is conspicuous by its absence here. Here he is nearly always a mass of intimations and premonitions, prophesying what is to follow rather than laying down the definitive doctrine. One of the few exceptions is his division of the habitat of the plants of Sweden in *Stationes Plantarum* (1754), where he makes out a table of the six different types of habitat: water, mountain, shade, meadow, rock, and organisms (the habitat of parasites). Water plants are grouped according to whether they grow in the sea, on the shore, in lakes, marsh, peat, or other wet localities; mountain plants may grow on open mountain or in "groves"; shade-loving plants, in groves or forests; plants of the field or arable land, on plantations, on wasteland, in meadows, in sand, or in clay; rock plants, on verges (road, ditch, etc.), slopes, or cliffs. The final group consists of what Linnaeus refers to, inaptly in some cases, as parasites, either of trees or of plants.

This division shows plainly that Linnaeus was aware of the importance of both climate and soil when he was dealing with the relationship of plants to their environment. This is in itself nothing remarkable. We meet this awareness in scholastic botany, and it goes right back to Aristotle and Theophrastus. But Linnaeus deepens this understanding by giving abundant examples, and by specifying in detail the way in which these factors operate in practice. The examples given in his work of the differential effect of soil are innumerable. The above list of habitats shows the extent of his experience in this sphere, much of it having been gained in the course of his dedicated work both in the Hartekamp garden and in that of the University of Uppsala. We see that Linnaeus considers that the soil affects the plant in two different ways: by helping to determine which species will be able to obtain nutrition in a given locality, and by having an effect on the size of the individual plant and on its appearance with regard to hairs, color, and so on. This is in line with his original views on the nature of varieties.

Linnaeus sees the world as having four climatic zones: the torrid with a winter temperature of 50°–70°F, the temperate with a corresponding temperature of 30°–40°F, the cold (which includes most of Sweden), and the frigid.[26] Regarding the frigid zone, he states that it is not only latitude which determines its extent, but also height from sea level, so that it may be found on the highest mountains in whatever part of the world these may be. His paradise theory depended on this being the case, as we have already

26. Linnaeus, "Rön om växternas plantering," *Vetenskapsakademiens Handlingar* (1739), 18 ff.

seen. It is also the basis of the grandiose plans to cultivate the Swedish mountains which he contemplated. There is no doubt, he considers, that useful plants from the Alps will establish themselves and even spread in the high mountains of northern Sweden once they are taken there. He believes that in principle all the mountaintops and all the cold regions of the earth are hosts to basically the same plants. On the other hand, he does not overlook the fact that geographical latitude could in itself constitute a differentiating factor. The length of the summer, and above all the length of the day, varies with its latitude. Admittedly, this means that the shortness of the summer in the north may be compensated for by the long, light nights; but in order to be able to make use of the summer light, the plants have to produce their seed very early, which is a limiting factor in their northward penetration. As was the case with soil, we see that Linnaeus considers that the climate has a differentiating effect both on the selection of species and on the appearance of the individual plant. He finds one explanation for the modest size of plants in the high mountains in the short time available for their seed to mature. They do not have time for any great vegetative growth.

In his studies of nature's household, Linnaeus also notes the interaction of different organisms, even if perhaps he does not entirely realize the extent of its importance. Nevertheless, he goes much further than his academic predecessors, who hardly did more than mention the mutual sympathy or antipathy of certain creatures in stereotyped examples with conspicuous strains of mythology and magic. He saw, for example, how an area could be better utilized if it was occupied by plants of different sizes. The trees extract their food from deeper levels of soil than the plants around them and develop their greenery high up in the air, where they have infinitely more room than down at ground level. He often commented on the way shade-loving plants were able to use the special light conditions of the forest glades. He also took note of the converse situation—that tall species which cast a large amount of shade or plants with other special characteristics may displace other forms of vegetation. Thus the beech forces the heather out of places where it grows in southern Sweden, something Linnaeus attributes primarily to the fact that beech leaves do not decompose during the first year, but instead cover the ground with a suffocating cover.

Linnaeus displayed a particular perspicacity in his division of topographical areas into biological zones of varying extent—in parts still very tenable. G. Einar du Rietz has noted how extraordinarily well he distinguished the alpine belts of the Swedish *fjäll*: the forest land, the *fjäll* birch forests, the low *fjäll*, the *fjäll* slopes, and the high *fjäll*, and how well he understood their characteristics. He also had an eye for zones in less dramatic contexts, such as, for example, the exceptionally instructive Västergötland hills. Hunneberg, for instance, is portrayed in a very illuminating fashion in *Västgötaresan (Västergötland Journey)*. From the village on the plain to the crown of the hill he sees ploughed fields, alder shrubbery, "narrow sunken meadows," steep slopes at the foot of the hill with oak groves, and so on, the vertical walls of rock "with grey crustose lichens and umbilicaria," and at the top, the forest of pine and spruce with scrub and forest mosses. The famous twentieth-century Swedish ecologist Rutger Sernander has drawn our attention to a passage in *Skånefloran* in which Linnaeus describes the zones of the shore in a manner which conforms almost exactly with the ideas of modern plant sociology.[27]

Urban Hiärne (1641–1724) was one Swedish scientist who had already realized that the vegetation we see today has not come down unchanged from the beginning of time. The landscape changes, lakes become overgrown with weeds, and different tracts of land gradually alter in character. This is due partly to the inherent mechanisms of plant life itself, such as the peat or humus which the plants produce, the shade thrown by trees, and the competition for light, food, space, and so on. Linnaeus came to hold a very dynamic conception of the development of species as the result of the hybridization of a relatively small number of original forms. His view of the history of vegetation was also dynamic. His theory of paradise is well known and has already been mentioned. Linnaeus conceived of his single island at the equator as having grown slowly in size as the level of the surrounding water sank, until all the land on the world's surface had risen out of the water. This was consistent with the much discussed theory of receding waters, which gained an increasingly firm hold among Swedish scientists during the eighteenth century. In this way the vegetation of Paradise Island was clearly spread over all the dry land, possibly helped by a variety of hybridizations. Linnaeus also thought about the sequence in which the organisms must have appeared when there was a new area for them to colonize. His observations on the subject have been summarized by Lindman: the bare cliffs rising from the sea are first covered by crustose lichens, the slight humus from which permits the spread of other lichen species with a more differentiated thallus, which in their turn provide humus for mosses, followed successively by herbaceous plants, shrubs, and trees.[28] Like Hiärne, he visualizes the overgrowing of minor watercourses by bog mosses, leading in time to firm ground with meadow vegetation. Occasionally, the process may be the reverse, he says: a rich layer of humus can be destroyed, either by the slash-and-burn cultivation or by becoming covered with peat, and the land therefore impoverished.

Before all of these processes can occur in practice, the plants must be able

---

27. R. Sernander, "I Linnés fotspår," *Svenska Linnésällskapets Årsskrift* (1921).
28. Lindman, op. cit., 94.

to spread from one place to another, often over comparatively long stretches. Linnaeus was already aware of the most important factors to be considered in the science of vegetable dispersion, and he went into them specially in *Coloniae Plantarum*. He mentions dispersion by wind, to assist which the fruits and seeds of many plants are equipped with down, which allows them to be borne over great distances. Water, in rivers in particular, may also carry seeds a very long way, and he is aware, too, of the role of birds in dispersing species with edible fruit. Man also plays a part: weeds are often inadvertently spread by the trade in corn and by the distribution of garden produce; many goods are packed in straw when transported by sea, which results in seashores and harbors often being the beachhead from which species are established in a new area.

These are only a few examples of Linnaeus's discussions of plant biology. Time and again, however, we can see the possible results of his suggestions, and also the isolation of his pronouncements among his contemporaries—they had enough to do in absorbing his taxonomy. But another reason for this loneliness is certainly the fact that Linnaeus never pushed his opinions on the biological subjects with anything like the persistence, discipline, and concentration that made him, externally as well as internally, such a successful taxonomist.

TORE FRÄNGSMYR

Linnaeus as a Geologist

The work of such an unceasingly active naturalist and writer as Linnaeus led him to take up geological questions on numerous occasions, as one would expect. With his keen eye for the processes of nature he made many perceptive observations, which he quickly noted down in his accounts of the provincial journeys, or in his botanical works, or as rough drafts for other projects.

The achievements of Linnaeus as a geologist have already been examined in a study by A. G. Nathorst.[1] The account which follows will discuss only a few of the more important aspects. One concerns the well-known dispute about the diminution of waters, in which the contribution of Linnaeus was a fundamental one. From this we inevitably come to the question of the stratigraphy of the earth and all the ramifications of this problem. But the idea of a continuous decrease in the waters of the globe was at the same time closely connected with Linnaeus's view of the first age of the earth, the blissful paradise recounted in Genesis, and this necessitates a detailed look at the ideas of the period on this subject. This, in turn, leads us to another ever-topical question of the time: how the events related in the biblical story of the Creation were to be interpreted. An introductory consideration of Linnaeus's immediate predecessor, Emanuel Swedenborg, will, therefore, be followed by a section on Linnaeus's concept of paradise and his views on the diminishing-waters controversy and, in conclusion, by an outline of his attitude toward the Bible as a scientific source.

---

1. A. G. Nathorst, "Carl von Linné såsom geolog," in *Carl von Linnés betydelse såsom naturforskare och läkare* IV (Uppsala, 1907). English transl. "Carl von Linné as a Geologist" (Washington, The Smithsonian Report for 1908).

When God had made Adam and Eve, he created the Garden of Eden for them. The second chapter of the book of Genesis describes this beautiful paradise idyll, where the first human beings lived in harmony with each other and with nature until the time of the Fall. This story made poetic material and was much used as a theme by poets in the hexaëmeron genre; but it was also employed in Christian religious art. When the story of the Creation came into conflict with empirical science, paradise became one of the key questions—the Flood was another—which often showed how the evidence of the Bible in general was regarded. The picture of paradise could be seen only as a poetic portrayal—although this was rare—or it could be considered the definitive documentation of the first age on earth. It could also be put on a par with other legends and fables of literature. The details given in the Bible were very scanty, however, which meant that the text had to be interpreted and explained to fill the gaps. There was discussion of the geographical location of paradise and its physical appearance.

The subject was also taken up in Sweden, on more or less the same lines as abroad. Before we deal with Linnaeus, it seems natural to look first at how Swedenborg, hardly ten years earlier, had seen the earthly paradise, for there are illuminating similarities between them.

The Earthly Paradise

Emanuel Swedenborg had portrayed the heavenly state of the infant earth in *Principia Rerum Naturalium* (1734). The purpose of the book was actually to describe the coming into existence of the universe and of the world, but Swedenborg wished to round it off by depicting the first time on earth.[2]

Swedenborg's description is basically the one which is found in his earliest works and which recurs later in his religious and literary writings.[3] Much of his theory of the orgin and development of the earth is taken from Descartes and Thomas Burnet. When the earth had begun to orbit the sun, a crust formed round it, disintegrating later so that its parts formed the present continents. As the earth moved farther and farther from the sun, a series of changes took place. The most important was that the earth lost speed, and this led to the periodic changes in climate, resulting in the seasons.[4]

2. E. Swedenborg, *Principia Rerum Naturalium* (Dresden, Leipzig, 1734), 445.

3. Cf. I. Jonsson, *Emanuel Swedenborg* (Twayne's World Authors Series 127) (New York, 1971), and T. Frängsmyr, *Geologi och skapelsetro* (Lychnos-Bibliotek, 26) (Uppsala, 1969), chap. 3.

4. Cf. Swedenborg, *Om jordenes och planeternas gång och stånd* (Skara, 1718); reprinted in *Opera* III (Stockholm, 1911).

While the earth was moving more rapidly in its orbit round the sun, it was characterized by an equable and constant temperature, an eternal spring. Swedenborg found this time of paradise in the descriptions of the golden age by the classical poets and, in particular, in the *Metamorphoses* of Ovid. This summons up an idyll of the never-ending reign of spring and of a fruitfulness beyond compare:

Then spring was ever-lasting, and gentle zephyrs with warm breath played with the flowers that sprang unplanted. Anon the earth, untilled, brought forth her stores of grain, and the fields, though unfallowed, grew white with the heavy, bearded wheat. Streams of milk and streams of sweet nectar flowed, and yellow honey was distilled from the verdant oak.[5]

But Swedenborg also considers that he finds support in Ovid for his theory of the earth's loss of velocity. With the close of the golden age the eternal spring ended, and in Ovid's poetic account, too, the slower revolutions of the earth give rise to temperature changes and seasons:

Jove now shortened the bounds of the old-time spring, and through winter, summer, variable autumn, and brief spring completed the year in four seasons. Then first the parched air glared white with burning heat, and icicles hung down congealed by freezing winds.[6]

Swedenborg sees further confirmation of his theory in Virgil, in the hexaëmeron poet Alcimus Avitus, and in other classical writers. He mentions, for example, the description given in Plato's *Phaedo* of "the true world," which was said to be in that area of space nearest heaven and to be adorned with gold and silver. In the beautiful climate men did not become ill, and they lived much longer than on earth.[7] Plato's picture belongs to the same genre as other pagan visions of paradise, such as the concept of a golden age or the myth of the Elysian Fields. Swedenborg claims further support from the mention by Hesiod of the Gardens of Hesperides, which were said to lie beyond the ocean, and from the passage in Genesis about the flaming sword which cut off the first man from paradise. He also notes that the ancients regarded paradise as being in a higher region than the present surface of the earth, and he interprets this as showing that the earth must once have been nearer to the sun.[8] Thus Plato's ethereal paradise would be not a different earth but our earth in another position. The flaming sword of Genesis would be an allusion to the heat of the sun. Interpreting them in

---

5. Ovidius, *Metamorphoses,* I:107–112, transl. F. J. Miller (Loeb Classical Library), vol. I (London, 1944).

6. Ibid., I:116–120.

7. Plato, *Phaedo,* transl. with introduction and commentary by R. Hackforth (Cambridge, 1955), 176 f.

8. *Principia,* 448.

this way, Swedenborg found that the poets of antiquity provided support for his theory of the slowing down of the earth.

Swedenborg obtained all of this evidence from Burnet. In the extracts he copied from *Telluris Theoria Sacra*, which long went unnoticed as a result of a misreading by the publisher, Swedenborg marked just these particular references.[9] He agreed with Burnet in the location of the earthly paradise, a question that was occupying many minds at the time. Burnet considered that the whole globe, its surface flat and smooth before the Flood, formed the paradise spoken of in the Bible. Swedenborg is of the same opinion. Everlasting spring made the whole earth a universal paradise, and nature was in her infancy, playing and smiling; it was in this golden age, according to the ancients, that the gods were born.[10] Everlasting spring was a prerequisite of the rich fertility. At God's command the earth brought forth plants and animals, the sea produced fish, and so on. Thus He perfected His work, using those elements which were already there, but the agreeable climate was an additional factor. Finally, man was created as the crowning glory. Swedenborg's account ends with a tribute to God in his infinite wisdom, the creator of the universe.

Two aspects of Swedenborg's concept of paradise are particularly important. One is that he finds support in the old myths for the theroy of the decelerating earth which he had presented earlier, and the other is that he puts the biblical story of the Creation on an equal footing with the accounts of the golden age contained in the poetry of antiquity. He recognizes no boundaries between the Christian and the pagan. Moses and Ovid appear as two comparable giants, who have described the same event from differing perspectives. Now this way of looking at the matter was by no means new; it formed the very essence of the *Philosophia Mosaica* of the Renaissance, represented in Sweden by the mystic Johannes Bureus and others.[11] But it is, nevertheless, worth emphasizing that the Bible is not accorded any special status as a historical source. We encounter the same point of view in Linnaeus, but here the parallel is more implicit and, therefore, needs to be elucidated in detail.

To a lover of nature such as Linnaeus, imagining paradise with its rich flora and fauna must have been a tempting mental exercise. He saw the

---

9. R. L. Tafel, *Documents concerning the Life and Character of Emanuel Swedenborg* II (London, 1890), has read "Ex Roumette" (p. 871), but Inge Jonsson has discovered that the correct reading must be "Ex Bournetto," i.e., "from Burnet" (*Swedenborg*, p. 34). Swedenborg's excerpts in the Academy of Sciences, Stockholm, Cod. 86–53, pp. 167 f., 171. Cf. Th. Burnet, *Telluris Theoria Sacra*, 1681 (Amsterdam, 1694), 126 f.

10. Burnet, pp. 127–133; Swedenborg, *Principia*, 448.

11. S. Lindroth, *Paracelsismen i Sverige till 1600-talets mitt* (Lychnos-Bibliotek 7) (Uppsala, 1943), 204 ff.

Garden of Eden as "the first and noblest botanical garden,"[12] but he saw it also as something which had a real part to play in his scientific argument.

In 1743, at Uppsala, Linnaeus gave his famous conferment address, "On the Growth of the Habitable Earth" (*Oratio de Telluris Habitabilis Incremento*). In it he set forth his theory that the dry land surface had gradually increased as the water had abated; to start with, only a small island had been visible above the water, and it was this small island which constituted paradise. He touched upon the question in other connections, but it is primarily this address, published the following year, which gives us our knowledge of his ideas on the infancy of the earth.[13] In this chapter we shall put the paradise island in its ideo-historical context, in order to be able to examine its relationship to Linnaeus's scientific theories at a later stage.

In a poetic vision, Linnaeus draws a picture of the extent and life of the habitable world in its infancy. The greater part of our present continents lay under water, and all that appeared above this boundless sea was a little island. This was all the land which God created in the beginning. Here He laid out the Garden of Eden, paradise, with Adam and Eve and all the plants and animals (*Oratio*, §§ 8–9, 16–18, 44). This little paradise island gradually grew, and eventually, as the waters receded, large coherent land masses developed (§§ 27–44). There was a high and imposing mountain on the island, which Linneaus uses to explain how a variety of climates could have occurred within a limited area: at the top of the mountain the climate was alpine, and proceeding downward warmer climates of various types were encountered, as was necessary if flora and fauna of all types were to thrive there. Linnaeus was, of course, of the opinion that God had placed one pair of each species of each plant and animal in paradise and that these had then multiplied. Where hermaphrodites were concerned, on the other hand, one individual of each species was sufficent (§§ 7–15, 19–25, 45–53). A large part of his exposition is spent on showing how plants have been able to spread from a restricted locality and appear in almost all parts of the world's vast surface (§§ 54–90). Exactly the same process was repeated after the Flood. Noah had taken one pair of each species with him into the ark, and when the Flood had exterminated all other life, new flora and fauna spread from these pairs (§§ 22, 97).[14]

Even from this brief outline is it evident that Linnaeus's description of the first appearance of the earth is, in part, the product of his scientific

12. *Fauna Svecica* (Stockholm, 1746), preface.
13. *Oratio de Telluris Habitabilis Incremento* (Leiden, 1744). English transl., "On the Growth of the Habitable Earth," *Select Dissertations from the Amoenitates Academicae*, vol. I (London, 1781).
14. Cf. N. von Hofsten, *Zur älteren Geschichte des Diskontinuitäts-problems in der Biogeographie* (Würzburg, 1916).

reasoning. Admittedly, Linnaeus chooses to justify the claim that paradise consists of an island by referring to the statement in the Bible that Adam would know and name all the animals,[15] but this idea also formed the starting point for his theory of diminishing waters.

Until now it has been most usual to refer only to these scientific ideas, as if they determined every detail of Linnaeus's concept of paradise. His biographer Bishop Elis Malmeström takes the view that "scientific interest contributed to this peculiar modification of the biblical notion of the Garden of Eden," and he appears to wish to explain every departure from the Bible in the same way.[16] This argument is based soley on the text of the Bible, without consideration of the wealth of ideas and conceptions that followed in the Bible's wake. In fact, the story of the Creation gives only a very brief account of paradise, and over the centuries this has been embroidered and embellished in keeping with folk and literary tradition, and it cannot be said that these traditions contradict the Bible. To use only the actual words of the Bible in determining whether a concept is "biblical" is, therefore, to take far too restrictive a view. Nor can the paradise myth in this form be considered in isolation from the classical tradition of the golden age, the dream of Atlantis, and other ideas of a long-vanished utopia. It is hard to imagine that an educated man such as Linnaeus could have been untouched by centuries-old notions which were still generally cherished in his day. It is rather probable that these notions colored his concept of paradise, and if this was the case, it can scarcely be described as peculiar. It may be appropriate, therefore, to recall something of the content and extent of these ideas.

Where was paradise? Since the earliest times there had been speculation about the location of paradise, which, according to Genesis, God prepared for the first human beings. Even if certain Jewish traditions were inclined to see Eden as a celestial abode— a "garden of the gods," in the words of Johannes Bureus, who held such a view—the usual opinion was that the place was to be found on earth. It may be noted that the question has been discussed even in modern times.[17] The natural starting point was, of course, the second chapter of Genesis, which states: "And the Lord God planted a garden eastward in Eden, and there He put the man whom He had formed" (Genesis 2:8).

This brief description is followed by the names of the four rivers. A spring rose in Eden and divided to form four rivers: Pison, which encircled

---

15. Genesis 2:19–20.

16. E. Malmeström, *Carl von Linnés religiösa åskådning* (Stockholm, 1926), 123, and *Carl von Linné* (Stockholm, 1964), 173, quotation, 174.

17. Cf. R. Hennig, *Wo lag das Paradies?* (Berlin, 1950).

Havilah where gold was found; Gihon, which flowed around the entire land of Ethiopia; Hiddekel, said to be in Assyria; and Euphrates (Genesis 2:10–14).

That was all there was to go on. The Fathers of the Church debated whether the account should be interpreted allegorically or literally, but in time the latter alternative gained the upper hand.[18] Generally, one proceeded from the information that paradise lay "eastward" and from the mention of the four rivers, but there were also a number of other suggestions. Paradise was pinpointed in virtually every continent and country, even in Sweden,[19] while some assumed that it was situated not on earth but on the moon or somewhere up in the firmament. In his discussion of the ideas of Linnaeus, Malmeström asserts that "the Bible places paradise in the land of the Euphrates and Tigris,"[20] disgregarding the profusion of speculative literature on the subject. The first point to make here is that even today it is extremely doubtful whether we can be as precise as this on the strength of the vague information contained in the Bible. The second is that even if we could, it would not be relevant in this connection, because Linnaeus's contemporaries were not at all unanimous on the subject. In the eighteenth century writers were still proposing a great many possible interpretations. The abundance of literature shows both the extent of the preoccupation with the question of paradise and the variety of opinions that were in circulation.[21] In Sweden the matter was dealt with in 1714 by Olof Celsius, Senior, in a dissertation bearing the frequently encountered title *De Situ Paradisi Terrestris*. He adheres to the traditional pattern set by authorities abroad and plumps for the Euphrates-Tigris area as the most probable alternative.[22] But other opinions are also reported. Linnaeus's hypothesis must be seen against the full extent of this background.

During the Middle Ages the belief in an earthly paradise was an established one. Maps showed the earth as a round disc, resting on the water,

---

18. E.g., J. Marckius, *Historia Paradisi* (Amsterdam, 1705), 1–11; L. I. Ringbom, *Graltempel und Paradies* (Stockholm, 1951), 256, and *Paradisus Terrestris* (Helsinki, 1958), 16 ff; J. K. Wright, *The Geographical Lore of the Time of the Crusades*, 1925 (New York, 1965), 71 f.

19. *An Universal History, from the Earliest Account of Time to the Present* I, 2nd ed. (London, 1740), 54.

20. *Carl von Linné,* 173 f.

21. See, for instance: P. Heylyn, *Cosmographie in foure Books,* 5th ed. (London, 1677), 112; T. Burnet, *Archaeologia Philosophica,* 2nd ed. (London, 1728), 375–476; P. D. Huet, *Traité de la situation de paradis terrestre,* 7th ed. (Amsterdam, 1701), 4 f.; Marckius, op. cit., 19–41, 133–154; J. J. Scheuchzer, *Kupfer-Bibel* (Augsburg, Ulm, 1731), 33 f.; *An Universal History,* I, 53 ff.; J. H. Zedler, *Grosses vollständiges Universal-Lexicon aller Wissenschaften und Künste,* vol. 26 (Leipzig, Halle, 1740), col. 743 ff. Cf. F. Delitzsch, *Wo lag das Paradies?* (Leipzig, 1881).

22. O. Celsius, *De Situ Paradisi Terrestris* (respondent E. Klint) (diss., Uppsala, 1714), 32.

and divided into three parts by an inscribed T. The upper half was made up of Asia, and the lower one was divided into two parts, Europe and Africa. Jerusalem was in the center—on the evidence of Ezekiel 5:5 and other authorities—and paradise was at the top, in the east; the upper part of the map was thus east, not north as it is today. This schematic picture of the world is found on maps and paintings virtually throughout the Middle Ages. All maps of the world contained information about the location of paradise, but it must, of course, be borne in mind that they were in the same tradition and often emanated from the same publishers. George Kimble maintains, for example, that the map of Isidore of Seville formed the basis of most of the maps of the world of the later Middle Ages.[23]

Even as a more complex picture of the world emerged, these ideas persisted. Paradise continued to be placed in the east, although east was gradually moved round to the right of the map. In both cases the four rivers were marked in, but here arose the difficulty that they did not reflect the present situation. The only one which it seemed possible to locate with certainty was the Euphrates; in consequence, Hiddekel, expressly assigned to Assyria, was taken to be the Tigris. Pison was often identified as the Ganges, as Havilah, with its gold, was believed to represent India.[24] Gihon was assumed to correspond to the Nile, as it was nearest to Ethiopia. This was not the only interpretation, but it was the commonest, and elements of it were almost always included. The problem was that these rivers, far from rising at the same place, were widely separated.

How, then, was the fact to be explained that the biblical description did not fit in with contemporary geography? There were generally three solutions to that puzzle. If one accepted the rivers named, of which only the Euphrates and the Tigris were in any way adjacent, then it was assumed that the course of the other rivers was largely underground. Others based their reasoning on the supposition that the surface of the earth had undergone such a cataclysm in the form of the Flood that the original watercourses had been altered—in some cases this line of argument was combined with the idea of subterranean rivers—and this was why the exact conditions narrated in the Bible could no longer be found. This was the view adopted by many eighteenth-century authorities, such as Whiston, Woodward, Scheuchzer, and Tournefort, who was cited by Linnaeus.[25]

23. G. Kimble, *Geography in the Middle Ages* (London, 1938), 24 f., 184, 197. Cf. Ringbom, *Graltempel*, 251, and *Paradisus,* 10 ff.; M. Letts, *Sir John Mandeville* (London, 1949), 26 f.

24. Zedler, op. cit., col. 767 ff.; Delitzsch, op. cit., 12, 15 ff. Cf. J. E. Terserus, *Annotationes in Genesin* (Uppsala, 1655), 13.

25. J. Woodward, *An Essay toward a Natural History of the Earth* (London, 1695), 266; W. Whiston, *A New Theory of the Earth* (London, 1696), 104 ff.; Scheuchzer, op. cit., 33 f.; P. de Tournefort, *Relation D'un voyage du Levant* III (Lyon, 1717), 179.

Linnaeus himself did not believe in this result of the Flood, but he reasoned along the same lines to the extent of holding the opinion that the earth no longer looked as it had at the Creation. A third solution was that paradise had extended over the entire area between the four rivers.[26]

Disregarding this latter idea, which appears not to have won any great favor, the most widespread opinion was probably that paradise had been in Mesopotamia. The area was accorded a variety of names—Armenia, Assyria, Babylon, Mesopotamia—but the area intended was above the Persian Gulf, around or between the Tigris and the Euphrates. This was the common view during the Middle Ages and into the eighteenth century; even those who believed that it was no longer possible to determine the area with accuracy accepted that it had been in Mesopotamia.[27]

As we have seen, Linnaeus takes a different view. He supposes rather vaguely that paradise was located below the equator, probably somewhere in Africa.[28] This opinion also occurred in the literature, whether Africa in particular was mentioned, or only the southern hemisphere. When Dante put the mountain of purgatory along with the earthly paradise in the southern hemisphere, he was deviating from contemporary opinion, which envisaged Eden in the east. In another respect Dante did what so many others had done: placed the Euphrates and Tigris in paradise and let them flow underground so that they could be in their regular places at the same time. During the latter half of the fourteenth century and the first half of the fifteenth, Dante's opinion became increasingly widely accepted as paradise began to be assigned to central or southern Africa.[29] Burnet was long undecided, but eventually he, too, came down in favor of the southern hemisphere. He believed, of course, that the whole face of the earth was in a paradisiacal state until the time of the Flood, but in a later English edition he also puts Eden in a particular geographical area below the equator and argues that it is the line of the equator itself which by its heat constitutes the flaming sword mentioned in the Bible. Huet, who was often quoted as an authority on this question, mentions in his summary that some wished to place paradise "in Africa below the equator," and a similar report is to be found in Olof Celsius.[30] Africa is nearly always included in the surveys of

26. E.g., Zedler, op. cit., col. 745.
27. Heylyn, op. cit., 266; A. Kircher, *Arca Noë* (Amsterdam, 1675), 22; Woodward, op. cit., 266; Whiston, op. cit., 104 ff.; Scheuchzer, op. cit., 34. Many works contain maps of Eden—e.g., Huet, op. cit., after preface, unpag., and S. Bochart, *Geographia Sacra,* 3rd ed. (Leiden, 1692), 9. Cf. also Zedler, op. cit., col. 747; Delitzsch, op. cit., 33 ff.; Wright, op. cit., 261 f.; Katherine B. Collier *Cosmogonies of Our Fathers* (New York, 1934), 107, 202, 458.
28. *Oratio,* § 46.
29. Cf. Kimble, op. cit., 243 f., illustration between 118 and 119.
30. Huet, op. cit., 5; Celsius, op. cit., 7.

current opinion which writers drew up when dealing with the question.

Linnaeus's geographical indication is too vague for us to be able to infer the direct influence of any particular author. We have, however, seen that similar statements crop up so frequently that his view can scarcely be regarded as at all eccentric or out of the ordinary. It should also be apparent that at the time of Linnaeus the question of the geographical whereabouts of paradise had long been and was still being so widely discussed that he was naturally aware of the common opinions. The same applies to the topography of paradise; his description can only be fully understood by seeing it in the light of the earlier tradition.

The flora of the accounts of paradise was luxuriant and ran wild, and it was by no means confined to the Christian religion. Popular and religious notions intersect and demonstrate not insignificant similarities. During the Middle Ages paradise was often conceived as a mountain or an island, sometimes both, sometimes only one.[31] In many cases there were variations on the theme—paradise as a magnificent castle on a mountain or some other lofty site, a parallel to Montsalvat, the castle of the grail—but it is the basic pattern that matters. The paintings of medieval Christian art have helped to give a concrete picture of paradise. Lars-Ivar Ringbom has shown that paradise mountain was a recurrent theme of Christian pictorial art, sometimes combined with other sacred mountains, such as Zion or Golgotha.[32]

There is, thus, no doubt that the mountain occupied an important place in the descriptions of paradise in the Christian tradition. True, it was not mentioned in the story of the Creation, but confirmation could be sought elsewhere in the Bible. A. J. Wensinck has pointed to Semitic ideas on the "navel of the earth," which was at times identified with mountains.[33] From various places in the Bible the conclusion was drawn that mountains occupied a special position, as the foundation of the earth's surface, or as the link between heaven and earth; but what is even more important is that the mountains were regarded as having been the first solid material to rise from the water at the Creation. An old Syrian legend puts paradise on a high mountain range, a "Mount Eden" higher than all the other mountains and completely encircling the earth, and there is a similar tradition in Armenia.[34] The link between Christian ideas and other traditions—the seats

31. Ringbom, *Graltempel*, 257 ff., 322 ff., and *Paradisus*, 9–52.

32. *Graltempel*, 331 ff., and *Paradisus*, 53–83. Ringbom considers it likely that this mythical paradise mountain is identical with the plateau of Takht-i-Suleiman in northwestern Persia (*Paradisus*, 287–399). Cf. critique by C. Nylander, *The Deep Well* (London, 1969), 111–126.

33. A. J. Wensinck, *The Ideas of the Western Semites concerning the Navel of the Earth* (Amsterdam, 1916), 1–10.

34. E. A. Wallis Budge, ed., *The Book of the Cave of Treasures* (London, 1927), 60 ff.

of the gods on the mountains of Nordic mythology, the golden mountain of Meru of the Indians, or the Greek mountain of the gods, Olympus—has been denied, but it would appear difficult to dismiss it entirely.

A good idea of the medieval concept of paradise may be obtained from the fantastic book of travels of John Mandeville, a book of wide renown and popularity. Mandeville, the pseudonym of a person who has never been identified with certainty, had not, of course, visited all the countries he described, and his accounts were based on earlier literature, in particular the writings of Vincent of Beauvais. As far as paradise was concerned, he admitted openly that he had not been there; it was not accessible to mortals, but, nevertheless, he knew a good deal about it. Paradise was in the east, at the highest spot on earth, so high that it approached the orbit of the moon and was not reached by Noah's flood. The four rivers rose in the center, but then went underground again in order to reappear in India, Egypt, and Mesopotamia.[35] When Columbus sailed west in search of the sea route to India, he had read Mandeville and others and thought that he could point out paradise. He believed he had reached the easternmost parts of India, "the farthest ends of the Orient," and in 1498, on the third journey, he talks about paradise at length in a letter to Ferdinand and Isabella. It consisted of an island in the form of a high mountain situated in the ocean in the southern hemisphere; the four rivers were also named.[36]

We have here the same picture as in Linnaeus: a high mountain on an island. The mountain appears, as we have seen, in a number of traditions, but the idea of an island was also a common one; what is more, the particular island was sometimes named. The most widespread opinion here was probably that Ceylon was the site of the earthly paradise. There seems to have been a legend on the island of Ceylon that Adam was buried there, high up in the hills. This information is included in many accounts. In Sweden it is referred to by the theologian and poet Haquin Spegel, among others,[37] but the subject had been taken up earlier, in the book by the Swedish traveler Nils Matsson Kiöping. "This island of Ceylon is one of the most fertile lands known on earth, and is therefore called the earthly paradise," he writes, and he also believes that the banana was the forbidden tree of whose fruit Adam and Eve partook. Linnaeus was of the same opinion, and as he read and quoted Kiöping at an early date, it is probable that he obtained the idea from him. Kiöping also speaks of a "high and

35. *Mandeville's Travels* (London, 1953), ed. M. Letts, 214 ff., 405 ff.
36. S. E. Morison, ed., *Journals and Other Documents on the Life and Voyages of Christopher Columbus* (New York, 1963), 287; cf. pp. 170, 282, 375. Björn Landström has reconstructed Columbus's view in his work *Columbus* (London, 1967), 147.
37. See, for instance, Burnet, *Telluris theoria*, 77; Huet, op. cit., 5. Marckius, op. cit., 32; *An Universal History*, 58; Zedler, op. cit., 744; Kimble, op. cit., 184; H. Spegel, *Thet öpna paradis* (Stockholm, 1705), 9.

mighty mountain, which the Christians called Adam's Peak and do maintain that Adam lies buried there."[38]

Linnaeus was thus well aware of this tradition, but he did not himself accept it. In 1747 he was commissioned to examine a collection of plants from Ceylon, and he referred to the subject in his introduction to *Flora Zeylanica,* which he published the same year. Ceylon is richer than other places in stones, plants, and animals, he says, and for this reason there has been a wish to place paradise there. Other, more perspicacious scholars believe, however, that our first forefathers chose to live on this particular island after they had been banished from paradise. He goes on to mention that the lemon tree has been regarded as the tree of knowledge which stood in the Garden of Eden. Linnaeus, who does not, in fact, appear to be sympathetic to this idea himself, mentions Olof Celsius, who dealt with the matter in his celebrated book on the plants of the Bible and who had also discussed it earlier.[39]

The notion of Ceylon as the Garden of Eden may seem a curious one, but it was spread assiduously, and strengthened the idea that paradise had had the shape of an island. One suggestion was that an island had formed between the Euphrates and the Tigris.[40] Milton formulated similar ideas in his own way in *Paradise Lost.* Adam tells Raphael what he remembers of his own creation, how he was led by an emissary of heaven to paradise, a mountain with a plateau upon which splendid fruit trees grew. When Adam and Eve were banished from the Garden after the Fall, an angel led them down the slope to the plain below. Raphael had previously shown Adam what was going to happen during and after the Flood. "This Mount of Paradise" is to be carried away by the torrent and deposited at its mouth, where it will take root as "an island salt and bare."[41]

This Christian legend of paradise must now be compared with the ancient traditions of a departed, happier time in human history.

Hesiod's poetry dealt with a golden age, and the theme was later taken up by Roman poets such as Ovid, Horace, and Virgil. Plato wrote on the wonderful island of Atlantis, which suddenly sank into the sea; the reality behind this picture has been discussed down to modern times. With time these ideas branched out into a number of different conceptions: the Elysian Fields, the beautiful gardens of Hesperides, the fairy island of Saint Brendan, or the Fortunate Isles, *Insulae Fortunatae.* There is no need to go into

---

38. N. Matson Kiöping, *Een kort beskrifning uppå trenne resor och peregrinationer* (Wisindzborg, 1674), 105, 107, quotation, 108.

39. *Flora Zelanica* (Holmiae, 1747), 11; Celsius, *Hierobotanicon* I (Uppsala, 1745), 158 ff.

40. Heylyn, op. cit., 112.

41. Milton, *Paradise Lost,* 8:300–305, 12:637–640, 11:825–830; ed. Th. Newton (Birmingham, 1758).

the connection between these utopian concepts at this point, nor shall we investigate the extent to which certain of them were based on a factual reality; Insulae Fortunatae seems to have been an ancient name for the Canary Islands, for example. The important thing here is the common characteristics of these visions in their concrete form: an island is often involved, the climate is delightful, fertility is great, people are happy—and this blissful state is long past.[42]

It is evident that the Atlantis myth and the dream of the golden age display obvious similarities to the paradise story, and they have undoubtedly left their mark on its later form. These concepts were brought together during the Middle Ages; during the Renaissance they were incorporated as a part of the *Philosophia Mosaica,* which, in Platonic circles in particular, strove to reconcile Genesis with pagan sources. Here, too, it is worthwhile to recall Burnet; he considers that pagan poets such as Hesiod, Ovid, and Virgil are referring to the same state of paradise as that described by Moses.[43] In the English translation, he dealt with the subject in greater detail in connection with his theory of the earth. The golden age, it is said there, refers to the state of the whole earth, whereas the islands of the blessed and other visions correspond to the more specific, restricted paradise which Burnet assumed in this later version:

That this parallel (the golden age–paradise) may the better appear, we may observe, that as we say that the whole earth was, in some sense, paradisiacal in the first ages of the world, and that there was besides, one region or portion of it that was peculiarly so, and bore the denomination of Paradise; So the ancients besides their golden age; which was common to all the earth, noted some parts of it that were more golden, if I may say so, than the rest, and which did more particularly answer to Paradise; as their Elysian Fields, Fortunate Islands, Gardens of Hesperides, Alcinous, etc. these had a double portion of pleasantness, and besides the advantages which they had in common with the rest of the earth at that time, had something proper and singular, which gave them a distinct consideration and character from the rest.[44]

Among other authors may be mentioned Robert Hooke, who, although he did not expressly draw a parallel with the bibilical portrayals of paradise, regarded the Atlantis myth of Plato and Ovid's poetry of the golden age as actual descriptions of the first time on earth.[45] The fact that these examples

42. E.g., W. H. Babcock, *Legendary Islands of the Atlantic* (New York, 1922); H. Pettersson, *Atlantis och Atlanten* (Stockholm, 1949); P. Svendsen, *Gullalderdrøm og udviklingstro* (Oslo, 1940), esp. 13–109.
43. Survey in J. Brucker, *Historia Critica Philosophiae a Mundi Incunabilis ad Nostram Usque Aetatem Deducta,* IV:2 (Leipzig, 1743), 610–643. Cf. Wright, op. cit., 47; Svendsen, op. cit., 42, footnote; Lindroth, op. cit., 204 ff. On Burnet, see *Telluris Theoria,* 72 ff., 127–133.
44. *The Theory of the Earth,* 3rd ed. (London, 1697), 121.
45. Hooke, *Posthumous Works* (London, 1705), 372 ff., 377 ff.

from classical literature are often named in surveys of the field in which the author does not himself opt for one particular view only serves to illustrate the diversity of opinion. Here the succinct account of Huet may be cited by way of example, for he was an authority who was without doubt known to Linnaeus; Tournefort refers to him in his book of travels, which was used by Linnaeus, and Huet is mentioned both in Spegel's poem of paradise and in Swedish dissertations on these matters. Huet considers that the pagan notions of happy isles, Elysian Fields, Hesperidean Gardens, and other bygone idylls, took their complexion from the Christian portrayal of paradise.[46]

In Sweden, Olof Rudbeck's grandiose patriotic work *Atlantica* certainly played a part. Rudbeck identified the Atlantis of Plato with the Scandinavian peninsula. It is true that this was not paradise but the new starting point for the human race after the Flood, but he breathed new life into the concept of an island as the beginning of the reconstruction of the earth. He combined ancient tradition and his patriotic dream and called the old Sweden by names such as "Atlantis," "the island of the gods," "the island of the blessed," and so on.[47] Echoes of Rudbeck's exposition are to be heard well into the eighteenth century, and even in the dissertation of Celsius, referred to earlier, it is taken as a matter of course that the ancient ideas of the happy isles allude to the biblical paradise. Some place paradise in the Americas, says the author, others on the island of Taprobana, others in the Fortunate Isles, and others in Armenia.[48]

This process of synthesis is most consistently accomplished in two dissertations on the four ages of the world, debated at Uppsala in 1729 and 1731 with Lars Arrhenius and Mattias Asp, respectively, as *praeses* (responsible professors). The respondent was Olof Burman, later deputy university librarian and eventually to become a minister of the church. The first part of this presentation recounts various traditions in detail, both those of antiquity and the theories of Rudbeck. The author takes up what is to be the main theme of the second part, the parallel between biblical and pagan accounts; old names have disappeared with the passing of time and been replaced by new ones, Saturn in place of Adam, Elysian Fields instead of paradise. In the second dissertation the author establishes from the outset that the golden age in the strict sense was the first period after the creation of the world and of man. The four eras named in Hesiod and Ovid find

---

46. Huet, op. cit., 193; Tournefort, op. cit., 178 f.; Spegel, op. cit., preface; O. Celsius, op. cit., 26; M. Asp, *De Quatuor Mundi Aetatibus* II (respondent O. Burman) (diss., Uppsala, pr. Stockholm, 1731), 86.

47. *Atlantica* I, 1679 (Uppsala, 1937), chaps. 8, 9, 14, 15, 23.

48. Taprobana or Taprobane was the old Greek name for Ceylon. See *Encyclopédie*, vol. 15 (Neufchatel, 1765), 899 f.

their corresponding epochs in Christian chronology. Thus the golden age was the time of paradise; the silver age was the time between the fall of Adam and the Flood of Noah; the bronze age was that between the Deluge and the Flood known to the ancients as that of Deucalion; and finally came the iron age. The place known by the ancients as the Elysian Fields and assigned to a number of different locations is equated with paradise, and the author does not consider it surprising that the pagans tried various places in their search for the Elysian Fields, in view of the fact that not even the Christians can agree on the definite whereabouts of paradise. In the same way much evidence is produced for the assertion that Saturn and Adam are the same person; one clue lies in the identity of their sons, Abel corresponding to Pluto, Cain to Neptune, and Seth to Jupiter.[49]

We have already seen that Swedenborg was of the same opinion: to him the accounts of Ovid and Moses were to be given equal credence. In other words, we have here a total merging on a broad front of the Christian paradise myth and the ancient dream of a golden age, which must have influenced Linnaeus. He was, moreover, well read in classical poetry, and in *Oratio* he himself draws the link with the golden age by quoting Horace. In the sixteenth epode Horace warns the Roman people of the decline and fall of the empire, but exhorts those who have courage to try to cross the ocean to the happy fields, to the islands of the blessed:

Us the encompassing Ocean awaits. Let us seek the Fields, the Happy Fields, and the Islands of the Blest, where every year the land, unploughed, yields corn, and ever blooms the vine unpruned, and buds the shoot of the never-failing olive; the dark fig graces its native tree; honey flows from the hollow oak; and from the lofty hill, with plashing foot, lightly leaps the fountain.[50]

Jupiter set aside these regions for the devout, concludes Horace, and dimmed the luster of the golden age with bronze and then with iron.

In his address Linnaeus quotes the first lines of Horace's poem, which assume that the earth in the beginning was only an island with all the flora and fauna (§ 16). This island is henceforth equated with paradise, the abode of Adam. The reference to Horace shows conclusively what would in any case have appeared highly probable, namely, that Linnaeus puts the paradise legend on an equal footing with the notion of the golden age and that the latter tradition of the ancients influenced him in his idea of paradise as an island. The short quotation also includes the actual expression "the islands of the blessed," *divites insulae*. It is clear that he wished to use

49. L. Arrhenius, *De Quatuor Mundi Aetatibus* I (respondent O. Burman) (diss., Uppsala, 1729), 28; Asp, op. cit., 71 ff., 80 f., 87 ff., 97 f.

50. *Epodes*, 16:41–48, transl. C. E. Bennet (Loeb Classical Library) (London, 1946). Cf. Malmeström, *Carl von Linné*, 29.

Horace to corroborate this particular concept of the first dry land as an island. The Bible says nothing of this, but it crops up all the more frequently in descriptions by the ancients, and Linnaeus did not see any objection to blending Christian and pagan, any more than did Swedenborg and other contemporaries.

There were difficulties in the idea that paradise had been an island in the great ocean, but they were of a practical nature. The same objections could be leveled against the hypothesis that the whole earth constituted paradise: in that case Adam had nowhere to go when he was expelled from paradise, observed Haquin Spegel.[51] This was no problem for Linnaeus. He thought in practical terms: whether, for example, it could have been possible for the plants to spread over all the earth; but the banishment of Adam from paradise does not seem to have troubled him. Paradise had a function in his scientific doctrine; he was able to use ready-made ideas. In other contexts he could offer other interpretations. For example, he gives the paradise story a sexual import in the early medical lectures, *Diaeta Naturalis,* in 1733. The forbidden fruits here stand for Adam's testicles, the treacherous serpent is the penis, and the delights of the fruit represent actual intercourse.[52] Linnaeus never put forward this viewpoint in writing; the idea was obviously too daring.

The "Diminution of the Waters" Controversy

In the 1740s a great controversy over the "diminution of waters" broke out in Sweden. This was a scientific dispute which was to continue for the next few decades without any definite conclusion being reached. It had been discovered at an early date that the shoreline, on the Gulf of Bothnia and the Baltic Sea coasts in particular, was lower than it had once been—either because the land had risen or because the waters had abated.[53] Linnaeus's address on the increase of the habitable earth was a contribution to the debate, but he was by no means the first in the field, Urban Hiärne and Swedenborg having stated their opinions earlier.

Hiärne took an overall view and remarked how everything on the surface of the earth had changed its form and been transformed into its opposite.

---

51. Spegel, op. cit., 7.

52. *Diaeta Naturalis* 1733, ed. A. Hj. Uggla (Uppsala, 1958), 111, 162, 169.

53. A.G. Högbom, *Nivåförändringarna i Norden* (Göteborgs Kungl. Vetenskaps-och Vitterhets-Samhälles Handlingar, Fjärde följden, XXI:3) (Gothenburg, 1920); H. Richter, *Geografiens historia i Sverige intill år 1800* (Lychnos-Bibliotek, 17:1) (Uppsala, 1959), 240 ff; S. Lindroth, *Kungl. Svenska Vetenskapsakademiens historia 1739–1818,* I:2 (Stockholm, 1967), 613 ff. Cf. also E. Wegmann, "Changing Ideas About Moving Shorelines," in C. Schneer, ed., *Toward a History of Geology* (Cambridge, Mass., 1969), 386–414.

But he had a simple explanation for the falling level of the water in the Baltic: it was attributable in part to silting by molluscs, marine plants, and other matter washed ashore by the sea, in part to the widening of the straits around Denmark, which enabled more water to pass out into the North Sea. Swedenborg attempted to give a more universal explanation, using his theory of the deceleration of the earth. According to this hypothesis, the alternation of the tides had earlier been so rapid that the water level had never had time to sink to its "normal position." Now that the intervals had become longer, the surface had naturally dropped further.

Hiärne and Swedenborg, therefore, gave different reasons for the diminution of waters, but they agreed about the fact that it had occurred. The true explanation—that the thick ice sheet had been pressing down the land, whose elasticity then caused it slowly to rise—was still far in the future. But the long train of pieces of evidence throws an interesting light on their scientific approach. The same applies to their two immediate successors, Anders Celsius and Linnaeus.

Celsius had noticed the phenomenon as early as 1724, he says, on a journey to Medelpad and Hälsingland. Moreover, he heard about it from "reliable men," which presumably includes his father, Nils, and his uncle Olof, who referred to the subject in dissertations in 1720 and 1721. He had further opportunity to confirm his impressions in the course of Maupertuis' expedition to measure the length of one degree along the meridian in 1736. His opinions are set forth in a well-known paper included in the Proceedings of the Swedish Academy of Sciences for 1743 (*Vetenskapsakademiens Handlingar*), just before Linnaeus's conferment address. Shortly afterward he himself delivered a conferment address on the topic,[54] which was published in 1744 in the same volume as that of Linnaeus. The three contributions were published within a space of three months, and it is likely that the aim of Celsius's address was to clarify his position after Linnaeus's entry into the field, as the views of the two men on the subject differed. We shall first consider Celsius.

In his paper Celsius develops the ideas of Hiärne and Swedenborg on the diminution of waters. His first concern is to prove the actual existence of the phenomenon by giving a number of striking illustrations, and in doing so he more or less repeats what his predecessors have said. He mentions the direction of the long ridges (eskers), the order of the strata and the fossils, the inland situation of onetime ports, the classical finds of anchors and wrecks far from the sea, and the fossil beds near Uddevalla. He thinks it not

---

54. A. Celsius, "Anmärkning om vatnets förminskande så i Östersjön som i Vesterhafvet," *Vetenskapsakademiens Handlingar* (1743), 35, and *Oratio de Mutationibus Generalioribus quae in Superficie Corporum Coelestium Contingunt* (Leiden, 1744).

unreasonable to suppose that the whole of Scandinavia was once an island, which was the cherished belief of Rudbeck. But this circumstantial evidence was not enough for the scientist in Celsius. He wanted to calculate the extent of the fall in the water level as exactly as possible, and by collating various pieces of information he came close to the true measurement, approximately one meter per hundred years. This farsighted man had a mark inscribed at Lövgrundet, near Gävle, to indicate the water level at that time and to serve as a reference for the measurements of future generations. The continued subsidence of the water would mean that the navigable channels would have to be remeasured and that the Baltic would be dry after three or four thousand years, "if events always followed the foregoing calculations."[55]

Celsius's paper makes only cursory mention of the causes of the decrease in the volume of water, but in the conferment address he expands his views into a general theory of the mutations of the planets, the earth included. The first idea to which he gives an airing in the paper is the old one that a certain amount of water is converted into earth by evaporating and being absorbed by plants as rain. As the plants decay they then become soil. The other cause might be that the water runs down "into the depths of the earth" through holes in the sea bed; here he mentions Hiärne, although without following the reasoning of the latter to its conclusion, which is that the water then continues to circulate and returns via rivers to the sea. He admits to being very uncertain on this point and stresses that it will be impossible to decide definitely one way or the other before a thorough investigation has been made over a long period.[56]

We may here look more closely at the first of these ideas, that of the transformation of water into earth, since it forms the basis of the more detailed theory. Celsius cites Newton, but Newton was by no means the only proponent of the doctrine, which had its roots in classical antiquity but which gained fresh currency during the seventeenth century as a result of the tree-growing experiments of van Helmont and others. Many devotees of the theory of the transmutation of water held their opinions on the strength of the chemical experiments of Boyle, disregarding the doubts expressed by Boyle himself, and it has been stated that Newton was also influenced by them.[57] It must be borne in mind, however, that two different kinds of transformation were involved, one in which water became soil by the agency of plants, and the other a true transformation by distillation. In

---

55. Four feet, five inches, according to Celsius, which is equal to 1.3 meters; "Anmärkning," §§ 22, 29, 32.

56. Ibid., §§ 26–28.

57. D. McKie, "Some Notes on Newton's Chemical Philosophy," *Philosophical Magazine and Journal of Science*, ser. 7, vol. 33 (London, 1942), 852 ff.

the present context it is the first of these which is envisaged. Newton takes up the topic in passing in the third book of *Principia,* where he discusses the orbits of comets. The vapors which form the tails of the comet rarefy and are attracted by other planets and taken up in their atmosphere:

So for the conservation of the seas, and fluids of the planets, comets seem to be required, that, from their exhalations and vapors condensed, the wastes of the planetary fluids spent upon vegetation and putrefaction, and converted into dry earth, may be continually supplied and made up; for all vegetables entirely derive their growth from fluids, and afterwards, in great measure, are turned into dry earth by putrefaction; and a sort of slime is always found to settle at the bottom of putrefied fluids; and hence it is that the bulk of the solid earth is continually increased; and the fluids, if they are not supplied from without, must be in a continual decrease, and quite fail at last.[58]

At the time of Celsius this was the subject of lively debate. Some years after his death the Academy of Sciences discussed the extent to which water could be transformed into solid matter, on which subject Newton and Celsius were invoked, and thus account for the diminution of waters. The idea was resisted by that indefatigable opponent of the diminishing-waters theory, Johan Browallius, who was president on this occasion.[59] In his *Skånska resa,* Linnaeus gives several ways in which water could be transformed. The sea is a mother to the earth, he says here. Its water evaporates, falls as rain, and is soaked up by the plants, which when they die "increase the humus." When the seawater is still, it "becomes slime" and precipitates a sediment; sea snails and mussels form their calcareous shells from the water of the sea. According to Linnaeus, all stagnant natural fluids are crystallized by degrees into a fine gravel, and the substance formed by crystallization in the case of the sea is a sand, which drifts to the shore and contributes to the process of aggradation. What Linnaeus is describing here was an intricate scientific question which was to be followed up by the chemist Johan Gottschalk Wallerius.[60] Celsius himself, however, appears to have been more hesitant than his contemporaries and posterity have realized. Newton was indeed cited in a popular work on comets as early as 1735, and again in the paper, but the original manuscript reveals an uncertainty in the author that does not come out in the printed version. After a

---

58. Andres Motte's translation: *Mathematical Principles of Natural Philosophy* (Great Books of the Western World, 34) (Chicago, 1952), 359.

59. Lindroth, *Vetenskapsakademiens historia,* I:2, 618.

60. *Carl Linnaei Skånska Resa, Förrättad år 1749* (Stockholm, 1751), 334 f.; Wallerius, *Tankar om verldenes, i synnerhet jordenes, danande och ändring* (Stockholm, 1776) 47 ff. See also my chapter on Wallerius in *Geologi och skapelsetro,* 228–291.

reference to Newton, we meet the following sentence, which was later deleted: "But as we do not yet know with certainty whether water can be transformed into soil by the decomposition of plants, it is not possible to say definitely whether this can explain the decrease of the seas."[61] In the conferment address the matter is not mentioned at all. Nor does Celsius appear to have tried to probe more deeply into the problem, and the lasting impression is that he raised the idea here because it suited his purpose and because it had the support of such an authority as Newton.

The basic idea is, however, that the water has diminished and is continuing to do so. Celsius placed the phenomenon in its wider context in his conferment address. All heavenly bodies, which includes the earth, go through three stages of a continuous process: one of inundation, one of "incineration," and, in between, an intermediate stage, a sort of interval between the two extremes. The earth is now in this intermediate position, but the fact that the waters are still subsiding demonstrates that it has recently been inundated. After a few thousand years the earth will have lost its water and the air its humidity. The combined effect of the sun and the subterranean fires will cause the greater part of the world's surface to begin to burn. As a result, vapor will rise and the atmosphere will become denser. The surface of the earth will be "turned to glass" by combustion. From this glassy material, sand will form and will, in its turn, mix with salt and water vapor to form the various soils. When the surface of the earth has cooled, large amounts of rain will fall from the humid air. Celsius here builds on the theories of Leibniz, who also included combustion and inundation as the most important phases in the world's development. The basic material of the earth's surface was a kind of glass, which had been broken down by fire and water to its minute constituents, which is just what Celsius also believed. The causes in both cases are to be sought in the constitution of the earth itself, the heat of the inner fire, and the cooling effect of the water.[62]

Celsius makes no mention here of the effects which Newton had attributed to the comets, namely that their vapors replace the fluid and the moisture which are consumed on earth. This idea had been paid special attention by Whiston, the successor of Newton, who took a comet to be the cause of the changes in the surface of the earth. Whiston made use of the newly acquired knowledge of comets which he gained from Newton and

---

61. A. Celsius, *Tanckar om cometernes igenkomst* (Stockholm, 1735), fol. 3ᵛ. Cf. manuscript "Om watnets affallande," Uppsala University Library (UUB), A 277, fol. 5ᵛ.

62. *Oratio de Mutationibus,* 93, 95 f. Cf. Celsius's notes on the same subject, UUB, A 533e, 9. He quotes from Leibniz's *Protogaea,* which means the first short draft, published in *Acta Eruditorum* (Leipzig, 1693), 40 ff. The final version was published posthumously in 1749, five years after Celsius's death.

Halley. The great flood occurs, he believed, when the earth passes through the tail of a comet which is on its way to the sun. Conversely, the newly acquired heat of the comet may set fire to the earth on its return journey, possibly with the help of the subterranean fire.[63]

Celsius was well aware of all this and seems at times himself to accept the same explanation. He deals with the question at length in a dissertation in 1743, debated after the publication of his paper on the diminishing waters, but before the conferment address. After a historical survey, in which Newton and Whiston figure prominently, he sets forth his theory that comets are the cause of these catastrophic events.[64] But he also takes up this favorite subject in two works of popular science, the first in 1735. After mentioning Newton, he refers to Whiston: "If the air of the comet has much water in it, we could, as Mr. Whiston believes, have an abundance of rain over the earth and a great flood." The question recurs in 1744 in *Bref om cometen*, the last work from Celsius's hand, in which he adopts a popular method of the time in explaining the nature of comets to an inquisitive lady. She is worried by the hypotheses of Whiston, whereupon Celsius allays her fears with an explanation of the workings of Newton's universe. A comet that came close to the earth could, by its gravitational pull, cause a flood or at least great humidity, but there is no cause to worry about such a disaster's being imminent. The wish to write a popular work—to explain to a wide audience and to still disquiet about a real comet—no doubt helps to account for the fact that Celsius does not speak entirely frankly. In *Oratio*, floods and fires are said to be a possibility on earth and a fact on the comets themselves. As all planets went through the same stages, which is clearly stated in the conferment address, this must also apply to the earth. When comets are inundated or catch fire, there is always some part of their surface which is spared. In these places some of the population can survive— Celsius assumes that comets and other planets are inhabited—and continue the species. In his conferment address he says exactly the same about the earth and about the chance that men and animals will survive.[65] That Celsius has omitted the role of comets in his address may have something to do with the composition of his audience; the work that came out the following year contradicts the idea that he might have abandoned the theory. It may be mentioned in parenthesis that Leibniz, the authority most frequently adduced in the address, was to renounce the idea in the book edition

---

63. Whiston, op. cit., 126 ff., 30 ff., 368 ff.

64. *De Influxu Cometarum* (respondent O. Floderus) (diss., Uppsala, 1743).

65. *Tanckar,* fol. 3ᵛ (quotation); *Bref om cometen* (Stockholm, 1744), 24 ff., 27 ff.; *Oratio de Mutationibus,* § 9, 93; *De Pluritate Mundorum* (respondent I. Svanstedt) (diss., Uppsala, 1743).

of *Protogaea,* but the version read by Celsius did not touch upon the question.[66]

There is one important difference between Whiston and Celsius to which some reference must be made. Whiston agreed that the great deluge caused by the comet was the biblical Flood, and that conflagration would represent the end of the world. Celsius is of a very different opinion. He declares emphatically that his description is not of Noah's flood or of the burning of the world on the final day, because these events cannot, theologians say, occur by natural means; the implication is that the processes being considered by Celsius follow natural laws and do not presuppose any divine intervention. The same perception shows through again when the curious lady wonders whether it might not have been a comet which foretold the destruction of Jerusalem, and this is denied by Celsius.[67]

Celsius thus takes a rational view of diminishing waters, clearly rejecting any connection with the Flood. Much of his work lends additional weight to this dissociation. For example, he ignores completely the six-thousand-year world of Christian chronology, according to which there ought in 1740 to remain about 260 years until the earth's destruction. Celsius envisages a considerably longer future, when, for example, he estimates that the Baltic Sea ought to run dry in three or four thousand years, and indeed adds that the period could be as long as ten thousand years.[68] Nevertheless, it is a surprising fact that Celsius was responsible on two occasions for theses which had a traditional biblical orientation. One is a chronological calculation of the date of the Flood, and the other takes up the familiar problem of the Flood's extent. The author expounds the view that the Flood really did cover the entire surface of the earth, and in evidence he brings out the usual arguments to support a diminution of the waters: fossils, anchors, and shipwrecks far from the sea. Burnet and Whiston, Swedenborg and Bromell, are among his authorities.[69] This is in direct conflict with Celsius's earlier accounts in which he distinguishes between the Flood and the diminution of waters.

How is this to be explained? The thought that Celsius might have moved toward a freer interpretation can be discounted, although there were five years between the dissertations and the conferment address, because by 1735 he was already quoting the comet theories of Whiston and Newton in his treatment of diminishing waters. The question of whose hand actually

---

66. *Protogaea,* ed. C. L. Scheidt (Göttingen, 1749), 11 f.
67. Whiston, op. cit., 368; Celsius, *Oratio de Mutationibus,* 89; *Bref om cometen,* 23 f.
68. "Anmärkning," § 32. Cf. UUB, A 277, fol. 6ᵛ.
69. *De Anno Diluviano* (respondent H. Neander) (diss., Uppsala, 1741); *De Universalitate Diluvii Noachii* (respondent A. Hallenberg) (diss., Uppsala, 1738), 3 ff., 24 f., 28 f.

held the pen on the occasions of these theses is of minor importance, for we may take it that the *praeses* (who was responsible) approved the content, especially in view of the particular subject. Was there a situation of conflict, or was it merely academic opportunism which made Celsius wish to avoid controversy about a sensitive issue? There was no need to deny a universal Flood, even if one envisaged other processes as more material to the development of the earth. In any case, Celsius concludes his conferment address by describing his speculations as an intellectual exercise, a common reservation when there was a risk of being taken as a critic of the Bible. For all that, it is impossible to escape the feeling that it must have been a difficult dilemma for him.

In view of his scientific orientation it was natural for Celsius to consider the surface of the earth from an astronomer's viewpoint. In the same way, Linnaeus was to contemplate the diminishing waters and similar natural phenomena from a biological aspect. But each of them proceeded from the observations gathered by Hiärne and Swedenborg from different parts of the country.

Linnaeus's famous and remarkable address on the subject of the accretion of the land has many interesting facets. We have already dealt with his vision of a paradise island growing into great continents. The large section on the dispersion of plants is important in its own right, but lies outside the scope of this study and must be bypassed here. We should, however, remember that his views on this subject had a connection with the diminishing-waters theory and the paradise concept and that they, therefore, undoubtedly contributed to the shaping of the latter opinions. This is what shows that Linnaeus looked at the question of the diminution of waters through the eyes of a biologist.

The advocates of the diminishing-waters theory usually enumerated a series of circumstances which combined to show that the water level had fallen. Linnaeus was no exception. His long list of empirical findings, or proof, as it was normally called, is based mainly on his predecessors Hiärne, Swedenborg, and Celsius. What Linnaeus does is to develop the argument, to go into the matter more deeply and with more precision. Once he had become aware of the problem, he started to make important observations on his own journeys. The Lapland and Dalarna journeys do not have much to offer in this respect, but they were undertaken as early as 1732 and 1734, respectively. The journey to Öland and Gotland was made in 1741 (the report being published in 1745), and here the notes are more numerous. The same is true of the two journeys he made after the conferment address, to Västergötland in 1746 (publication in 1747) and to Skåne in 1749 (publication in 1751). Linnaeus does not claim to be putting forward ideas which are entirely original, and he quotes the figures of Celsius on the falling level of the Gulf of Bothnia.[70] The fact that the ports of Österbotten and Västerbotten had become farther and farther from the sea was being repeated with great monotony, and Linnaeus did not fail to point it out too. But what he saw with his own eyes was more tangible, and for this reason the travel books make a fresher impression than do the examples in the address. This is what he writes about the east side of Gotland:

The annual rise in the land was here so clear to our eyes that we had never seen a better example, and this was especially so on the east coast, before the land began to narrow, and before the farm was reached. The land, which appeared gently undulating, was like a ridged field on the east side, with the ridges running parallel to the shore. Each ridge was some 1–3 fathoms wide, and the side of each ridge which was toward the sea was always the broader. On the very shore we saw how these ridges were formed, one each year, from the gravel thrown up on the shore by the sea. These ridges were quite clear nearer to the sea, but the farther up on the land one progressed, the smoother and more difficult to discern they became.[71]

Linnaeus counts no less than seventy-seven layers of deposited shingles. The last is said to be at least three hundred yards from the sea, and he wishes that he had been able to take a measurement of the height of the final ridge above sea level; since he imagined that the deposits had occurred annually, this would have given him the amount by which the sea had dropped in seventy-seven years. Linnaeus does, however, appear to have harbored some doubts about the extent to which each ridge really would represent one year, because this would mean "that this point becomes much younger than one would otherwise be inclined to imagine." On the other hand he finds it difficult to think of any other explanations. Here Linnaeus touches upon the sensitive question of the duration of the geological processes, and ultimately of the age of the earth. He was to return to the subject in another connection, as we shall see later.

Linnaeus finds evidence for the fact that Gotland has lain under water in the stone pillars, or "raukar," on the shore, an example which was not remarked upon by his predecessors and the origin of which he correctly describes. In his address he mentions briefly that at Slite and Kyllej there are enormous blocks of stone, resembling tall churches, giants and colossi in size, which have been carved out of extremely hard rock. Torsburgen and Hoburgen have vertical limestone sides, he goes on, which have been grooved and hollowed out by the swell during the time when the sea covered the whole of Gotland except for the two hills.[72] In the book of his journey he tells in detail and in his characteristic style of these "stone giants" and

70. Linnaeus, *Oratio*, § 33.
71. *Öländska och gothländska resa* (Stockholm, Uppsala, 1745), 256 f.
72. *Oratio*, §§ 30 f.

includes a drawing which makes full use of the scope for seeing fantastic figures in the shapes of the "raukar." When one sees them from a distance, they look like "statues, busts, horses, and I do not know what kind of spirits," and he proceeds to explain:

It is unmistakable that all of these were at one time one limestone mountain, but later, when the sea was still almost as high as they and further until it left their feet, they have been polished and hewn and formed by the surging, roaring waves into the shapes which they now possess; there is no doubt that as its level has fallen the water which has given the sides of these stones such a riffled appearance and tapered them off toward the bottom, has been able to cut away and erode the soil between them.

Once he had begun to think about the diminishing waters he made frequent notes of associated phenomena in his writings, particularly in the descriptions of his travels in Västergötland and Skåne.[73]

Linnaeus the traveler was able to give a concrete and vivid picture of the powerful forces of nature. Many of his predecessors were perhaps equally mindful of the effect of such dynamic processes on the earth's surface, but naturally the descriptions of those phenomena which they had not seen with their own eyes became vague and diffuse. Urban Hiärne, for example, was extremely perceptive about changes in nature, but he was obliged to rely far too much on secondhand information and hearsay. When he mentioned that much of Öland and Gotland had once been submerged, he was relying on information obtained by letter from the architect Abraham Swanskiöld.[74] Linnaeus was in a far better position to make his observations more specific.

For the most part there is consistent agreement between his conferment address and the descriptions of his journeys, particularly in the case of the journeys made before the address was delivered. On one matter, however, there is a discrepancy. This is the question of whether it is possible that the large erratic boulders he had seen on Gotland were carried to their position by the water. He has wondered about the huge blocks of stone near Hoburgen, which cannot be shifted by either the might of beasts or the devices of man, but which have, nevertheless, been carried there from the offshore islands of Stora and Lilla Karsö by the weight and force of the water. Another block nearby must have been transported from Sweden or Russia by the waves at a time when Gotland was still submerged beneath the salt sea. He has found a third example on the estate of a Privy Coun-

73. *Öländska och gothl. resa,* 218, 258 ff.; *Skånska resa,* 16, 125 f., 264; *Wästgöta-resa* (Stockholm, 1747), 40, 43, 63.
74. Hiärne, *Den korta anledningen, til åtskillige malm och bergarters, mineraliers och jordeslags, etc., efterspörjande och angifwande, beswarad och förklarad* I (Stockholm, 1702), 99 f.

cillor Cronstedt at Fullerö, where the lake has left a boulder on the shore in a position which, unquestionably, it did not occupy before. The conclusion is clear: "If Lake Mälar moves stones of such size that they can hardly be dragged by many pairs of oxen, what, may I ask, might we not expect of the ocean?"[75] We encountered the same opinion in Swedenborg, who tried on several occasions to show that deep seas had sufficient force to move large boulders.

Nevertheless, doubts gradually formed in Linnaeus's mind, for in the Gotland journey he says that he cannot understand how the water could have rolled such large blocks of stone from the Karlsö Islands to Hoburgen. Nor does he still believe that they could have been borne from Sweden or Russia as he earlier suggested. The observation at Fullerö is no longer significant. Linnaeus has quite simply changed his mind. The journey to Gotland took place two years before the conferment address was given, but the report was published two years after. If we refer to the original diary of the Gotland journey, we find that the first impression was not what was later reported in print. We know, he writes here, that the boulders are not rock which has fallen from Hoburgen: "from this we can judge the force of the sea, which has been able to throw up such striking weights."[76] On first seeing the spot, Linnaeus presumably formed the same opinion as Swedenborg—possibly he was to some extent influenced by him—but he changed his views on reflection, before publication.

Swedenborg had written about the fossil beds at Uddevalla back in 1716. Magnus Bromell commented on the example, Celsius mentioned it in his paper, and Linnaeus referred to it briefly; but that was before he had made his journey to the west coast.[77] In Darlarna and Hälsingland, on the other hand, he had seen petrified molluscs himself. It is common knowledge, he writes in his address, that among the many things washed up on the shore are the shells of dead shellfish. From this he draws the conclusion that there must once have been a shoreline at the places where such shellfish have been found. In the case of Dalarna, this would mean that the sea once extended one hundred and twenty miles or even more inland from the present coast. He rounds off his comments with the familiar quotation from Ovid about the sea changing into land, about the mussels far from the sea and the anchors up in the hills.[78]

Up to this point Linnaeus is speaking in very general terms. It was

75. *Oratio*, §§ 38–40.

76. *Öländska och gothl. resa*, 260, 263; manuscript "Iter Gotlandicum" (Linnean Society), 363. Cf. S. Fries, "Linnés resedagböcker," *SLÅ* (1966), 28–64.

77. *Geologi och skapelsetro*, 165; M. von Bromell, *Lithographia svecana*, I (Uppsala, 1726), 59 ff.; Celsius, "Anmärkning," § 17; Linnaeus, *Wästgöta-resa*, 197 ff.

78. *Oratio*, §§ 34 f.

particularly common to bring out these details and to refer to Ovid—the quotation is a persistent motif running through our first geological accounts both before and after Linnaeus. It is true that Linnaeus made his own field observations, but generally they served to confirm the views he already held. He does not produce anything new here. It suited him very well to quote Ovid, both because of the authority still conferred by a classical writer and because the awareness of constant change is the main theme of *Metamorphoses*. Linnaeus had sufficient insight to be unable to adopt a static view of the earth's history. Beyond that, details were of less importance. Like many of his contemporaries, he quotes Ovid's assertions of anchors being found on high mountains, although as far as was known, nobody had seen or received firsthand information of any such discovery. But the item was included as part of the armory.

That fossils were of organic origin was the accepted view of almost all natural historians of the mid-eighteenth century. It was also a matter of course to Linnaeus. He had become acquainted with fossils and rocks earlier as the pupil of Kilian Stobaeus at Lund, who had acquired a substantial collection over the years and who enjoyed a fruitful correspondence with Bromell. Linnaeus appears never to doubt that fossils are the remains of what once were living plants and animals. His journeys gave him the opportunity to extend his knowledge of the subject, on the islands of Öland and Gotland and in Bohuslän in particular.[79]

Unlike the "diluvians" and his former mentor Stobaeus, however, Linnaeus did not believe that the fossils had been washed up by the Flood.[80] The deposits had formed in the open ocean, which at the dawn of time had covered almost the entire surface of the earth and was still receding. Mud and silt had settled to form a bed for plants and animals on the sea bottom, but for this to happen the sea must have been calm. And here Linnaeus puts forward his very original theory of the importance of the sargasso weed. Waves are broken and water is stilled if there is enough seaweed or wrack; such vegetation would thus be highly favorable to sedimentation. This idea is not contained in the conferment address, and first occurs in the Västergötland journey. Linnaeus saw "floating grass" on Lake Torrvarpen, where it so kept down the waves during even the fiercest storm that the surface of the water became mirror smooth. "It is remarkable that the floating waterweeds can subdue the waves in this way, and we know that out in the Pacific Ocean also the wind seas are permanently calm wherever *Fucus Sargazo*

---

79. C. M. Fürst, *Kilian Stobaeus d.ä. och hans brefväxling* (Lund, 1907), 15, 18 f., 74 f. Cf. Nathorst, op. cit. (n. 1, above), 38 ff. A modern standard work is M. Rudwick, *The Meaning of Fossils* (London, 1972).

80. Stobaeus, *Monumenta Diluvii Universalis ex Historia Naturali* (respondent J. H. Burmester) (diss., Lund, 1741).

dictus is floating," he says.[81] He adds as a parallel that whalers are in the habit of pouring oil on the waves when seas are heavy, something which he had learned from Gronovius in Leiden.

By the following year, 1748, Linnaeus had already developed the brief outline of a theory in the sixth edition of *Systema Naturae*. It is taken further in the Swedish translation of *Oeconomia Naturae* (1750), of which the Latin original does not contain a word on the subject. Linnaeus believes that the sargasso weed has played the biggest part in the emergence of the "many new countries and mountains" which have come into existence. When the water is still, silt and mud are deposited on the sea bottom, where they form a bed for various kinds of fishes, mussels, and snails. These are mixed with the mud and gradually transformed into limestone. Linnaeus considers that the sargasso weed has been widely distributed and that it has consequently contributed to stratification in Sweden as well. He takes Kinnekulle as an example. The lowest of the series of strata here is sandstone, compacted from silt, directly above which is slate, formed from vegetable mold: "Above this is a thick layer of limestone full of strange petrifications perchance brought down by the sargasso. On top of this lies slate, again of decomposed sargasso, and the top layer is granite."[82] The sargasso weed has thus made two contributions to the layers of rock: first, by calming the waves of the sea indirectly causing the bed of limestone to be formed, and second, by decomposing, itself, to produce a stratum of slate. This was no casual suggestion. Linnaeus stuck firmly to his theory. In his Skåne journey he stressed that the strata had been formed not in the Flood but in sargasso-filled water. Torbern Bergman's famous description of the world includes a commentary revised by Linnaeus, which says the same.[83]

A fuller description, not markedly different from the foregoing one, is to be found in Linnaeus's lectures on the animal kingdom given in the later 1740s and early 1750s. Here Linnaeus builds on a description of the East Indies by the Dutchman François Valentijn and gives his views on mussels and the sargasso weed. The deposits beneath the weed and the crystallization of the water into the sand lead to the gradual formation of a sandbank, and when this rises above the surface of the water, moss begins to grow on it. The moss decays into humus, in which other plants take root, until finally we have dry land. This is how all dry land has arisen, "excepting that inhabited by our forefathers in the beginning."[84]

---

81. *Wästgöta-resa*, 263 f.

82. *Systema Naturae*, 6th ed. (Stockholm, 1748), 219, footnote 5; *Oeconomia Naturae* (Uppsala, 1749), 3 f.; Swedish transl. in *Skrifter af Carl von Linné*, vol. 2, ed. Th. M. Fries (Uppsala, 1906), 2, 8 f.

83. *Skånska resa*, vii, 87; Bergman, *Physisk beskrifning öfver jordklotet* II, 2nd ed. (Uppsala, 1774), 287 f.

84. F. Valentijn, *Beschryving van Oud en Nieuw Oost-Indien*, 5 vols. (1724–26); Linnaeus, *Föreläsningar öfver djur-riket*, ed. E. Lönnberg (Uppsala, 1913), 307 f.

How Linnaeus arrived at his sargasso theory is uncertain. The idea is not found in its entirety in any of his contemporaries, but he may well have obtained the inspiration for it from Valentijn or some other author who had described the plant kingdom of the East Indies. The sargasso weed itself was well known, however, mention of it often being made by botanists and travelers. Linnaeus describes its appearance by saying that "it looks like a green meadow," and the same image can be found in the account of the Swedish sea captain Willman, published in Kiöping's much-read travel book: "Here we came to the Sargasso or Grass Sea, as it is called by the Dutchman, the whole sea was overgrown with green, it was as if we sailed through a green meadow, although we could feel no land."[85] On his Västergötland journey Linnaeus saw for himself how water plants could spread and "bind" the surface or at least reduce the waves. It is possible that an observation of this kind was decisive. Moreover, he has learned from Gronovius that oil can calm rough waters, and he then draws a parallel with seaweed. The second step in his argument—that sedimentation is most inclined to occur in calm water—is a quite natural conclusion. The same thing has been maintained by Swedenborg in connection with the origin of Kinnekulle, but he believed that the calm was due to the protection of the surrounding hills, Hunneberg and Billingen, which acted as windbreaks.

As was to be expected, Linnaeus encountered opposition, and we shall examine some of the objections. The sharpest tilt at the diminishing-waters theory was made in a work by Johan Browallius in 1755. Browallius, who was an old friend of Linnaeus', became professor of natural history in Turku in 1737, and later bishop of the same city. When the diminution of waters was discussed by the Academy of Sciences in 1747, Browallius was president and attacked the theory. He also played an active part in the preparation of the unfavorable report of the clergy on the Swedish history of Olof Dalin in the same year.[86] Dalin had used the diminishing-waters theory to show that Rudbeck's patriotic view of Sweden's glorious history could not be correct. According to the diminishing-waters theory, Sweden must have been under water at the time of the birth of Christ.

In his presidential address, Browallius criticizes those who speculate on the origin of the world, because they "search out a fable of the world from their own heads." The criticism is also directed at those who have added hypothetical reservations to their theories, for the Creator has not put us here to teach "how a world might come into being." Browallius expresses his respect for Newton, but adheres to the traditional belief in a world that is six thousand years old. The Bible is still the basis of all science; it gives us

85. *Oeconomia Naturae*, 9; *Skånska resa*, 87; Matsson Kiöping, op. cit., 227.
86. Browallius's letter to Linnaeus in *Bref och skrifvelser af och till Carl von Linné*, I:2, ed. Th. M. Fries (Stockholm, 1908), 328. Cf. Högbom, op. cit., 51 ff., 66–76.

advice and instruction on, for example, animal husbandry, cultivation of the land, metallurgy, chemistry, astronomy, and other matters.[87]

Browallius rejects the diminishing-waters theory on theological grounds and disapproves of the fact that Linnaeus so casually dismisses the role of the Flood in the process. Browallius also sees the series of strata described by Linnaeus as being formed by the winds and not by water. In addition to the biblical argument, he makes an objection of a different kind, wishing to show that Linnaeus and those who share his opinions have drawn the wrong conclusions, even if their premises were to be accepted. Accordingly, he points out that the hills at Helsingborg, which Linnaeus regards as having been formed over an unconscionable period of time, are only forty feet high. According to the measurements of Celsius to which Linnaeus refers, they ought to have taken nine hundred years to form, and this is no longer so remarkable: "nine hundred years is no boundless infinity of time to make our minds whirl." The time factor is what divides them; biblical chronology remains the ground on which Browallius ultimately rests his case. The sargasso theory is rejected because it would take an even longer time than that suggested by Linnaeus.[88] According to this hypothesis, all mountains ought to consist of limestone at the bottom, followed by the same sequence of strata above, which is what Linnaeus clearly asserts, but which Browallius considers not to be demonstrated in nature. He believes rather that the mountains have been formed in different ways and at different periods. Some must stem from the Creation, others from the Flood, and still others from particular changes in the earth's crust at a later date. Another objection is that the sargasso weed grows only "between *tropicos*" and that nobody has been able to explain how in that case the climate changed in the Nordic countries. If no part in the changing of the surface can be attributed to the Flood, neither can such an effect be ascribed to subsiding waters. For Browallius the conclusion was evident from the outset: the Flood did cause the changes. It deposited the strata and it buried the fossils, whose organic origin Browallius had never doubted. But the lowest layer of limestone, which is believed to emanate solely from crustaceans, was presumably formed in the Creation: it is "much more reasonable and consistent with the wisdom and goodness of the Creator to say that He made most of it beforehand, and laid them in the first fresh stratum of the earth, than that He employed a method which would mean that the earth and its inhabitants would lack such a large, essential, and necessary part of the globe for hundreds of thousands of years to come."[89]

---

87. Browallius, *Känningar af Guds försyn och nyttiga vetenskapers främjande* (Stockholm, 1747), 4 f. 16, 26, 35.

88. Browallius, *Betänkande om vattuminskningen* (Stockholm, 1755), 9, 25, 48 f.

89. Ibid, 151 f., 156 f., 175 ff., 181 f., 188 ff.

Browallius could not neglect to do what he regarded as his duty as a servant of God, that is, defend the Bible. But he was uneasy lest his old friend Linnaeus should take offense. In a letter written in the spring of 1755, he hopes anxiously that their friendship will not be affected and suggests that Linnaeus read through the manuscript before publication so that certain passages might be modified; he even cherishes the hope that Linnaeus will write a foreword to the book.[90] Some months afterwards, in July, Browallius died. The book came out posthumously and bore the author's name, instead of being anonymous as Browallius had evidently intended. Whether Linnaeus replied, and if so, in what vein, is not recorded, but obviously he did not write a foreword. True to his habit, he did not engage in polemics either, but there was only one way in which he could react. In November of the same year he writes to his pupil Peter Jonas Bergius: "The lamented Browallius will be held to be right about the diminishing waters as long as nobody dares to reply to him. But mark my words, he will be defeated in a few years.[91]

Linnaeus was clearly correct. After Browallius's writings, which are not without rationality as critical studies and a certain authority, the question seems no longer to have had the same urgency. The dispute about the diminution of the waters was to continue, albeit in a less impassioned form, for a long time, but Linnaeus no longer took part.

A few words should be added here to fill in the background of Linnaeus's view. Felix Bryk has implied that Linnaeus obtained the idea of diminishing waters from *Telliamed,* the work of the celebrated Frenchman de Maillet. Although this book did not appear until 1749, its contents were known much earlier from transcripts, one of which was said to have been in the possession of Antoine de Jussieu in Paris, who was visited by Linnaeus during the time Linnaeus spent abroad. Maillet died in 1738, and in the foreword to his description of Egypt, published in 1735 and 1740, his treatise on the diminishing waters is mentioned as being already known in learned circles.[92] The possibility that Linnaeus knew Maillet's book cannot be discounted, it is true, but on the other hand there is no need to assume any direct influence, as was, incidentally, soon being asserted by Browallius. The argument of Maillet is much more detailed than that of Linnaeus and relies upon exhaustive empirical investigation of sea currents, deposits on the sea bed, various kinds of fossils and stones, the sequence of rock strata, and so on. He also cites some of the findings of

90. Browallius's letter to Linnaeus, 20 Mar. 1755, *Bref och skrifvelser,* I:3, 327 f.

91. Linnaeus's letter to Bergius, Nov. 1755, ibid., 123.

92. F. Bryk, "Benoist de Maillet und Carl von Linné," *SLÅ* (1949), 99–111; De Maillet, *Description de l'Egypte,* ed. Mascrier (Paris, 1735), viii; Browallius, *Betänkande,* 29.

Jussieu,[93] which makes a connection with Linnaeus plausible. But the similarities between Maillet and Linnaeus are hardly sufficient to demonstrate any influence. By comparison with *Telliamed* the conferment address is little more than a draft, even if it is supplemented with brief interpolations from the accounts of the journeys. Linnaeus's own reference to Celsius shows that he was aware of the Swedish tradition, as mention is made there of predecessors such as Hiärne, Bromell, and Swedenborg. On the whole, Linnaeus produces exactly the same arguments; the only new one, the sargasso theory, is to be found neither in his first exposition of diminishing waters—the conferment address—nor in Maillet's work. In these circumstances there seems little to suggest any close connection between the two.

Something should be mentioned here of Linnaeus's views on the traprock of Västergötland. In a paper presented to the Academy of Sciences before *Västgötaresan* was published, Linnaeus listed the sequence of strata in Kinnekulle. He was helped by Johan Svenson Lidholm, a volunteer of the Fortifications Corps. The strata had been described earlier, by Swedenborg and by Kalm, but not so meticulously as was now done by Linnaeus.[94] Some brief comment is in order at this point on Linneaus's reflections on the fact that the top of Kinnekulle was composed of a layer of granite. Beneath lay sandstone and limestone, containing fossils, but at the top was granite or traprock with no fossils whatever. A common belief at this time was that primary rocks, alps, and other high mountains had been formed at the Creation or by the Flood, whereas lower hills and ridges had developed later from the action of water, and so on. Precisely this account of the origin of mountains is given by Hiärne. Swedenborg could not accept such a solution in the case of the hills of Västergötland. The uppermost layer of granite must have been sedimentary, as the lower strata contain marine fossils. The absence of fossils in the granite indicates, he believes, that the material in it was initially so finely powdered that heavier substances sank through to the layer below or that small marine creatures fled from this pulverized mist before it hardened. Kalm had noted the puzzling structure, but he was reluctant to utter an opinion on the matter, which he handed over to the mineralogists.[95]

Linnaeus approaches the problem in the same manner as Swedenborg:

It is remarkable that there should be only granite here at the top of the hill. From this it is to be seen that not all granites did exist in the beginning, and that they, too,

93. De Maillet, *Telliamed* (Basle, 1749), 84, 94.
94. Linnaeus, "Kinne-kulle aftagen i profil," *Vetenskapsakademiens Handlingar* (1747), 54 ff.
95. Kalm, *Wästgötha och Bohusländska resa förrättad år 1742* (Stockholm, 1746), 279 f.

are the children of time, like other forms of rock, because the sandstone layer is come of sand; the limestone layer is of clay, with its fossils; the slate is from humus, and the humus from plants; above all these lie the granites, which cannot therefore have been created in the beginning.

Later he states that granite arises from ground moraine and must, consequently, be a child of time, *temporis filia*.[96] This idea is repeated with only minor variations in *Oeconomia Naturae*. The granite "is produced from gravel," he says here, and would appear to be the same as that "washed up by the sea, when the rock began to form a shore." It is clear that Linnaeus means that this upper layer is the result of the sea having thrown up gravel as it receded, and the gravel having then hardened. Linnaeus's views on the stratification of rock and its origin in sedimentation were adopted and developed by Torbern Bergman and other writers on geology.[97]

Another question to be answered concerned the extent to which the sequence of strata could be regarded as generally applicable—whether it was true only of a particular hill, or whether it was the same all over the globe. Linnaeus was always inclined to jump to conclusions, and he did so here. He gets no further than the foreword to *Västgötaresan* before saying "I have described Kinnekulle, where nature has laid before us the anatomy of the earth's crust and shown how *strata terrae* were piled up in ancient times." He finds the sequence of strata in Kinnekulle repeated in the surrounding hills and also on Öland and Gotland. Even in Estonia the pattern is the same, according to oral testimony, as it also is in the Kingsberg silver mine in Norway. Therefore, says Linnaeus, "the profile of Kinnekulle holds the key to *strata terrae* or the anatomy of the earth's crust, not only here in Västergötland but maybe in most parts of the world." We find Linnaeus still clinging to this position in the later 1760s, in the twelfth edition of *Systema Naturae*.[98]

Linnaeus's conclusions were premature, founded as they were on all too fragile empirical evidence. Indeed, it was not unusual at that time for a few examples to be interpreted as representing the universal order of all rock strata.[99] In the case of Linnaeus it may also be possible to point to a psychological motive: his well-known striving to bring order and system to the world of nature. This would explain the inherent contradiction to be discerned in his view of the history of the earth. He does not believe that the earth started with a definite structure which was later modified either in detail only or suddenly by the Flood—which was more or less the attitude

96. Linnaeus, *Wästgöta-resa*, 35, 78.
97. *Geologi och skapelsetro*, 306 ff.
98. *Wästgöta-resa*, preface, 77 f.; *Systema Naturae* III, 12th ed. (Stockholm, 1766–1768), 10.
99. A. Geikie, *The Founders of Geology*, 2nd ed. (London, 1905), 194.

of Browallius. On the contrary, he realizes that the face of the earth has altered, and that it has been built up by gradual processes, mechanically. His favorite expression is "child of time," *temporis filia*. But then Linnaeus assumes that these processes have conformed to a fixed pattern from which there have been no accidental or unpredictable deviations. He suddenly sees the structure of the entire surface of the earth in the sequence of strata on Kinnekulle, and the vision gets the better of him. The outcome was rather similar when Linnaeus wanted to explain life as a mechanism. Nordenskiöld has shown how he attempted to embrace topical mechanistic theories, but allowed himself to be carried away by his own poetic imagination when he could not fit them together into a coherent whole.[100]

The description of the sedimentation process and of the nature of fossils bears witness to Linnaeus's scientific insight, but his doctrine of the sargasso weed, nevertheless, seems strange. It is one of the speculative flights of a rich scientific imagination, which is, in fact, how it was regarded even at that time—Linnaeus was asked many questions to which he never gave an answer.

The Bible as a Scientific Source

Linnaeus always manifested a deep and religious feeling for nature. He felt dizzy, as he puts it in later editions of the *Systema Naturae,* when he saw the eternal, omniscient, omnipotent God "on his back." He traced God's footsteps across the field of nature and observed, even in those which were scarcely discernible, "an infinite wisdom and might, an inscrutable perfection." The whole of nature bore the divine stamp, and it had been given to Linnaeus to interpret the gospel; the study of nature became an act of devotion and a religious ritual. But although the picture of God the Creator is always vivid in Linnaeus's writings, he does not emerge as an orthodox Christian. Not only did he read the Bible; he was also familiar with the classics. Malmeström has demonstrated how he could quote pagan authors such as Aristotle, Pliny, and Seneca, even when he was conveying his ideas about the way the world came into being and about its Creator: "If one will call him *destiny,* one is doing no wrong, for all things hang from his finger; if one will call him *Nature,* one is doing no wrong either for all things are originated from him; if one will call him *providence,* one is also right, for all things happen at his sign and at his will."[101]

Malmeström is reluctant in his commentary to accept Linnaeus's philos-

100. E. Nordenskiöld, "En blick på Linnés allmänna naturuppfattning och dess källor," *SLÅ* (1923), 22 ff.

101. Quotations from Linnaeus, published with commentary by Malmeström, "Linnés religiösfilosofiska betraktelser," *Kyrkohistorisk Årsskrift* (1925), 16.

ophy as deeply felt, and sees it rather as an expression of the ideas of the Enlightenment. Consequently, he considers that that part of Linnaeus's concept of God which is at all linked to his scientific opinions has this "general, somewhat insipid air of Enlightenment rationalism." He then draws the following conclusion: "But neither are these opinions an adequate expression of Linnaeus's deeper religious perception." And in his later writings Malmeström emphasizes that "fidelity to the world of the Bible is more truly characteristic of Linnaeus's 'basic outlook' than respect for Seneca and Pliny."[102]

It is not easy, nor perhaps very interesting, to try to put one's finger on Linnaeus's fundamental theological philosophy, if indeed he may be said to have had one. He had a religious outlook on life, which he shared with most of his contemporaries; according to the physico-theological way of looking at things, the principal aim of the study of nature does not seem to make a distinction between religious convention and "deeper" feelings. In the eighteenth century, belief in God and the Bible was still a matter of course for all educated men, but naturally there could be differences of expression and emphasis in this belief. Christopher Polhem interpreted the story of the Creation symbolically, but he allows it an important function—it is to reveal to man the greatness of God—and may be said in this sense to believe in the Bible. It was possible to hold an independent opinion, as long as one expressed oneself with caution and professed respect for the Bible. That Linnaeus was deeply religious—he believed in God, in the Bible as the Word of God, and in himself as God's interpreter of Nature—is so apparent as hardly to need mentioning. It is also well known that he was very conversant with the Old Testament and quoted from it frequently.[103] But this does not mean that he was an orthodox Christian. The aphorisms on Destiny and Nature bore the imprint of pagan philosophy and were scarcely looked upon kindly by orthodox theologians. Nor, for his part, was Linnaeus particularly well disposed toward them. Wherever one may think and write as he will, study flourishes, he declares as early as 1733: "Where religion is free, the land flourishes. Where theology reigns, there is nothing but wretchedness."[104]

There is undoubtedly a conflict in Linnaeus between the Bible and science, but it is hardly possible to resolve it by looking for a basic theological attitude, a kind of deeper insight. It would, therefore, appear more profitable to examine how Linnaeus the scientist sees individual events and phenomena that are reported in the Bible, and his opinion of them as

102. Malmeström, ibid., and *Carl von Linné*, 203, 216 ff.
103. Malmeström, "Linnés bruk av bibelord i Nemesis divina," *SLÅ* (1963), 42–51. On Polhem, see my *Geologi och skapelsetro*, 94–119.
104. *Diaeta Naturalis*, 199.

scientific texts. The concrete questions that will be looked at here concern the Creation, the Flood, and the age of the earth; mention will also be made in this connection of the conclusions arrived at earlier with respect to paradise.

In addition to his general statements about the Creator and the infinite wisdom of nature's order, Linnaeus gives at one point a direct interpretation of the book of Genesis. This is to be found in a summarized draft, preserved by the Linnaean Society, and must be of late date, since the hypothesis of the hybrid appears in its final form; Linnaeus did not publish this until the late 1750s or the early 1760s.[105] The exegesis was written for the express purpose of demonstrating that there was no contradiction in Moses:

All naturalists who have also been free thinkers have believed that they have discovered a clear contradiction in the story of the Creation, in that there was light, with day and night, before there was the sun (v. 3) and that plants existed (v. 11) before the sun was created. But this, to them, complete impossibility, seems capable of explanation when the matter is more closely considered.

What Linnaeus is referring to here is the old problem that light was created and a division made into day and night before the appearance of the sun, moon, and stars, which came only on the fourth day. According to Linnaeus, the explanation lies in the fact that the Bible deals only with the genesis of the actual earth. Moses is describing "the creation of this *globus terraqueus*, and there the whole argument falls," says Linnaeus, for there is no doubt in his mind that the elements were created previously. The planets contain a core of heavier material, Linnaeus writes, quoting Anders Celsius among his authorities.[106] Such a core or *molecula solida*, that is, the inchoate earth, having floated around in the universe and attracted water, then "chanced to come into the planetary system around the sun." As the earth approached the sun in this state, the water evaporated to a mist, which "made a thick cloud." The mist obscured the sun, just as it does in autumn, but the light of the sun was able to penetrate sufficiently to mark day and night. On the second day it began to rain, and then to clear, whereupon the firmament became visible. During the third day water formed around the core of the planet, covering it. Beneath this sea the surface of the earth was very rugged, with rocks and skerries and banks; the highest peak soon

105. Manuscript "Om skapelseberättelsens tolkning" (Linnaean Society) "God created classes, ex his mistis ordines, ex ordinibus genera, ex generibus species." Cf. J. Ramsbottom, "Linnaeus and the Species Concept," *Proceedings of the Linnaean Society,* Session 150 (London, 1938), 192–219.

106. Cf. Linnaeus's conferment address "Skaparens afsikt med naturens verk" (1763), ed. A. Hj. Uggla, *SLÅ* (1947), 73.

began to dry out, and here paradise was created. On the fourth day the firmament became quite clear, so that the sun and moon began to shine.

This commentary is sufficient to show that Linnaeus's interpretation was conventional and characteristic of the period. The commonest explanation of the contradiction was this very argument that the story of the Creation related only to the origin of the earth, and that the sun and other heavenly bodies existed earlier, but were hidden until the fourth day. We can find other examples too to illustrate the continued currency of this view in the mid-eighteenth century. The details may vary at times, but the basic idea is the same. God created matter, or chaos, from nothing, but this unarranged mixture of all kinds of elements prevented the sun from being visible, although the sunlight was able to penetrate it. Gradually the various elements settled according to their density, and this led, among other things, to the separation of land and water on the second day. When the elements had taken their places in this way, and the atmosphere around the earth had cleared, the sun, moon, and stars appeared. In addition to Burnet, Whiston, and other writers already mentioned, Collier has named many other examples: the atomist Edmund Dickinson (1703), the anti-Cartesian John Witty (1724), and the theologian Tobias Swinden (1714, translated into French as late as 1757). [107] A work as general as *An Universal History,* of which several editions were published and which was translated into German and French, contains many different opinions, but the author himself also states his viewpoint.[108]

The book of Genesis referred to the origin of the solar system, not of the earth alone, or of the entire universe. The earth and the other planets were each formed from their own chaotic mass as parallel events. The elements began to arrange themselves according to their density, and when the atmosphere had cleared somewhat, the rays of the sun were able to filter through with their imperfect and flickering light, which was, nevertheless, sufficient to banish the total darkness and distinguish day from night. This explanation of the first daylight is, the author maintains, much more reasonable than the idea that the substance of which the sun is composed could have arisen from the earth's chaos, for more than 90 percent of the matter in the universe consists of flaming particles, and if they had first been present in the chaos, it would have been impossible for there to have been darkness and a shroud of mist. The irregularities of the surface of the earth arose when the particles of earth settled unevenly because of their differing densi-

---

107. Collier, op. cit., 151 f., 161 f., 168 ff., 176 ff., 180.

108. The first seven volumes of *An Universal History* were published in London, 1736–1744 (Collier's statement, p. 193, is wrong). Although work was published anonymously, the authors are known. The articles on creation were written by the famous orientalist George Sale (cf. *Dictionary of National Biography,* vol. 50, 179 ff.).

ties. Linnaeus similarly assumes that the earth's crust acquired its unevenness in the beginning—not from the Flood, as Burnet and many others believe—but he does not describe how this happened. Regarding the third day, he notes in his draft: "The earth beneath the sea is very rugged, with rocks and skerries and banks." In *An Universal History* the author continues to reflect contemporary thinking. On the fourth day the air becomes free of foreign particles and fog; with this the moon and the planets appear, having kept in time with the earth in their development, as does the sun, working on the earth with its light and heat and helping to clear the atmosphere, and the stars, which play no part in this creation.[109] We may recall Linnaeus's brief note relating to the fourth day: "The sky became clear and the sun and moon started to shine, for *astra* existed before, although they were not visible until there was clear air."

The foregoing may suffice to show that Linnaeus used one of the commonest explanations of the time to solve his problem. The idea behind it was no doubt apologetic, but apparently he had not devoted any great amount of attention to the subject. What is more, he permitted himself many obscurities in his draft. In the sentence just cited, for example, it is not clear whether the stars have been created separately, as averred by the account in *An Universal History,* or whether they are counted along with the sun and the moon; the latter is more probable, however.[110] Nor do we gain any clear picture of the way the earth originated. Linnaeus assumes that a *"molecula solida"* floated along with the other astra out in *"systemate universi"* and that it "chanced to come into the planetary system around the sun." This has a vague air of the cosmogony of Descartes and of others inspired by him, which differed from that of Swedenborg in asserting that the earth had moved inward toward the sun rather than outward away from it. Linnaeus also writes about the origin of the plants and animals, but he says little of note, and we shall not go deeply into his comments here. He indicates that one plant of each species was created and that all plants originate from a seed, at the same time that he denies abiogenesis. As far as the beasts are concerned, he follows the biblical description of the fifth day faithfully by saying that the sea brought forth fish, insects, and birds; this is supported by the old idea of water as the origin of all things, as he cites Thales, Cicero, and Seneca.[111].

What Linnaeus has to say elsewhere on the subject of Creation takes the form of a general eulogy, without any definite details of the actual process of creation. "That the wondrous edifice of the earth was brought forth and shaped by the eternal Master, we are told not only by the Holy Scriptures,

109. *An Universal History* I, 41 f.
110. See "Systema naturae, introitus," in Malmeström, *KHÅ* (1925), 7 ff.
111. "Skaparens afsikt med naturens verk," 78.

but also by common sense,"[112] is a typical example of his pronouncements on the matter. Even more frequently, he expresses his constant admiration for the all-wise order of nature, which does more than anything else to point to a higher power as the origin of all things. By the agency of the Creator the grass which feeds the cattle has appeared; fish, which do not have the warmth to be viviparous, have instead "by the providence of the Creator" been made capable of producing roe. Nature exists to show us the genius and greatness of our Lord; this is its main business. All is done to the glory of God, which is attested not only by moralists and theologians, but also by Nature herself, and man has been put here to reflect this, his Creator's wisdom. Here we meet the well-known physico-theological philosophy of the period; one should infer God's existence and greatness by studying nature and its complicated coherence. Linnaeus also sees clear signs of the hand of God in the chain of being which fills the whole of nature. One link differs so little from the next that if one could see the whole chain at once one would hardly be able to distinguish the links.[113] All levels and forms of life, the manifoldness and the variety, were necessary expressions of the omnipotence of God.

Linnaeus does not, therefore, doubt that the Bible has in essence described the way the process of creation came about. Nature and the Scriptures can tell the story, each in its own way; both the Holy Writ and natural history show clearly that there was a creation and a paradise that was the abode not only of man but of all the beasts. But the scantiness of the biblical portrayal left room for theories about the more detailed course of events; the version of Moses was often seen as a deliberate simplification, a popular description for the benefit of his own people. *An Universal History,* for example, states that the Creation story is

the substance of what Moses has delivered concerning the creation of the world; which being short, and rather suited to the capacities of the people he designed to instruct, than written for the satisfaction of a philosophic enquirer, has left room for various explications, and the setting up of several very different hypotheses.[114]

So when Linnaeus comes near to Descartes' theory of the first stage of the earth's development, this is not contrary to the Bible, even though these phases were not mentioned by Moses. The implications of the Creation story are merely being interpreted in greater detail and rewritten in scientific terms.

112. *Oratio,* § 1.
113. Many examples in *Oeconomia Naturae, Curiositas Naturalis, Politia Naturalis,* and other dissertations, translated into English in *Miscellaneous Tracts relating to Natural History* (London, 1759) and *Select Dissertations from Amoenitates Academicae* (London, 1781).
114. *An Universal History,* 35.

We saw in an earlier chapter that the position is exactly the same with regard to paradise. Linnaeus allows himself great freedom in relation to the literal biblical text, but he remains loyal to a biblical tradition. From the rich world of ideas he picks up those which best fit in with his scientific thought. The use of pagan poets as witnesses to the nature of the biblical paradise had been common since the Middle Ages; it was not regarded as contradicting the Bible. The same could be said of a Cartesian description of the origin of the earth.

But what line did Linnaeus take about the sensitive question of the geological significance of the Flood, particularly with regard to fossils and stratigraphy? It is quite evident that he recognized the organic origin of fossils. This is often implicit in his writings, and at times it is expressly stated.[115] He regards it as equally obvious that the Flood did at some time occur and takes its universal extent as an argument in favor of his theory of paradise. It would have been pointless to create the earth as large as it finally became and to give it a complete plant and animal life, if everything was shortly to be obliterated by the Flood.[116] On the other hand, Linnaeus will not allow the Flood any radical geological effects. The diluvial theory did not hold sway unchallenged, even if it did dominate. We need only recall Swedenborg, who, admittedly, assumed a prehistoric sea covering Scandinavia, but who, nevertheless, did not exclude the possibility of certain changes being caused by the Flood. Linnaeus is unusually unequivocal on this point. In as early a work as *Oratio,* he writes, after announcing that petrified molluscs show that the shoreline was once as far inland as Dalarna: "He who attributes all this to the Flood, which suddenly came and as suddenly passed, is verily a stranger to science, and himself blind, seeing only through the eyes of others, as far as he sees anything at all."[117]

Linnaeus makes the same objection to the view that the strata of the earth's crust were formed during the Flood. He adduces instead the sargasso theory, which we have already considered, and insists that deposition took place over a long period. Here, too, the argument is that the biblical flood was over in such a short space of time that it could not have had any profound effects. He becomes even more convinced when he examines series of strata and mollusc shells on the spot. He maintains in particular that the finds on Balsberget in northeast Skåne originate from shellfish which have lived on the deepest seabeds and not along the shores, and that it may be difficult to explain how they arrived on land:

They have to state that the shellfish were brought here by the Flood, and are thus witnesses to this remarkable change in the earth. But those who insist that this is so

115. *Öländska och gothl. resa,* 40, 141 f.; *Wästgöta-resa,* 41.
116. *Oratio,* §§ 21 f.; cf. § 97.
117. Ibid., § 36.

seem to me to have little understanding of mathematics; for how could the rising water throw the shells to a particular spot many thousands of miles away and lay the other strata on top of them in such order?[118]

No, the answer must be that the earth has lain under water, and, he implies, the period of submersion must have been a long one, and stratification must have occurred with the assistance of sargasso weed. After the waters receded, silting continued with the aid of gravel hardened to stone. Linnaeus alludes obliquely to the long period of time which nature must have required in order to carry out the process: "Thus we see here the rarest shells in the greatest profusion . . . the most obvious results of alluvial depositions . . . how many thousands of forms of life Nature must have produced before it could fill this little area."[119]

Linnaeus dismisses the Flood as a geological factor for two reasons. For one thing, it lasted for such a short time, and for another, an inundation of this kind could not have had such a widespread and consistent effect on the earth's crust. A process of deposition by stages, with time playing a major role, would be a much more feasible explanation of the stratified construction of the earth. In one of his autobiographies Linnaeus summarizes his contribution to the debate :

Linnaeus said he had not seen *rudera diluvii universalis, sed successiva temporis.*
Linnaeus tried attentively and ingeniously to explain *strata montium.*
Linnaeus said he had still never got through *rudera aevi* to *terram primogeniam.*[120]

The time factor here is contrasted with the Flood; he has not seen any trace of the universal Flood, but he has seen the results of the gradual workings of time. But these "traces of time," *rudera aevi,* have still not led him to the newborn earth, the original crust of primary rock, if we will. Another pronouncement from the same source shows more clearly that by *terra primogenia* Linnaeus was referring to the surface of the earth and not to the earth as a whole. Here he explains how the "basic soils," which later formed the rocks, arose: limestone from the animals, humus from the plants, clay from the sea, and sand from the air; then he adds: "He could not see the earth created in Archean times, nor any trace of the Flood." Elsewhere he similarly maintains that the earth's surface had become so thickly covered "that no one has yet been able to pierce the *rudera* of the earth and see its first aspect."[121]

All ideas of Noah's Flood as a factor in geological processes are dismissed. But that need not mean any dissociation from the Bible. There is

118. *Skånska resa,* 87.
119. Ibid., 88.
120. *Vita Caroli Linnaei,* ed. E. Malmeström and A. Hj. Uggla (Uppsala, 1957), 172.
121. Ibid., 189. See also "Skaparens afsikt," 73 f.

nothing in Genesis about the Flood having washed up mussels and snails onto the land or having been the cause of the earth's structure. These additions were made by later commentators, who found it difficult to explain how petrified marine remains had been found on high mountains, and combined this with the biblical information that the Flood rose fifteen cubits above the mountains (Genesis 7:20). Linnaeus seizes upon the information that the Flood lasted for a year (Genesis 7:6, 8:13), which he finds incompatible with his own scientific observations. It cannot, therefore, be said that Linnaeus opposes the Bible, but possibly he may be said to be more loyal to science than to the word of the Holy Scriptures; because of the powerful position of the diluvians, it was common to consider their opinions as being those most true to the Bible, despite the fact that they had little support from the actual text.

From what has already been said about the Flood, it can be seen that Linnaeus was not satisfied with biblical chronology, which was a key problem in the conflict between the story of Creation and geology. In the autobiography referred to earlier, he makes a remark that has often been quoted without ever really being elucidated: "Linnaeus would gladly have believed that the earth was older than the Chinese had claimed, had the Holy Scriptures suffered it."[122] Consideration of the opinion of the Chinese on the age of the earth was no quaint flight of fancy on the part of Linnaeus, since Chinese history, in fact, played a leading part in the discussion of the chronology of the Bible during the seventeenth and eighteenth centuries, and it is, therefore, necessary to sketch in the background.

Chinese history began to be known in the West during the seventeenth century, mainly through French Jesuit missionaries. During the next century there was, as is well known, a steady flow of information concerning China's history, religion, and morality. It was soon noted that the table of emperors did not agree with the chronological information given in the Bible. According to the Bible, approximately 4,000 years had elapsed between the world's creation and the birth of Christ; the Flood was calculated to have occurred in about the year 1656 after the Creation.[123] The period between the Flood and the birth of Christ would thus be approximately 2,350 years (the figure is a round one, since there were differences of a decade or so between the figures of even the strictest Biblicists). But now the missionaries came up with the information that the Emperor Fu Hi (also spelled Fou-hi or Fohi) ascended the throne, according to Chinese annals, some 3,000 years before the birth of Christ (2,952 was the exact figure most often reported). China would thus have been not merely inhabited but even

122. *Vita*, 172.
123. About chronology, see O. Linton, "Skapelsens år, månad och dag," *Lychnos* (1973), 271–312; F. C. Haber, *The Age of the World* (Baltimore, 1959).

a kingdom several hundred years old before Noah's Flood. The table of rulers did not appear to have been interrupted by any universal flood, whereas according to the Bible everything had been obliterated with the exception of Noah and the Ark. Moreover, there was no clear account of the time before Fu Hi, but there was an implication that this, too, might have been longer than the Bible conceded.[124]

Some authors accepted the implications of Chinese history, and of the history of the Chaldeans and the Egyptians, and rejected biblical chronology. Isaac de la Peyrère, the French traveler and ambassador, is often regarded as one of the first skeptics. He caused a considerable stir with his book on the preadamites;[125] Adam was merely the ancestral father of the Jews, but there had been other people before him. He also implied that the world was eternal, a heretical idea of Aristotle's, which had always been repudiated by Christians. But there was a much more usual way of resolving this dilemma—one which was particularly common among Jesuits—and this was to turn to the Greek Septuagint instead of the Hebrew version and the Vulgate. This allowed longer intervals, both between the Creation and the Flood (606 years longer) and between the Flood and the birth of Jesus (780 years longer). Those who favored this interpretation were thinking in terms of a total period of from 5,000 to 6,000 years, rather than 4,000, which enabled them also to claim the support of St. Augustine. In this way it became possible to include the Chinese emperors in Christian chronology, and it was then tempting to identify them with biblical personages. Some took the view that Fu Hi, as the first emperor, must represent Adam, while Yao, being the seventh and ruling at the time of the Flood, was Noah. Others identified Fu Hi with Noah.[126] Whiston, for example, appears to have been influenced eventually by Chinese history, and his later works and editions to have been converted to the belief that Noah—identified with Fu Hi—had lived in China, returning there after the Flood was over. The preeminent Sinologist of the period, the Frenchman Du Halde, states it to be the "common" opinion that the sons of Noah populated China; the first generations lived in the Orient, but their descendants continued into China. These various traditions are reported by Pehr Osbeck, a Linnaean apostle who traveled in China, but who does not take up a definite position himself.[127]

124. Chinese chronology and its influence in V. Pinot, *La Chine et la formation de l'esprit philosophique en France (1640–1740)* (Paris, 1932), 189–279.

125. Ibid., 192, 195 ff.

126. Pinot, op. cit., 208; Linton, op. cit., 273, 281, 292; S. Shuckford, *The Sacred and Profane History of the World Connected*, 2nd ed. (London, 1731–1740), I:29, 102 ff.; II:60; III:398 ff.

127. J. B. Du Halde, *Description de l'Empire de la Chine* I (Paris, 1735), 263; P. Osbeck, *Dagbok öfwer en östindisk resa* (Stockholm, 1757), 121.

It is possible, although it does not seem likely, that Linnaeus was thinking of the chronology of the Septuagint when he referred to the Chinese. A
difference of one or two thousand years would not have had very much
effect on his geological timetable. He must have had other facts in mind, or
perhaps he was merely referring to the well-known notion that the Chinese
thought in terms of an ancient history, stretching considerably farther back
than that of the Bible, without being more precise; this general tradition is
the basis of many of the arguments which feature in the controversy. Johan
Browallius refers to it in his work on the diminution of waters. Chaldeans
and Egyptians are renowned for "their fabulous age," and some Chinese
claim to go even farther back, although the more reasonable of these go only
as far as Yao. Browallius is unimpressed by the Jesuit's parallel between
the Chinese and biblical chronology, which, he says, has no bearing upon
the main issue with which he is concerned, for "in the countless aeons of
diminishing waters, one thousand years more or less hardly makes any
difference to the question."[128] The Rudbeckian alchemist Gustav Bonde,
who was interested in these matters, collated his thoughts on the subject in a
work which displays little originality. He relied entirely on the work of
foreign writers, in particular that of Shuckford, and believed that one
would arrive at a date "many thousand years before the creation of the
earth" if one went by the table of the rulers of China. He repeats without
objection the arguments of the Jesuits in support of their calculations and
asserts that the purpose of the Bible is not that of establishing chronology,
"but solely that of increasing our knowledge of God and our duty to him,"
which means that we may make use of secular chronologies with a clear
conscience. In this way we may agree with the Chinese "and at the same
time make them content." One of the passages in Bonde's work which may
probably be considered his own is the odd comment on Enoch (Hanoch),
the son of Cain: "It is extraordinary that when Hanoch or Hanich is read
backwards, it becomes China."[129] The Chinese legends which were repeated in the West also included the story of the way the earth was created
with a temporal framework corresponding to the twelve hours of the clock,
each lasting for between eight and ten thousand years. The heavens were
created at the twelfth hour, or midnight, and the earth, the first hour after
midnight. We are now living in the seventh hour, making the time which
has elapsed since the Creation between sixty and seventy thousand years.
But some assume a longer period, adds the English history of the world
which reproduces this information. A period of a different length is indicated in a work on the countries of Asia which was translated from French

128. Browallius, *Betänkande*, 50 f.
129. G. Bonde, *Utkast til en jämnförelse emellan den bibliska och werldsliga historien*
(Stockholm, 1760), 28–34.

into Swedish. The period between the colonization of China and the Emperor Fu Hi is given here as thirty or forty thousand years, a piece of information which is included only to show "how far these conceited Asians will go with their claims."[130]

When Linnaeus cited the age of the Chinese, he must have been thinking of figures of this order, figures that were five to ten times greater than the six thousand years of the Bible. The main question, then, becomes the meaning which is to be attached to Linnaeus's remark. Malmeström's opinion on this point is that "the piety with which he was inculcated at home and his understanding of the Bible prevented him from allowing reason and the results or suppositions of research to be the sole determinant in questions of fact which were of scientific significance."[131] Linnaeus may express a reverence for the Scriptures, but he does not put forward any strenuous defense of them; it is not possible to infer a greater loyalty to the Bible than to science. He "would gladly have believed" that the earth was older if the Bible "suffered it."[132] He hesitates to say so directly, which is in no way surprising in view of the sensitive nature of the question, but it seems that he does want to believe in his assumption. The following sentence, not quoted by Malmeström, describes how he has been able to find continuous traces of the effect of time, but not of that of the Flood. This is undeniably of relevance in the context.

Time is a key concept in Linnaeus's outlook on the development of the earth's surface, as it was in his later doctrine of the formation of the species, where the species is characterized as the child of time, *temporis filia*. It was no coincidence that he was inclined to credit the earth with a longer history. We have seen how he rejects the Flood as a geological factor on account of its insufficient duration. When he contemplates nature, he is more than conscious of all the forces which affect and alter the face of the earth, provided there is enough time. He is fascinated and becomes lyrical when he examines the rock strata north of Helsingborg and thinks of the age that has been required for this work: "I feel dizzy when I stand upon this hill and look down upon the long period of time which has passed like waves in the Sound, leaving behind only these faintest traces of the former world, and which can now only whisper when all else has become still." This was new and radical thinking in eighteenth-century geology. His insight into the importance of the time factor points ahead to the geological theories of the nineteenth century. And this is a perspective that recurs frequently in the writings of Linnaeus. He experiences the same feeling when he sees the

---

130. *An Universal History*, 34; [Marcy and Richer], *Nya historien, om chineserne, japanerne, etc.* I, 2nd ed. (Stockholm, 1759), 5.
131. *Carl von Linné*, 175.
132. *Vita*, 172.

distinct layers of shifting sand which have hardened into standstone, at Skillinge, east of Ängelholm; when he remembers the hills at Helsingborg and reflects upon the time which these processes have taken, he "feels dizzy" again.[133] In Västergötland he observes the mechanical erosive and weathering effect of water. Nature is forever changing. Bogs may form and then be transformed into dry meadows.[134] The sequences of rock strata "are the most ancient of antiquities, placing before our eyes the changes of the world gone by," and the fossils bear witness to our earth "longer ago than any *historicus* can follow." In all of these transformations he sees processes that succeed each other in a continuous circle, a sign that "in former times, as now, nature built up the land, tore it away, and built it up again."[135]

As we have seen, Linnaeus was cautious about questions that might bring the Bible and science into conflict. He was true to the Bible to the extent that he took a favorable view of the biblical tradition, even in the broader sense, and that he paid frequent respect to the Scriptures. But if his writings are examined more closely, it becomes clear that he disregarded the Bible completely as a scientific textbook. There was a place for paradise in his view of things, it is true, but only as the starting point for a dynamic process, leaving aside his bold interpretation in sexual terms. He entirely discounted the Flood as a geological factor and never accepted the main theme of the story of the Creation—that everything was created in a week. On the contrary, he maintained repeatedly that he had never seen the original surface of the earth; the present one consisted of different layers, formed over an immense period of time. Nature was in a state of continuous change. All this bears witness to an outlook quite different from that expressed in the description of the world and its surface contained in Genesis.

133. *Skånska resa,* 309, 348.
134. *Wästgöta-resa,* 86, 114.
135. *Skånska resa,* 318.

GUNNAR BROBERG

Homo sapiens •
Linnaeus's Classification of Man

One of Linnaeus's last students, the physician Sven Anders Hedin, drew attention in a memorial sketch to the way in which the beloved teacher gave new clarity to the proposition "Nature makes no leaps" by placing man at the very end of the chain of nature. But Linnaeus maintained, and "perhaps rightly so," that more than one link was missing immediately below. According to Hedin, the uncivilized ideas of the Iroquois and the dull imagination of the Greenlander were cited in vain; Linnaeus pointed to the perfection of the human brain, taking into account also the exalted and divine spirit that guides us. Where can this capacity for wisdom be found except in man? Man is a mixture of the transient and the infinite; he represents the first link in the chain that leads up to the world of angels. The brain was one of the parts of the body that particularly interested Linnaeus. He himself had devised a theory of the functions of the different parts of the brain and was not infrequently found examining the skulls of favorite students in order to determine the nature of their talents. Pressures of time and distaste for controversy made Linnaeus unable and unwilling to pursue his research further. Intolerance was the order of the day, and Linnaeus was careful not to attract the suspicion of theologians for spreading materialist delusions. But sometimes, in the inner circle among his pupils, he would reveal something of his investigations.[1]

Hedin's account is inaccurate on most points and may first of all be taken as an indication of a not inexplicable confusion about Linnaeus's view of

1. S. A. Hedin, *Minne öfver von Linné far och son* (Stockholm, 1808), 90 ff.

the nature of man. Linnaeus's achievement, and that is what concerns us here, was that he was the first to place man in a system of biological classification, namely, among the primates, as *Homo sapiens,* and that he made the first serious attempt to divide mankind into a number of races. This much is to be found in every work of reference. And having placed the ape in close proximity, he has, hardly surprisingly, been included among the precursors of Darwin. Ernst Haeckel, having received an honorary doctorate at the Linnaean anniversary celebrations at Uppsala in 1907, dedicated his speech of thanks to the memory of "the founder of the biological system, the inventor of the binomial system of nomenclature, the distinguisher of the primates." The science of primates and the question of man's origin began with Linnaeus, according to Haeckel.[2]

Linnaeus is a part of the process which John C. Greene has called "the death of Adam" in his well-known book dealing with the growth of evolutionism and the decline of the doctrine of the Creation.[3] The evolutionary perspective is inescapable, but it requires only a brief mention in the present context. In the eighteenth century man was already being seen as a natural being, like any other, and this created an upheaval that was having consequences in many fields. Physical anthropology was born as a science, and Linnaeus served as one of the most important sources of inspiration in this new subject, the natural history of man. His contribution was his descriptive method by means of which man could be described in the same way that a dog or a cat could be. The old controversy about man's position in nature may be said to have been set in motion in a scientific sense in 1735 in the first edition of *Systema Naturae,* where man takes his place in Nature, on the top rung, to be sure, but nevertheless on the same ladder as the rest of Creation. "The die was cast," says Greene. The Age of Enlightenment gave the subject no rest. Major works were devoted to the various implications of the basic fact that man is an animal and must be seen as such. Not only nations but man himself now had history, and this history no longer consisted solely of the customary genealogies starting with Adam. Linnaeus had a crucial role here as an arbiter, and both his sound and his less sound judgments obviously had their repercussions. Not the least exciting of these reports were those which resulted in his setting up a number of human species other than *Homo sapiens.*

As a pioneer and key figure in anthropology, Linnaeus is the subject of frequent references in the literature, but the only really detailed treatment

2. E. Haeckel, *Das Menschen-Problem und die Herrentiere von Linné* (Jena, 1907).
3. J. C. Greene, *The Death of Adam* (Ames, Iowa, 1959), chaps. 6–8. Cf. G. Gusdorf, *Dieu, la nature, l'homme au siècle des lumières* (Paris, 1972), 355–423.

is Thomas Bendyshe's "On the Anthropology of Linnaeus," which was published as early as 1863.[4] It has been much used and gives the majority of the essential texts, together with translations of the Latin. But the broader grasp of the subject and the richer source material that we possess today are sufficient to warrant a new examination. The basic texts are, in fact, neither many nor voluminous, consisting of the relevant sections of *Systema Naturae* and the dissertation *Anthropomorpha*.

Background: The Scholastic Definition and Comparative Anatomy

The concept of man is hard to define, and no less so when so specialized an aspect as the emergence of a more rigorous biological classification is concerned. Terminology, definitions, and nomenclature may sometimes seem a dry and superficial form of learning, but this is, in fact, far from being the case. So Linnaeus asserts, at least. "If you do not know the names of things, you lose the knowledge of them," was one of his maxims. There is a reciprocity between names, definitions, and knowledge which is more important and therefore more difficult in the case of man than in any other.

The fact that man is an animal was no secret in 1735, when Linnaeus published the first edition of *Systema Naturae*. The innovation lay in expressing this view without reservation, as a fact of natural history. For a number of reasons it is best to begin with Aristotle. Not even after the most fleeting contact with his zoological writings can anyone doubt that man is here regarded as an animal. He is referred to as such throughout. As the foremost in rank, it is man whose description opens *Historia Animalium*, and as the best known of the animals, man becomes the yardstick by which everything is measured and understood. Starting from our physical organs and bodily functions, Aristotle proceeds by way of analogy to what may be considered their equivalents in other creatures. Aristotle does not produce a zoological taxonomy, but he does offer various suggestions. Time and again he points to the difficulty of dealing with such a diversity of criteria according to the rules of logic. For example, if we use the appearance of the foot as a criterion, it is true that we can distinguish man from many animals, but not from all. A single dichotomy is not enough: we have to work with many differentiae, which then brings in the problem of priorities, a problem that Aristotle does not seriously attempt to tackle. However, the idea of the chain of being is also implicitly available to bridge the gap between man

4. T. Bendyshe, "On the Anthropology of Linnaeus," *Memoires of the Anthropological Society of London* 1 (London, 1863–1864). Bendyshe's account is incorporated, e.g., in P. Lester's *L'anthropologie et la paleontologie humaine*, in *Histoire de la science* (Paris, ed. Pleiade, 1957).

and the animals; its origin is to be traced in part to some classic pronouncements in *Historia Animalium*, although man is not expressly included.[5] But *De Anima* gives the well-known physical characteristics of a three-stage hierarchy based on type of soul, with the rational soul reserved for man. In the treatises on logic—*Categoriae, Analytica Priora*, and *Posteriora*—we find a superfluity of discussion and distinctions on the subject of the status of our kind. The thesis "man is an animal" becomes something of a paradigm to illustrate all the syllogistic figures against which all statements may be tested. It is used to show how the definition is to be made up of the next higher concept, the genus, and the essential predicate, the attribute or differentia. "Genus summum" must include the attributes of all lower species right down to "infimae species," which is why we should begin at the top if we want to be sure that the series will hold good throughout. Aristotle proposes several essential attributes for man, but he often does so in order to polemicize against them, and he states nothing definitely. He refuses to incorporate man in a logical table.

Scholastic teaching was less equivocal. Textbooks in logic hammer away at the proposition "Homo est animal" in order to develop mental agility. The *predicabilia* are exemplified by the assumption that "animal" as a genus includes both *homo* and *bestiae* (or *bruta*). This dichotomy was for a long time definitive, but it does not appear to derive from the writings of Aristotle. It may be mentioned in passing that the Germanic languages, unlike English and French, lack a natural pair of words with the same value as the neutral *animal* and the lower *brutum* or *bestia*. The statement "man is an animal" may, therefore, have sounded and may still sound more offensive in, for example, Swedish than in Latin.

An extremely important line had been drawn, one which was regarded as final. The differentia distinguishing man from *bestia* lies in his reason, in the fact that man possesses a higher soul. *Animal* is thus divided into *rationale* and *irrationale*, a *divisio per se,* a genuine division rather than an accidental one such as the differentiation between *animalia* large and small, or friendly and hostile. A complete definition of man according to the rules of scholasticism from *summum genus* runs as follows: Man is a "substance." But so are the angels. So substance must be divided into corporeal and incorporeal. Man has "body," whereas the angels are incorporeal. But stone is also a "body." So "body" must be divided into "living" and dead, that is, with or without a soul. Man is a living bodily substance, stone a lifeless one. But a plant also lives. Hence corporeal living substances must be divided into sentient and insentient. Man can feel, but the plant cannot. But a horse can also feel. So living, corporeal, sentient substances must be

5. Aristotle, *De Partibus Animalium*, 644a; *Historia Animalium*, 491a; ibid., 588b.

divided into "rational" and irrational. Only man is *rationalis*. Here we stop, at the outermost branch of the tree of creation. The series sets out the definition of man as *substantia corporea, vivens, sentiens, rationalis*—or, more concisely, *animal rationale*.[6]

It is a hierarchy with uncrossable boundaries. If nature is a chain, then it is one that is broken at important points. The attribute *rationale* raises man to a level unattainable by other terrestrial creatures. Hardly more than a brief reminder is needed of how the Aristotelian doctrine of the soul was received by Christian metaphysics, how the definition "rational" led to "equipped with an immortal soul," and so on. *Homo est animal*—the proposition was fundamental and was widely used to introduce textbooks in physics, in which the division of animal into *homo* and *bruta* was a normal arrangement. The rational animal was dealt with first (or last), and the boundaries between it and the others were clearly marked by division into different chapters or books. Man had been taken out of natural history and given an isolated position of his own. For example, Johann Sperling, highly esteemed in his time as a writer of zoological handbooks, gives the following definition of zoology in the mid-seventeenth century (the term appears not to have been in common use at that time): "zoologica physica est scientia brutorum quatenus corpora naturalia sunt."[7] It was this view in particular, that "zoology is the science of *bruta*," neither more nor less, that was to meet with Linnaeus's opposition. Before that, however, the isolated status of man was emphasized even more by Cartesian dualism, which denied animals even a lower soul and reduced them to automata.

In addition to mental superiority, several points of physical superiority had been claimed for our kind. According to the definition attributed to Plato, man was the only two-legged naked animal. In *Timaios* it is explained that the soul, located in the head, lifts our head toward heaven in a kind of homeward longing, thus keeping our body upright.[8] Man, unlike other creatures, can direct his gaze toward God and burst out in thanksgiving before the majesty of heaven. Our two-legged stance gives us a better view of our surroundings and makes us superior to the rest of nature; our posture also allows us to keep our hands free. Aristotle ascribes this teleological argument in an extreme form—that man thinks because he has hands—to Anaxagoras, but he himself believes that the argument should be reversed: as man is the most intelligent animal, he knows how to use his hands.[9] Galen, too, dwelt on these remarkable implements, which had made us such unrivaled housebuilders, and gave us the name *Homo faber.*

6. Cf. F. Burgersdicius, *Institutionum Logicarum Libri Duo*, ed. alt. (Lugduni Batavorum, 1634), 240–241.

7. J. Sperling, *Zoologia Physica*, ed. G. C. Kirchmajer (Wittenbergae, 1669), 1.

8. Plato, *Timaios*, 90 A.

9. Aristotle, *De Partibus Animalium*, 687a.

The brain could be regarded as both bigger than that of other animals and different in kind. There were other peculiarities concerning human life. Man is the longest lived of animals, and was said to be the one which carries its young for the longest period. The hymen and the menstruation of women could also be adduced, if need be, although their significance was less unequivocally positive. Both internally and externally man's body generally matched his soul and his intellect, being in a class of its own. Our body was seen to be ideally suited for its task, a miracle of practicality, a compendium of the Creation in its entirety, a microcosm, something at which truly to marvel, and a theme for countless treatises.

There was another side, of course: Man is a wretched creature, born naked, with a shriek, and subject to a thousand torments. The difference between human and animal reason is a question not of kind but of degree; it is not essential but accidental. The wisdom of animals was a popular subject when paradoxes about our kind were called for. Descartes' opinion was regarded on most sides as unreasonable, and his attempt to place the human soul in the pineal gland failed almost at once. The controversy about the reasoning of animals and the nature of the soul, nevertheless, heated up in the wake of Cartesianism, and rather curious stories were apt to circulate. For instance, a Swedish thesis of 1708 maintains that the soul of *bruta* is corporeal. Reference is made to Thomas Willis, the famous brain anatomist, and also to the Bible. The ancient belief was that the soul, or "life," of animals consisted of the blood, a view which is linked here with a vaguely implied mechanistic physiology. But in that case, what of the power of speech? That the serpent spoke to Eve (Genesis 3:4–5) and that the ass of Balaam complained of Balaam's cruelty (Numbers 22:28–30) may be satisfactorily explained as being due to the intervention of the Devil and God, respectively. But hyenas, parrots, magpies, and ravens are reported from time to time to have this power, and these are cases of a different kind. Henry VIII had a parrot that said "Give the knave a groat," and, indeed, Cardinal Ascanius had one that could recite the whole Creed. But this, like the aptitude for learning possessed by dogs, is dismissed as imitation. In other words, it is wrong to say that animals talk, because they do not understand what they are saying. But at the same time, they are not merely automata, but possess a lower form of soul. How their much attested intelligence was to be described was a tricky problem, but a common suggestion was to speak of *analogon rationis*.[10] Animals ranged, of course, from the simplest creatures to those which were almost human: the horse

10. J. A. Bellman, *De Loquela Animantium Brutorum*, resp. G. Halsenius (diss. Uppsala, 1708). Cf. H. Hastings, *Man and Beast in French Thought of the Eighteenth Century* (Baltimore, 1936); L. Cohen Rosenfield, *From Beast-machine to Man-machine* (New York, 1940); G. H. Bougeant, *Amusements Philosophiques sur les languages des bêtes* (1739), ed. H. Hastings (Genève, 1954).

was cited particularly frequently. But while there was evident delight in these higher qualities, the distinctions had for the sake of common decency to be maintained: they might be questioned, but not obliterated. Animals that offered a particular challenge to man's time-honored definition were the dog, the elephant, the parrot, and the ape.

Comparative anatomy gave a somewhat ambiguous answer to the question of man's distinctive nature. Pierre Belon's comparison of the human skeleton and that of a bird in the mid-sixteenth century is well known and of fundamental importance. This showed with instructive clarity the great similarities and an apparent uniformity of design, which Belon and others were, in fact, inclined to exaggerate. The progress made by anatomy from the Renaissance onward kept step with the discovery of many new species of animal. Approaches were a little haphazard, it is true, but the more important of the works that attempt to collate the material, those of Blaes, Severino, and Perrault, for example, gave much food for thought. If structure was really regarded as showing function, and man's structure, especially the structure of the human brain, indicated our exalted purposes, then the anatomy of the apes constituted a major problem.[11] In *Historia Animalium* Aristotle makes observations that attest to the fact that he studied the question with interest: the ape's face is like ours; he has similar nostrils, ears, and teeth; and, unlike quadrupeds in general, he also has lashes on his lower eyelid, albeit thin ones. He has two nipples, arms, fingers, and nails like those of a man, and toes like fingers, with the middle one longest. But the upper part of the ape is larger than the lower in the approximate ratio of five to three, and the hands have a structure that includes a part resembling a heel. From this it follows that the animal goes more often on all fours than upright, and consequently it lacks buttocks—the argument is in customary teleological style. The sexual organs of the female are similar to those of a woman, while those of the male correspond more closely to those of a dog. Dissection reveals that there are also internal similarities.[12] It is well known that Galen dissected pigs and Barbary apes, which were much more numerous in the Mediterranean region then than they are now, in order to clarify certain questions regarding man. Renaissance anatomists, such as Eustachio, Coiter, and Riolan the younger, also examined species of ape and reached the same results, without really going to the heart of the matter. Willis, however, embarked upon a study of cerebral anatomy with amazing success, and was able to show that the human brain was not unlike that of the other higher animals in structure. Parisian anatomists, led by

---

11. Cf. F. J. Cole, *A History of Comparative Anatomy* (London, 1944).

12. Aristotle, *Historia Animalium* 502a-b. Cf. W. McDermott, *The Ape in Antiquity* (Baltimore, 1938), and A. A. H. Lichtenstein, *Commentatio Philologica de Simiarum Quotquot Veteribus Innotuerunt Formis* (Hamburg, 1791).

Claude Perrault, demonstrated at the same time—the second half of the seventeenth century—that the speech organs of apes were identical with those of man. In 1699 another brilliant anatomist, Edward Tyson, published his celebrated monograph on a young chimpanzee (*Anatomy of a Pygmie*), an exceptionally important work, to which we shall refer again, and one which clearly showed the great similarities in both external and internal form. In the early eighteenth century the comparison of ape and man was fully established, indeed almost inescapable. An illustration published by the botanist Richard Bradley in 1721 may be seen as a counterpart to the comparison offered by Belon, although Bradley's is less well known,[13] showing a human skeleton alongside that of a monkey.

Herein lay, of course, a problematic truth—if the similarity was real. Either there was no unequivocal difference between man and animal, or, if there was one, it was of a different nature. In other words, cerebral structure, for example, did not reveal function and purpose: speech and spiritual qualities could not be supported by any material characteristics. Or, expressed in another way, the distinctive nature of man could not be proved by science. This opinion led of necessity to the conclusion that there was something specifically immaterial in man, a conclusion that could, of course, be used as an argument against materialism. Willis was aware of this, and Tyson found that "the nobler faculties—soul, reason, and understanding—cannot be produced by matter organized, but must have a higher principle." Quoting these words, John Ray wishes to emphasize that "things did not make uses."[14] But with this statement Ray is really questioning whether science can prove "higher" truths, at least about a point which had been regarded as particularly urgent in the physico-theological genre he himself fostered. To sum up, these anatomical studies led to the conclusion that science could not deal with man's ultimate differentia.

The idea of a hierarchy and a continuity in nature, of a scale and a chain, gained in popularity, particularly after the higher apes came on the scene. It hardly requires a new presentation here, and one example may for the moment suffice, taken from Tyson's flattering dedication to Lord Falconer: "The animal of which I have given the anatomy coming nearest to mankind, seems the nexus of the animal and the rational, as your Lordship and those of your high rank and order for knowledge and wisdom approaching nearest to that kind of beings which is nearest above us."[15] But this popular perspective could not in the long run replace the need to classify the animal

13. R. Bradley, *A Philosophical Account of the Works of Nature* (London, 1721), 170.

14. J. Ray, *The Wisdom of God* (1714), 6th ed., (London, 1714), 363 ff. Cf. W. F. Bynum, "The Anatomical Method, Natural Theology, and the Functions of the Brain," *Isis* 64 (1973).

15. Tyson, *Orang-outang sive Homo Sylvestris or the Anatomy of a Pygmie* (London, 1699), Ded.

kingdom in accordance with zoological taxonomy, which eventually had to have an effect on the conception of man's status.

The first really thoughtful attempt in this science is found in the mid-sixteenth century in a work by Edward Wotton, who collected the statements of Aristotle and arranged them in a manageable form. As usual, quadrupedia form a division of the "animals provided with blood," and quadrupeds are divided into the viviparous and oviparous. Mammals and reptiles are thus dealt with under the same heading. *Quadrupedia vivipara* are then divided on the basis of the shape of the foot.[16] Man is not included in the table, but is, nevertheless, described in the introduction, although according to other criteria. This was not, however, the way the matter was treated in the major natural histories of Gesner, Aldrovandi, and Jonston, where taxonomy is generally neglected. The thread was picked up again by the English country parson John Ray. Admittedly, Ray's *Synopsis Quadrupedum* (1693) is traditional in its juxtaposition of mammals and reptiles, but it contains a large number of major and minor improvements. In an introductory survey *quadrupedia vivipara* are divided into *terrestria* and *aquatica*, which means that the true nature of whales is recognized, although this does not entitle them to a place in the discussion that follows. Hirsuteness is a characteristic of terrestrial quadrupeds, with the possible exception of the manatees, which also posed a challenge to the quadruped concept by appearing to lack rear legs, an irritating exception that always necessitated comment. There is a further division between hoofed animals (*ungulata*) and clawed animals (*unguiculata*), major groups which were then split up by a series of subdivisions into the various species. Among the clawed animals, in the "separate fingers" group, we thus find the group "bearing nails" or "anthropoid," *Anthropomorpha,* including the apes.[17] Somewhat later Tyson produced a special classification of the unguiculate animals, but he, too, refrained from allowing man to appear in the context, despite his unique knowledge of our points of physical correspondence with the apes.[18]

Ray was aware of the criticism of the scholastic method and of the arbitrary criteria underlying it which was contained in the Lockean epistemology.[19] Locke himself speaks his mind about various attempts to define

16. E. Wotton, *De Differentiis Animalium Libri Decem* (Lutetiae Parisiorum, 1552). A history of mammalian classification is found in W. K. Gregory, "The Orders of Mammals," 1, *Bulletin of the American Museum of Natural History* 27 (1910). Cf. H. Daudin, *De Linné à Jussieu. Methode de la Classification et l'idée de serie,* 1 (Paris, 1926).

17. J. Ray, *Synopsis Quadrupedum Animalium et Serpentini Generis* (Londoni, 1693), 50 ff.

18. M. F. Ashley Montagu, *Edward Tyson, M.D., F.R.S., 1650–1708* (Philadelphia, 1943), 352 ff.

19. Cf. P. R. Sloan, "John Locke, John Ray and the Problem of the Natural System," *Journal of the History of Biology* 5 (1972).

man when he critically examines genus and the differentia method in the important sixth chapter of the third book in *Essay Concerning Human Understanding*. If anything, he champions a clear nominalism, showing at the same time that he is a supporter of the idea of a chain of nature. There are presumably higher spirits above us, he says, and in the visible world there are "no chasms, no gaps." Descending from man in tiny steps there is a continuous series of creatures, each quite insignificantly different from the next. There are fish with wings, for example, and credible reports have been received of mermaids and mermen. The great interest of the eighteenth century in semi-human species is no doubt to a large extent connected with this epistemological discussion of essence and with the relativity of definitions. As far as the definition of man is concerned, opinions vary: whereas some speak of *animal rationale,* others refer to "a biped without feathers and with broad claws." But "man" is a complex idea, and a single characteristic such as upright posture can never constitute an essential differentia. External criteria must be considered insufficient, since they leave undecided a problem such as the right of a monstrosity to the sacrament. We cannot know anything of the nonphysical, and the criterion of reason does not give any guidance as to the status of idiots. Confronted with such cases, both the clergyman and the lawyer must abandon their "sacred definition" of man, that is, *animal rationale.* Locke's survey is studded with examples from natural history—he was trained in medicine—and even the ape (the baboon) figures: "This is of the blue, that the red regiment; this is a man, that a drill, and in this, I think, consists the whole business of genus and species."[20] The pronouncement may stand as a classic summary of the criticism of the arbitrariness in natural history taxonomy as leveled from the standpoint of an increasingly relativistic view of man.

The Taxonomic Criteria of Linnaeus

Systema Naturae encompasses the whole of nature, in principle without omissions, and bears witness to an uncommon zeal for thoroughness. This being so, we may be sure that the inclusion of man within its covers cannot have caused any great agonies of indecision. Linnaeus sees nature as a whole, united by the same life, and he finds no justification for setting man apart in this context. It was obvious to him that man is an animal, but it was also a fact of the greatest importance. Man should not, therefore, deny his nature, but should in the medicinal sense live as an animal, he declares in the early medical treatise *Diaeta Naturalis.* Linnaeus asserts the right of his

20. J. Locke, *An Essay Concerning Human Understanding*, ed. A. C. Fraser (Oxford, 1894), III:6, §§ 12, 26–27, and 36.

science to treat man according to the laws of natural history—like any other natural object.

It is reasonable to assume that Linnaeus, like every other scholar, had had the proposition *Homo est animal* drilled into him in his school-days. Petrus Aurivillius's widely used textbook, for example, clearly states the traditional division of the substances from *genus generalissimum* to *species infima—bestia* and *homo*—and to *individua*: Peter, Paul, John.[21] This was how Linnaeus was later to construct his botanical method. If Svicerus's *Compendium Physicae Aristotelico-Cartesianae* was used in the gymnasium at Växjö, he could read the definition, "Man is a rational animal, or rather: man is a substance composed of *mens finita* and organic body." Human *mens* is "restricted" by comparison with the divine *Mens*, which not only thinks all the time but thinks about everything. But *Mens* is clearly distinguished from the body in the Cartesian manner, being composed of a special substance lacked by *bestiae* or *bruta*.[22] There are, however, frequent indications that Linnaeus never embraced such an opinion. Putting aside the language of philosophy for a moment, one may say that he loved animals. "One should not vent one's wrath on animals," he declares in a special paragraph in *Diaeta Naturalis*. "Theology decrees that man has a soul and that the animals are mere *automata mechanica,* but I believe they would better advise that animals have a soul and that the difference is in its nobility."[23] We feel greater compassion for a dog than for an insect, and even greater for an ape, which is emotional evidence that soul and reason occur throughout the animal kingdom. As a distinguishing attribute, Linnaeus considers, the difference is a matter of degree, not of kind. The apes alone are enough to refute the view that animals are robots. A note to a late edition of *Systema Naturae* states quite frankly that "Carthesius certe non vidit simias." In other words, man need feel no shame at being an animal: even though he is called *rationalis,* the animals cannot be called *irrationalia.*

The fascination which the apes held for Linnaeus is often evident. He must have been able to obtain firsthand knowledge of them in Holland, center of the trade in exotic animals. His employer, Cliffort, had a small menagerie that included apes. Linnaeus himself was to accumulate a not insignificant collection of animals in Uppsala, including several apes and monkeys donated by voyagers to the East Indies and by the king and queen. The charming description of his beloved guenon Diana has become a minor classic. The collection of his royal patrons included both live and preserved specimens, and at their palace, Drottningholm, he was able to observe a

21. P. Aurivillius, *Elementa Logicae Peripateticae* (Stockholmiae, 1738), 14.
22. J. H. Svicerus, *Compendium Physicae Aristotelico-Cartesianae* (Scaris, 1714), 268 ff.
23. *Diaeta Naturalis* 1733, ed. A. Hj. Uggla (Stockholm, 1957), 136–137.

menstruating guenon; also, the unusual event of a birth in captivity was recorded there.[24] Monkeys were kept in a number of places, which in two cases led to descriptions being sent to Linnaeus: one of the guenon of the Mayor of Västerås, reported by Pehr Osbeck, and the other sent by Anders Tidström and dealing with the pet of Lady Tessin. The *Proceedings of the Royal Swedish Academy of Sciences* contained a further contribution in the form of a colorful description of a mandrill by Claes Alströmer.[25] Determining the species in this comprehensive genus was just the sort of problem that suited Linnaean science. The material grew steadily; from an unstated but small number in the first edition of *Systema Naturae*, knowledge of the genus grew to such an extent that thirty or more species were described in the last one.

But this growing knowledge of the subject still did not produce anything to gainsay the basic similarity between the ape and man. A quotation of quite late date may serve to illustrate Linnaeus's line of reasoning:

I well know what a splendidly great difference there is [between] a man and a *bestia* when I look at them from a point of view of morality. Man is the animal which the Creator has seen fit to honor with such a magnificent mind and has condescended to adopt as his favorite and for which he has prepared a nobler life; indeed, sent out for its salvation his only son; but all this belongs to another forum; it behooves me like a cobbler to stick to my last, in my own workshop, and as a naturalist to consider man and his body, for I know scarcely one feature by which man can be distinguished from apes, if it be not that all the apes have a gap between their fangs and their other teeth, which will be shown by the results of further investigation.[26]

The apes resemble us in a number of ways, continues Linnaeus; the face has no hair; the bone of the upper arm spreads out into the clavicle; the breast has two nipples; the hands divide into fingers, which bear nails; and the eyelids have fringes of hair.

Indeed, in the uvula, the womb, and the muscles they are similar to us—even though they do not talk—and different from *bruta*. They often walk upright, standing only on their hind legs. They also take their food in their hands and carry it to their mouths, they drink from their cupped palm, and where there is no water they dig wells.[27]

Linnaeus was convinced that neither physical criteria nor even other characteristics permit a boundary to be drawn between man and ape. He finds

24. Cf. O. von Dalin, "Tal öfwer den första i Swerige födde markattan," *Witterhetsarbeten* 5 (Stockholm, 1767), 286 ff.; "Markattan Diana," *Vetenskapsakademiens Handlingar* (1754).

25. C. Alströmer, "Beskrifning på en sällsam babian, Simia mormon," *Vetenskapsakademiens Handlingar* (1766); Mss. in Linnean Society, London, for Osbeck and Tidström.

26. *Menniskans Cousiner*, ed. T. Fredbärj (Valda avhandlingar av Carl von Linné nr 21) (Ekenäs, 1955), 4.

27. Ibid., 5–6.

cause to quote the ancient Roman poet Ennius: "The ape is much like us, that ugly and disgraceful creature" *(Simia, quam similis turpissima bestia nobis)*. But for the sake of decency a nominal distinction has to be maintained.

Then follows the purely taxonomic side: how was the place of man to be described in terms of natural history? Two Swedish predecessors may be mentioned. In the early eighteenth century Magnus von Bromell gave lectures in medicine at Uppsala, and used to begin them with a survey of the kingdoms of nature that bore the stamp of Ray and Tournefort. Ray's version divides *vivipara* into *aquatica* and *terrestria* or *quadrupedia,* the latter group being split in turn into *bestiae terrestres* and, says Bromell, *ipseque homo,* man himself. It was thus permissible to call man a quadruped, but the reference is so brief that it should not be seen as any more than a symptom of the coming expansion of natural history.[28] A more important contribution is that of Petrus Artedi. Linnaeus must no doubt have discussed this question with his friend, who was to meet such an untimely death. Artedi left an *Idea Institutionum Trichozoologiae,* dating from the early 1730s, which in broad outline followed the system of Ray, but which, in a final section, included man, with the ape close behind. The character of our genus is drawn up thus:

1. Five long fingers, on both hands and feet. Smooth claws, broad, and almost straight. The inner toe of the feet longest.
2. The teeth are thirty-two in number, of which the five innermost ones in each jaw are molars, the remainder being front teeth plus two canines in each jaw. The three innermost molars are the biggest.
3. Tail not present. Locomotion supplied purely by the hind legs.
4. Two breasts and an equal number of nipples, both on men and, of course, on women.
5. Dominates by virtue of the power of speech, which the apes lack.[29]

This is all very Linnaean in style and content; indeed, Artedi's description is clearer and more detailed. Linnaeus's early comments on the subject of the quadrupeds stem from the same period. These are contained in *Pan Europaeus,* a small notebook on zoology, and also in lectures to his private

28. Royal Library (Stockholm), Ms X 511, M. von Bromell, *Praelectiones in Regnum Animale* (1714), unpag.
29. "Tvenne opublicerade Artedi-manuskript," ed. O. Nybelin, in *Svenska Linnésällskapets Årsskrift* (1934), 16–17.

pupil Mennander, in 1730.[30] Compared with Artedi, these treatments are both less exhaustive and also less faithful to Ray. Two years later, in *Systema Naturae*, man is included with the ape and the sloth in the order of *Anthropomorpha*, a designation borrowed from Ray, under the brief characteristic "four front teeth or none," but with the generic description replaced by the exhortation "Nosce te ipsum."

Division by the appearance of the foot has thus been exchanged for a division based on the arrangement of the teeth. In outline, Linnaeus's system is not so very different from Ray's, but it involves the first break with the old and misleading *quadrupedia* concept; moreover, from a modern point of view the teeth are the most resistant and may, therefore, be considered the most important distinguishing features of the animal. And in addition to the dental criterion, Linnaeus stipulates the importance of the number and position of the nipples. This is first announced in the *Lapland Journey* of 1732:

By the road hung a *maxilla inferiori equi,* which had 6 *incisores sat obtusos et detritos,* 2 *caninos et distincto spatio,* 12 *molares utrinque.* If I knew how many *dentes et quales,* and how many dugs each animal had, and *ubi,* I think I could devise a *methodum naturalissimum omnium quadrupedum.*[31]

The passage may give the impression of sudden inspiration, but there was undoubtedly a considerable amount of reflection behind it. Linnaeus has presumably proceeded from a general view, "picked out" various groups, and found correspondences in them with regard to teeth and nipples. What particularly appealed to him was the possibility of an animal classification based on numerical criteria on the same lines as the sexual system of the plants. In addition, there may also have been a theological aspect in that the teeth provided the best evidence for the way things were arranged at the Creation; they showed the form of life for which man was intended.

In this the man and ape relationship is construed from the respective diets:

Let us go to our class. If you look at *notas classicas,* at the teeth, at *manus et digitos,* then it is possible that you will see how closely related we are to *babianos et simias,* to *satyros sylvestres.* Consider whether they are not *carnivora,* they confirm the answer.[32]

It may strike us as odd to use the apes as evidence for declaring that man is a carnivore, but the explanation is that Linnaeus draws a comparison with

30. Mss. in Linnean Society, London, resp. Mennander in Royal Library, X 508 (copy Uppsala Univ. Libr., W 35).
31. Linné, *Iter Lapponicum,* ed. T. Fries (Stockholm, 1913), 121–122.
32. Ibid., loc cit.

the diet of the Lapps, which he took to be pristine. But elsewhere, in the lectures to Mennander, for example, man and ape are brought together, and the name *Fructivora* is given to their order. A similar division is also found in earlier literature: the physics textbooks sometimes spoke of quadrupeds as *animalia carnivora, herbivora,* and *omnivora.* Examples of the interest in different types of teeth may be found in, for example, Bromell, whose treatment of the subject includes the comment that "the guenon, which in everything else resembles man, also has teeth similar to those of man, and they are similarly placed, enabling him to eat every kind of food."[33]

The Jurisdiction of Natural History over Man

The foreword to *Fauna Svecica* (1746) goes to some lengths to justify the step which has been taken. "No one is right to be angry with me," asserts Linnaeus. Man is neither stone nor plant, but animal. And among the animals, he is not a worm, for he has a head, not an insect, for in that case he would have antennae, nor a fish lacking fins, nor a bird without wings, but a four-footed animal. He has teeth like theirs and four feet, two to walk upon and two to grip with. "And the fact is that as a natural historian I have yet to find any characteristics which enable man to be distinguished on scientific principles from the ape." There are apes which are less hairy than man, which walk upright, and which do such things with their hands as to lead less informed travelers to doubt the evidence of their eyes. Speech, admittedly, would appear to distinguish man from other animals, but when all is said and done, this is merely a capacity (*potentia*) or a result (*effectus*)—of upbringing, we are to understand. *Nota characteristica,* on the other hand, are taken from number, appearance, proportion, and position. In other words, it is extremely difficult to discover man's specific differentia. There is, however, something invisible in man from which our self-knowledge arises, namely, reason, the noblest of all that in which man so immeasurably surpasses all other animals.[34]

This is followed by a rhetorical eulogy of man, which, however, is hardly sincere in the light of other known utterances. This foreword was, in fact, a defense. It did not take long for objections to be heard from several quarters to the designation of man as a quadruped, and to our genus being judged by the same yardstick as the brutes.

Johan Gottschalk Wallerius, the chemist, had brought the question of the apes out into the open in his well-known dissertation directed against

33. Royal Library (Stockholm) Ms. X 36, 252.
34. *Fauna Svecica* (Holmiae, 1746), praefatio.

Linnaeus, who was a rival for a professorship in medicine in 1741. Deep down he was really a Linnaean himself, since they were both possessed by the same desire for systematization; but as soon as they came to particulars, their opinions differed. Wallerius begins his attack by saying that both anatomy and physiology show that man is not a quadruped at all. It is true that apes and satyrs sometimes rise up on their hind legs, but there is no doubt that their rough skin, their flattened nose, and their tail consign them to the quadrupeds. They lack the ability to bend their knees, neither do they have flesh on their hips, and so on. The name *Anthropomorpha* may be applied to them perhaps, but not to man, who can scarcely be said to resemble himself. And the definition "hairy body, four feet, four incisors or none" is repugnant to our genus.[35] Similar objections came from Jacob Theodor Klein, now forgotten, but at the time an authority of some standing. He devoted a special pamphlet (1743) to certain aspects of the Linnaean zoological system, which was widely circulated at the time. According to him, "hirsute" is misleading in the definition of the class; bear in mind the armadillo, the rhinoceros, and the hippopotamus. Recommending the old association of warm-bloooded and cold-blooded quadrupeds, he wonders where the turtles and lizards are. The place of man among the *Anthropomorpha* is also discussed. The exhortation *Nosce te ipsum* appeared to Klein to have been included in order to make readers lacking a sense of decorum wonder whether they were human or merely "anthropoid." Perhaps della Porta's pungent designation "bestial" will be found more apposite, Klein suggests.[36]

Linnaeus was sensitive to writings of this nature. That the lines in *Fauna Svecica* are a response to Klein's criticism is evident from some of the phrasing. He also asked Abraham Bäck for the loan of Klein's work. Bäck had offered to speak in Linnaeus's defense, and Linnaeus showed himself equally loyal when his friend came under the German's attack on another matter.[37] Linnaeus had a notorious dread of polemics, but he breathes fire and brimstone over his ignorant critic in a little draft that has survived. No better definition than *Nosce te ipsum* is possible; the characteristic is that of Solon rather than of Linnaeus and signifies the first step toward wisdom. If Klein had taken it, that is, if he had learned to know himself, "he would not have had to be discounted as *inter simias*"—among the quibblers—he would have recognized the obvious foolishness of all his writings, whereas now, in his blissful ignorance, he can hardly be classified as human.[38] The

35. J. G. Wallerius, *Decades Binae Thesium Medicarum*, resp. J. Darelius (diss. Upsaliae, 1741), 1 ff.

36. J. T. Klein, *Summa Dubiorum Circa Classes Quadrupedum et Amphibium in Linnaei Systemate Naturae* (Gedani, 1743), 1 ff.

37. *Bref och skrifvelser till och från Carl von Linné*, I:4 (Uppsala, 1910), passim.

38. Linnean Society, London, Ms. *Contra Kleinii animadversationes*.

key phrase *Nosce te ipsum* will not be discussed here, but what Linnaeus obviously means is that his description also does justice to the other, unquantifiable side of man. In context the comment *Nosce te ipsum* can also be taken as a witty appeal to the reader to look for man's physical peculiarities himself, which will be in vain.

The objections of Wallerius and Klein may reasonably be taken to indicate concern for the spiritual position of man in the traditional sense. A few more examples may be added. The selfless Johan Frederick Gronovius, who sponsored the first printing of *Systema Naturae*, had reservations on this particular point: "For man is truly the leading animal among living creatures, and, if we pause to reflect, he is also above all the others, which God in his omnipotence has created for man's amusement and benefit."[39] Albrecht von Haller, with whom Linnaeus maintained an increasingly strained correspondence, took a dim view of this reform. In a brief anonymous review of *Fauna Svecica*, he waxes sarcastic about the Linnaean role as a second Adam, nomenclator of the animals, and declares: "Kaum kann er sich enthalten den Menschen zum Affen, oder den Affen zum Menschen zu machen."[40] Despite his general admiration for *Fauna Svecica*, Johann Georg Gmelin in Petersburg is also compelled to question man's place among *Anthropomorpha*. According to Holy Scripture, we are created in God's image, and if a comparison is to be drawn, we ought to be called instead "guenon-like," *cercomorpha*.[41] In his reply to Gmelin, Linnaeus clearly refers to Haller's review:

Yet man does recognize himself. Perhaps we should now remove those words. But I ask you and the whole world for a generic differentia between man and ape which conforms to the principles of natural history. I certainly know of none. . . . If I were to call man ape or vice versa, I should bring down all the theologians on my head. But perhaps I should still do it according to the rules of science.[42]

Some works on natural history omit man without comment, which is, of course, also a standpoint. Klein's other works and the *Règne Animale* of Brisson (1756) adopt this course. Thomas Pennant, a major name in the genre and otherwise an admiring correspondent of the Swede's, evaluates the various systems of animals in his *Synopsis of Quadrupeds* (1771), lamenting the fact that the Linnaean system varies from edition to edition and includes the cetaceans among the mammals. He also states: "I reject his first division, which he calls Primates, or foremost in Creation, because my

39. J. F. Gronovius to Linné 1 Sept. 1735 (Linnean Society, London, *Letters* V: 363–364.)

40. A. von Haller, *Tagebuch* 2 (Bern, 1787), 201.

41. J. G. Gmelin to Linné 19 Dec. 1746 (Linnean Society, London, *Letters* V: 41–42).

42. Linné to Gmelin 14 Jan. 1747, in *J. G. Gmelini Reliqua quae Supersunt Comercii Epistolici*, ed. G. H. T. Plieninger (Stuttgartiae, 1861), 55.

vanity will not suffer me to rank mankind with apes, monkeys, maucaucos, and bats."[43] Pennant chooses to follow Ray's method, with certain modifications. His good friend in Sweden, Samuel Ödmann, later recommended the exclusion of man from the edition of *Fauna Svecica* which he was planning.[44] Toward the end of the century, Johann Friedrich Blumenbach, the great physical anthropologist, proposed a separate order for our genus, *Bimana*, as distinct from the *Quadrumana* of the apes, and in due course the order *Nocticolae* was added for the bats. These were the terms which were to be used by Cuvier and by others. The changes were the result, not only of a greater knowledge of anatomical differences, but also of a polemical desire to identify clear dividing lines between man and the rest of Creation.

Buffon gave man his own comprehensive volume of *Histoire Naturelle* (1753), with many later amendments which specifically stress man's distinctiveness. He, too, dealt with the term *quadrupedia,* which he criticized as a misleading designation, like others of the same type; according to him it served only as an aid to memory. The manatee does not fit, nor the ape, nor the bat. Man alone has two arms and two legs, whereas the manatee has only two arms, and the ape has four arms. Terminology of the Linnaean sort may be correct, but it gives only superficial knowledge, if that. Buffon stands for a nominalism in the spirit of Locke, and defends the loftiness of human reason in a manner that appears Cartesian. As another example of a similar dualistic conception of man, we may mention a longer chapter entitled *Homo duplex*: we can generalize, we have awareness and memory, we can create beauty, and grasp profundities.[45] Resorting to a convenient simplification, we may say that the intellectual aristocrat, Buffon, defends the elevated position of humanity against the less sophisticated Linnaeus.

Not dissimilar motives inspired La Mettrie, who made a short attack on Linnaeus in *Ouvrage de Penelope* (1748), a compendium of the great men of medicine of the age. All are declared almost equally incompetent, even if they are divided into those involved in useful disciplines and those engaged in useless ones. Linnaeus is the exponent of unprofitable botany, whereas Artedi's ichthyology happens to have been included in the useful occupations. La Mettrie jokes crudely with the terminology of the sexual system, which makes the knowledge of plants the most agreeable study in the world: botany is certain to be popular with the ladies from now on. But while he is, like Buffon, the sworn enemy of scholastic definition, he is fascinated by the formula which represents man. He twists it this way and that in various works, not always consistently, but usually in a most offen-

43. T. Pennant, *Synopsis of Quadrupeds* (Chester, 1771), v ff.
44. Cf. H. Wijkmark, *Samuel Ödmann* (Stockholm, 1923), 350 ff.
45. Buffon, *Histoire Naturelle* 4 (Paris, 1753), 69 ff. Cf. 14 (Paris, 1766) "Nomenclature des singes."

sive manner. Here *Fauna Svecica* gives rise to the observation that "man has become four-legged who was two-legged." However, one ought to argue as the author of *L'homme machine* does, states La Mettrie, namely that man becomes an ape by virtue of not one but a series of points in common. For a natural historian to proceed solely from the nature of the teeth is a logic that befits only an absurd pedant.[46]

Linnaeus is similarly honored in the little pamphlet *L'homme plante*, which is less well known, but which also dates from 1748. The original edition contains a description of this plant-man according to all the rules of Linnaean botany. Man belongs to the class *Dioecia,* and the order *Monandria* or *Monogynia,* with one stamen or one pistil. It is not surprising that La Mettrie chooses to describe a female specimen and shows obvious delight in the scope for ambiguities which is afforded. "The nectary is double" (i.e., the breast) and "is delectable to the touch"; the "pistil" and the "stilus" (vagina) are given measurements and definitions, the "stigma" (clitoris) is said to exude a fragrance like *Hypericum* in flower, and so on. The *essentia* consist of just the nectary and the pistil.[47] The parody plays boldly on the old *Homo est planta inversa* theme, but the main inspiration is provided by Linnaeus, who may well be imagined to have smiled on this occasion.

Klein, who suspected that Linnaeus had played into the hands of the freethinkers, was right. From now on the idea of man could be turned round, our animal side could be more unconditionally acknowledged, and the ape could for that matter be called man. A *Monachologia* (1783), reprinted several times and the work of the Austrian mineralogist Ignaz von Born, a former Jesuit who became an advisor to Joseph II, offers a further example. The arrangement is that of a dissertation in natural history: *monachus* is defined as "animal anthropomorphum," "equipped with cowl, wailing at night, avaricious," and the species, that is, orders, are described with precision in accordance with the table devised by Linnaeus. The motto is taken from his *De Noxa Insectorum* ("On the Harmfulness of Insects") and tells of the best way to exterminate vermin.[48] It is no coincidence that Born's irreverent work was published at just the time when religious freedom was being introduced into Austria and many of the riches of the monasteries were being confiscated for the benefit of general educational reform.

---

46. "Aletheius Demetrius," [de la Mettrie], *Ouvrages de Penelope ou Macchiavel de medicine* 1 (Genève, 1748): 25–45; 2: 18–38, 68–76.

47. La Mettrie, *L'Homme Plante* (Potsdam, no date [1748]), 29 ff. There is a modern edition by F. L. Rougier (New York, 1936).

48. "Johannes Physiophilus," [I. von Born], *Specimen Monachologiae Methodo Linneana* (Augustae Vindelicorum [Augsburg], 1783).

Homo sapiens, Other Terms and Other Human Species

Linnaeus felt that he had to explain himself to his critics and improve his description of man. In the tenth edition of *Systema Naturae* (1758), which contains much that is new, the terms *Mammalia, Primates,* and the designation *Homo sapiens* are introduced. All of them are still in use. In addition, Linnaeus created new, now-forgotten human species.

To start with the largest unit, the term *Mammalia* is to be found in the previous year, in the dissertation *Natura Pelagi*.[49] The search for a better designation than *Quadrupedia* was in itself nothing new. Ray had advocated hirsuteness to supplement the criterion of the number of feet. He had also half-included cetaceans in the group. The very title of Artedi's proposed division, his *Trichozoologia,* or "science of the hirsute animals," bears witness to the same insight. Given the extent of his knowledge, it is likely that he knew that the whales did not belong among fishes, but, nevertheless, he included them in his celebrated *Ichthyologia*. The old pattern was obviously difficult to break, and Linnaeus followed it in the earlier editions of *Systema Naturae,* but in his general restructuring of the fish class he took the opportunity to transfer the whales to *Mammalia,* a significant innovation that finally rounded off the higher animals into a natural unit. Some saw formalism and madness in this, it is true, but the new order was quickly accepted by most. It has been said, however, that it was the problem of whales that led directly to the change of terms; but a different explanation is more probable. An earlier remark may well be considered: "*Cetacei* may thank God that they can stand in their own *ordo*; they will never get a class of their own from me, much less will I have them among cows and oxen."[50] It was rather the complaints about man's being a quadruped that Linnaeus wished to acknowledge. He often brought up Klein's attack in his lectures, declaring bitterly that after the change of name in 1758 nobody should have any more objections. Even if his critics did not believe that man originally starts by walking on all fours, Linnaeus adds that every man born of woman must admit that he was nourished by his mother's milk.

The year 1758 also saw the name of the order changed: *Anthropomorpha* became *Primates*. With this change, Linnaeus acknowledged the fairness of the criticism that man could not simply be called "manlike"; that designation was also inappropriate for the sloth and the bat, which earlier were included in the group. The presence of these animals could naturally lead to objections to the designation *Primates,* "of the first rank," but that point was disregarded. Previously, *Magnates* had been tried, in *Museum Adolphi*

---

49. *Natura Pelagi*, resp. J. H. Hager (diss. Upsaliae, 1757), 13–14.
50. Linné to Bäck 12 May 1744 in *Bref och Skrifvelser,* I:4, 27. Cf. T. Gill, "The Story of a Word, Mammal," *Popular Science Monthly* 61 (1902), 434 ff.

Frederici (1754), and in the Swedish version *folklynniga* ("of human temperament"), which is a reminder of *Anthropomorpha.*

One could argue, of course, about the appropriateness of the name *Homo sapiens,* usually interpreted as "wise man." The choice of *sapiens,* or "the knowing man," must have quickly suggested itself, however; we are immediately reminded of the old definition of man as *animal rationale.* What is more, *sapiens* and *Nosce te ipsum,* which is given a long footnote, may be said to presuppose each other. The choice of name appears to have been made as an affirmation that man is indeed essentially different. On the other hand, *sapiens* is, according to the rules of taxonomy, only a specific epithet (trivial name) and not a definition, and not necessarily descriptive either. Linnaeus may not have been implying any definite meaning by his choice of name. The direct reason for this appellation is, of course, that man, like everything else in nature, had to have his specific epithet when binary nomenclature was introduced.

In some ways the choice appears rather arbitrary, or at least it might have turned out differently. Linnaeus actually uses the epithet *sapiens* not about man but in lectures given in 1753 on a species of monkey referred to as *Simia sapiens.* This undeniably gifted animal is said to be able to learn to play backgammon admirably, and for fear of tigers to keep watch so that others in the group could sleep safely and soundly.[51] Of course, it is no coincidence that it is a monkey which has been given this epithet. But there is also in *Systema Naturae,* rather remarkably, a parallel designation to *Homo sapiens,* namely, *Homo diurnus.* Drafts from this period show Linnaeus undecided between the two names; first one is crossed out, then the other. To correspond to *Homo diurnus* there is *Homo nocturnus,* also called *Homo troglodytes.* This is the real sensation: a new human species, literally "caveman," a name that could suggest to later generations some prehistoric creature. From the typography it is possible to see which designations are to be regarded as official, but Linnaeus himself continues to use the "unofficial" ones, *diurnus* or *nocturnus,* intermittently. "Day man" and "night man" are a truly odd pair and testimony to Linnaeus's weakness for antitheses.

Precisely what Linnaeus meant by the name *Homo sapiens* has been discussed elsewhere by the present writer.[52] However, Linnaeus did introduce other members into the human genus. It contained the *troglodyte,* or night man, for example, *Homo caudatus,* or tailed man, and eventually also *Homo lar.* It is a motley collection, and one realizes that Linnaeus had allowed himself to be led astray. New myths were formed from the rem-

51. Uppsala University Library, Ms. N 558, "Quadrupedia privatim föreläste" [1753], 37ᵛ.

52. *Homo sapiens L. Studier i Carl von Linnés naturuppfattning och människolära* (Lychnos-bibliotek 28) (Uppsala, 1975), chap. 6.

nants of old ones, ancient traditions were mixed with more recent reports. It was often in this weird light that writers attempted to clarify the phenomenon of man. This and other closely related questions are the subject of a work by the Frenchman Franck Tinland, *L'homme sauvage* (1968), which devotes a considerable amount of space to Linnaeus and which can in general be recommended.

Reports of strange animals might, of course, raise suspicion, but when there was a conceivable natural explanation, they were accepted. Providing such explanations was one of the tasks of natural history. This was certainly the opinion of Linnaeus, who is not slow to display a certain condescension when considering the gullibility and confusion persisting in the earlier literature. Under the title of *Paradoxa*, the early editions of *Systema Naturae* contain a number of old and unnatural curiosities for which he offers a natural explanation with the intention of discarding them from the files of zoology. They include the hydra, frog fish, unicorn, satyr, tailed man, Scythian lamb, phoenix, barnacle goose, dragon, and deathwatch beetle; the manticora, lamia siren, and even antelope were added later. Linnaeus tidied up nature after the barbarisms and darkness of the Middle Ages. Medieval monasticism is conveniently made to take the blame for all kinds of foolishness. He is throughout the man of the Enlightenment fighting old follies. The progress of science is illustrated by the fact that cases of this sort need no longer cause any difficulty. This type of outlook is exemplified in the introduction to the dissertation *Siren Lacertina* (1766), in which the loaded word "siren" is transferred to an amphibian two feet long, known nowadays as the mud iguana.[53] Thus, according to Linnaeus, modern natural history could demystify a world previously populated by superstition and fabulous creatures.

But if we dig deeper into the material, the siren is, in fact, an illustration of another feature, a credulity which is often to be observed in Linnaeus. An adherence to fragments of folklore in a critical and scientific mind should no longer occasion surprise. His *Skånska resa*, for example, includes an account of the finding of a calf on the seashore, thought to belong to the cattle of the undines, but which Linnaeus decided had been born prematurely, commenting that a calf hardly has the respiratory organs suitable for a life on the seabed.[54] This may be compared with Linnaeus's belief that swallows, contrary to all anatomical and physiological indications, winter on the lake bottom.[55] The example from Skåne also exhibits a popular and enticing parallel of the elements: the sea contained all that was to be found

---

53. *Siren Lacertina*, resp. A. Österdam (diss. Upsaliae, 1766) (also in *Amoenitates Academicae* 7).

54. *Skånska resa* (Stockholm, 1751), 79–80.

55. *Migrationes Avium Sistens*, resp. G. D. Ekmark (diss. Upsaliae, 1757) (also in *Amoenitates Academicae*, 5).

on the shore. Of course, such parallels were simply a case of using analogy to describe something that would otherwise be difficult to illustrate—designations such as sea cow, sea lion, catfish, sea hog (porpoise), may be mentioned—but it was also possible to take it all fairly literally. In Linnaeus's own native tracts, for example, it was believed that when the wind blew on Lake Möckeln the undines were doing their washing, and also that they owned fields where their cattle grazed.

We may perhaps regard the undine as having been disposed of under the designation of "siren" among other absurdities in the *Paradoxa* group. The siren is found, however, under the name of "syrene" in the most prominent position in *Pan Europaeus*, the early notebook on zoology, where it appears in the same group as man and the ape. What Linnaeus is building on here is the portrayal of a *Homo marinus* given by Thomas Bartholin, the Danish anatomist. A leading authority on the New World, Johan de Laet, had sent his Danish fellow physician, Ole Worm, a rib and a hand belonging to an unknown creature, which had been caught off Brazil.[56] The siren appeared in print in Artedi's *Ichthyologia* as a final genus after the manatees, but not in *Systema Naturae*.[57] However, Linnaeus's opinion was not so decided as to prevent him in 1749 from taking a consuming interest in a Danish mermaid, who was displayed, and who attracted large crowds in Nykøbing in Jutland. "Linnaeus has been quite wide-eyed," states a sarcastic letter mentioning the affair.[58] In a letter to the Royal Swedish Academy of Sciences he wrote in solemn style that science was still unsure about the existence of such a being. If the Academy could obtain this specimen, either alive or preserved, it would be one of the greatest discoveries ever made, "because this is a phenomenon which does not occur more than once every 100 or 1,000 years."[59] But when an inquiry through a Swedish emissary in Copenhagen elicited a negative reply with regard to the reliability of the dispatch, Linnaeus remained silent, possibly out of embarrassment.

It is not easy to pin down the significance of this interest in all the oddities of nature, and the question is one which has been neglected by students of the history of ideas. Linnaeus's strange uncertainty is accompanied by a clear understanding of the laws of biology. The description by Bartholin is said to have gained in credibility because it does not give a traditional description, mentioning tumbling locks of hair quite untypical of a water

56. T. Bartholin, *Historiarum Anatomicarum Rariorum Centuriae* (Hafniae, 1661–1667), Cent 2, 186 ff.

57. P. Artedi, *Ichthyologia, Genera Piscium* (Lugduni Batavorum, 1738), 81. The Siren might be, of course, an addition by the editor, i.e., Linnaeus.

58. D. Tilas to F. Cronstedt 18 Sept. 1749, in Royal Library (Stockholm) Ms. *Ep. T. 14D.*

59. Linnaeus to K. Vetenskapsakademien 29 Aug. 1749, *Bref och Skrifvelser* I:2, 129–130.

178

creature.[60] On the other hand, the human appearance of the face ought to have given rise to doubts, as ought the large number of extremely dubious articles in Bartholin's work. In any case, the riddle should not have been so very difficult. Countless reports of mermaids were, in fact, descriptions of manatees, as was Bartholin's, or of seals, or perhaps dolphins. The temptation to anthropomorphize these animals that were different from other marine creatures may be briefly illustrated by a note in *Iter Lapponicum* referring to the intercourse of seals: the female lies "wide open" and the male "ut homo" embraces her.[61] But the interest of Linnaeus and, for example, of Robinet also shows, of course, the power exercised by the idea of a chain of being.

The question remains of the degree to which Linnaeus and his time really regarded the siren and the satyr, for example, as resembling man. Or did they rather view the matter in a spirit of rationalism and consider that they had more or less identified and explained away some ancient mythical creatures? The whole of classical mythology appears to be on the way into Linnaeus's genus *Simia,* judging by his trivial names: satyr, sylph, sphinx, silenus, faun, even Diana and Bacchus (Jacchus). But if this treatment could be interpreted as explaining away the creatures of fable, it also necessarily had the effect of loading the apes with myth and semi-human characteristics. And this meant that there were new species of man around the corner.

The Dissertation *Cousins of Man:* The Apes, the Tailed Man, and the Troglodyte

The siren occurs in the later editions of *Systema Naturae* as a final note to the animal class, not unwarrantably supplied with a question mark. Its place has been taken by *Homo troglodytes,* "the cave-dwelling man." The classification is commented upon in the well-known dissertation *Anthropomorpha* (1760), of which an earlier version in Swedish, *Cousins of Man,* has come down to us; another title, *De Troglodytes,* may well refer to yet another version, now lost.[62] The title of the dissertation should be taken literally: it is indeed the species resembling man which are in question, the group between *Homo sapiens* and the monkeys, and it is to these we now

---

60. *Carl von Linnés föreläsningar öfver djurriket,* utg. E. Lönnberg (Uppsala och Berlin, 1913), 174–175.

61. *Iter Lapponicum* (1913), 211.

62. *Anthropomorpha,* resp. C. E. Hoppius, diss. (Upsaliae, 1760) (also in *Amoenitates Academicae* 6); *Menniskans Cousiner,* ed. T. Fredbärj (Ekenäs, 1955); the title *De Troglodytis* is found in Linnaeus to Bäck 16 July 1759, *Bref och Skrifvelser* I:5, 71.

turn. It may be appropriate to begin with some snapshots of this newly acquired knowledge of the apes. During the eighteenth century, we may say, the ape leaped forward from being, at most, a convenient symbol of human vice to the position almost of our brother and equal.[63]

This was another subject about which the expansion of seafaring afforded new knowledge. The first acceptable description of the chimpanzee was given in 1641 by the famous Amsterdam physician Nicolas Tulp, from a specimen owned by the Prince of Orange. Although the animal referred to is *Satyrus indicus,* Tulp states that Angola was the country of origin. This satyr is a quadruped, he says, but on account of its manlike appearance it is called "orang-outang," that is, "man of the woods" in Malay, latinized as *Homo sylvestris.*[64] This was the start of a persistent confusion of names and species. (Tulp's satyr has, in fact, recently been identified as a pygmy chimpanzee, officially described only in 1929!)[65] The illustration, many variations of which soon appeared, shows a woebegone female who is undoubtedly a trifle too rounded in appearance. It was said to resemble man in its habits, drinking water from a ladle, and drying itself thoroughly afterward. From Borneo it is also reported that the males (orang-outang this time!) are noted for their lechery; they attack women and rape them, as did the satyrs of old. The name seemed, in other words, not inapposite, and it inspired many similar presentations. But the first proper examination had to wait until Tyson produced his *Orang Outang sive Homo Sylvestris,* or *The Anatomy of a Pygmie* (1699). This is one of the classic works in biological history and has earned its author the title "father of primatology." The methods of comparative anatomy are applied in an admirable fashion. Tyson gives a list of forty-eight points showing that the difference between his pygmy and man is less than that between the pygmy and other apes, and also thirty-four points of difference between man and the pygmy. Excellent illustrations lend extra clarity. It may be observed that the name "chimpanzee" is found for the first time in 1738 on an engraving depicting an animal shown in London. The reports gradually increase in frequency, but far from all of them give firsthand evidence.

The orang-outang had been briefly and quite inadequately described by Jacob Bondt (1658), who also appended an odd illustration.[66] A hundred years later George Edwards gave another reproduction on the evidence of a badly stuffed skin, whose pinkish color makes it impossible to regard the

---

63. Cf. especially H. W. Janson, *Apes and Ape Lore in the Middle Ages and the Renaissance* (London, 1952); also the works by Greene and Tinland.

64. N. Tulp, *Observationes Medicae,* ed. nova (Amstelodami, 1652), 283–291.

65. V. Reynolds, *The Apes* (London, 1968), 43 ff.

66. J. de Bondt, *Historia Naturalis et Medica Orientalis* (Amstelodami, 1658), 84–85.

illustration as representing a chimpanzee.[67] The first acceptable description was provided by Buffon in 1766 and was followed by accounts by Arnout Vosmaer and Pieter Camper toward the end of the century. The profusion of names often makes it bewilderingly difficult to know which species is being referred to: orang-outang, chimpanzee, *Homo sylvestris, homme sauvage, satyrus indicus,* pygmy, *bari, smitten,* drill, pongo, jocko, "a sort of baboon," *troglodyte, Homo nocturnus,* and maybe more names— all are found. Buffon created order temporarily by differentiating between two kinds of orang-outang, a larger Pongo and a smaller Jocko (the names are taken from Battel's travels), but he suspected that Jocko was actually an immature Pongo.[68] The detailed illustrations in *Histoire Naturelle,* to which Daubenton contributed many anatomical descriptions, represented a great step forward in the investigation of the simian genus. Because Tyson was often quoted, his work became better known outside England. Much material, both living and dead, was brought to the celebrated Jardin Royal, including a new anthropoid ape, the gibbon, which Buffon was the first to present to the world of learning.

The main aspects of the subject are well known, but some Swedish snapshots may be added. Holland, which was visited by so many Swedes, medical men in particular, offered the chance to view many splendid exotica. In the crowded marketplace of Amsterdam, Carl Tersmeden (c. 1735) saw "an oran utan which is a kind of baboon," which was tethered by a strong iron chain around its neck because it is "one of the fiercest of wild animals."[69] Voyagers with the Swedish East India Company not seldom were capable natural historians. Carl Johan Gethe (c. 1745), for example, tells in the unpublished description of his travels of "the wild animal orang hotan," which he had seen tethered aboard an English ship in Canton. It bore a close resemblance to a man and had a large mouth, which protruded like that of a Negro, and arms long enough for it to lay its hands flat on the deck while standing upright. It could also walk on two legs, although it preferred to go on all fours. The length of the arms and the sharp nails indicated that in the forest the animal was arboreal, Gethe points out.[70] Naturally, plans were made to take such a rarity home to Sweden. Carl Fredrik Hornstedt gives an account of his tribulations in the 1780s with an orang-outang captured in Borneo, which he had acquired through the Society of Sciences in Batavia. Unfortunately, it drank a basin of broth,

---

67. G. Edwards, *Gleanings of Natural History* (London, 1758), 6 ff.
68. Buffon, *Histoire Naturelle* 14, 96 ff.
69. C. Tersmeden, *Memoarer,* utg. N. Erdman (Stockholm, 1915), 141.
70. Royal Library (Stockholm), Ms. M 280, C. J. Gethe, Dagbok hållen pa resa til Canton, 95–96, tab. XII.

which fatally aggravated a virulent fever from which it was already suffering. It was, therefore, put in a keg of arrack to preserve it for transport. Hornstedt asserts that his specimen will at any rate be the first of its kind in Sweden.[71] Nevertheless, it is possible that he was anticipated by Anders Sparrman, who prides himself in a memorial upon having procured an orang-outang for the museum of the Royal Swedish Academy of Sciences; in Holland it would certainly have commanded a price of twelve to fifteen ducats, but it cost the Academy nothing, Sparrman claims.[72] And in 1759, Linnaeus himself had received from George Edwards "a chimpanzee skin in excellent condition"; it differed in color from Tyson's specimen, and thus can hardly have been correctly identified.[73] The skin is now missing from the Linnaean collections, but it seems that Linnaeus had it stuffed. It may be mentioned that in the course of his long educational tour in the early 1780s, Linnaeus the younger saw a chimpanzee (*Simia jocko*) in Paris and made a drawing of its hand and foot, and that he also made a thorough examination of a gibbon (*Simia lar*) in the menagerie at the Tower of London.[74] These travels were by way of preparation for an intended new edition of *Systema Naturae*, which he never completed.

It was up to Linnaeus to evaluate and bring order to this information, allot names, and draw up references to the literature. He included two tailless species of ape, *Simia satyrus* and *Simia sylvanus,* the latter being the Barbary ape. In the 1758 edition of *Systema Naturae*, *satyrus* is constructed from Tulp's description, that is, from a chimpanzee, but by 1766 Linnaeus was using the illustration supplied by Edwards—in other words, the orang-outang, as the type specimen, while the satyr of Tulp is included as a variety. This has an important bearing on the question of names, and to be consistent with the nomenclatorial reference point of the 1758 edition, the chimpanzee (the pygmy chimpanzee) ought to be called *satyrus,* and definitely not *troglodytes*.[75] The confusion is understandable, since in 1766 *Simia satyrus* (i.e., the orang-outang) was said to live in Africa. The statement is repeated in *Anthropomorpha*, with the difference that it is now called *pygmaeus*, Tyson's name for his young chimpanzee. But, as he regretfully tells Edwards, Linnaeus never had the opportunity to study Tyson's work. Linnaean science is full of puzzling anomalies of this nature.

71. C. F. Hornstedt, "Anteckningar under en resa til Östindien," *Skrifter utgifna af Svenska litteratursällskapet i Finland* 10 (1888), 155.

72. Cf. Y. Löwegren, *Naturaliekabinett i Sverige under 1700-talet* (Lychnos-Bibliotek 13) (Uppsala, 1952), 281.

73. E. M. daCosta to Linnaeus 5 Oct. 1759, *Correspondence* 2, ed. J. E. Smith (London, 1821), 494.

74. Linnean Society, London, Linn. fil. *Diagnoses of Animals.*

75. Cf. W. Stiles and M. B. Orleman, *The Nomenclature for Man, the Chimpanzee, the Orang-utan, and the Barbary Ape* (Washington, 1927).

The pygmy, a representation of which is given by Edwards, "is farthest from us in the generic line," declares Linnaeus in *Anthropomorpha*. The head is relatively round, as in man, and the forehead is clean and bare, but the nose is somewhat depressed, as in a Hottentot. It is the hindmost extremities that display "closer alliance with the apes than with us." The description generally follows that of Edwards, but in the meantime Linnaeus had obtained some clarification of the dental arrangement in a letter, although no reply to his questions about the possible labia (*nymphae*) and the clitoris, as the specimen was a stuffed one. These characteristics were otherwise regarded as important. Edwards had been of the opinion that there was a difference of species, but in his answer Linnaeus ventures the suggestion that the differences lay in the fact that the individuals described were of opposite sex.[76] Nevertheless, he explains in his dissertation that the satyr differs from the pygmy in having an almost hairless face, bare abdomen and arms, and also a larger abdomen, even when young, and thus is well "distinct from the mademoiselles of our genus." As the satyr has "hands for hind feet," it is impossible to speak of any very close affinity with man. The size corresponds to ours, it generally walks bolt upright, it does not fear to do battle with our genus, and it is so lustful that women in the vicinity of the animal's haunts dare not walk alone in the forest. But like Tulp's, this satyr had good table manners, and it went to bed at night with its head on a pillow, pulled its quilt up to its shoulders, and slept like a "respectable old lady."

We now come to numbers three and four in *Anthropomorpha*, in which the boundary of the human genus has been crossed. *Homo caudatus*, or the "tailed man"—called Lucifer in *Systema Naturae* (1766), where it is not treated as a separate species—is a man with a tail and would appear to "rank as a fairly close cousin of ours." He is said to live on the island of Nicobar, between Sumatra and Bengal, and in Java. There does not appear to be a proper reproduction—the only one known to Linnaeus was one which he found in Aldrovandi's outdated work—but various travelers supplied details. Bondt certifies that there are such men in the mountains of Borneo and that many of his countrymen had been able to see them at the Royal Court. A hairless tail four fingers or more in length grows as a protuberance from the coccyx.[77] And Nils Matsson Kiöping, a Swedish traveler of the mid-seventeenth century, Linnaeus continues, saw the tailed man with his own eyes. He tells a gruesome story. A number of quarrelsome natives had boarded Kiöping's ship at Nicobar. They wanted to trade parrots for nails and other ironmongery, but when this was not accepted,

---

76. Linnaeus to Edwards 20 Mar. 1758; Edwards to Linnaeus 2 June 1758; Linnaeus to Edwards, in *Correspondence* 2, 497 ff.

77. Bondt, 85.

they wrung the necks of the parrots and ate them raw. They ran boldly "all over the place," taking with them every removable piece of ironware. "Big, fierce people, dark yellow in color," they were. "They had a tail at the back, hanging like a cat's tail." Later the mate and some of the men went ashore to look for food, but they did not return that night, and a rescue party was sent out. Shots were fired onto the shore from two small cannon, frightening the natives off into the woods. First the boat was found, smashed and with the nails removed, and then the mate's party, of whom only the bones remained.[78]

Finally, and most important of all, there is the troglodyte, that is *Homo troglodytes* or *nocturnus:* "the child of darkness which turns day into night and night into day and appears to be our closest relative," to quote Linnaeus. The troglodytes, he continues, are reported as early as the time of Pliny and live in Ethiopa, Java, Amboina, Mount Ophir in Malacca, and the Ternate Islands, usually in caves in the ground. Bondt described them and also provided an illustration. They grow little taller than a nine-year-old boy and are as white as snow, never becoming sunburned, since they are active at night. They walk upright and have short "fuzzy" hair like a Negro, although it is as white as chalk. The eyes are round, with orange pupils and irises, while the upper eyelid partially covers the lower one, giving the appearance of a squint. They differ completely from our species in having a transparent nictitating membrane, like that of bears and owls. A traveler to the East Indies whom Linnaeus met in Holland told also of a fold of skin which fell forward over the sexual organs of the female, as in the Hottentot. He further reported that there were no gaps between the teeth, which was a characteristic that distinguished man from the apes. In his notes to *Systema Naturae* Linnaeus had written quite simply: "vidi cranium in Hollandia." By day the troglodytes lie, half-dazed, in their holes, but they see excellently at night, when they steal everything they can find. The local population are unsparing in their efforts to stamp them out. The troglodyte has his own language, which is guttural and difficult to learn, but he cannot learn our language, other than "yes" or "no." According to the testimony of certain authors, he believes that he once ruled the earth and was driven from power by men, and that in the future his former ascendancy will return. Linnaeus refers here to an address by the Swedish writer Olof von Dalin in 1749.[79] In *Systema Naturae* Dalin is also quoted as the source of the information that troglodytes do not live beyond their twenty-fifth year. Kiöping's account of his travels is used once again for the details of the thefts and the language of the troglodyte. "They are regarded and

78. Kiöping, *En kort beskrifning uppå trenne resor* (Wisingsborgh, 1667), 112–123.
79. Dalin, *Om Swerige i sitt ämne och Swerige i sin upodling* (K. Wetenskapsakademien, Presidietal 1749) (also in *Witterhetsarbeten*, Stockholm, 1767), 123.

exterminated as vermin," Kiöping had written, claiming to have seen examples of this species in Amboina. The description is again very graphic: "And they are quite blind by day, as if their eyes were put out. For when they are dug out during the day, they crawl around like young dogs before their eyes are open." Kiöping goes on to relate that on board his vessel there had been such a creature of the female sex, who had no idea of how to cover herself because she could not see at all; when forced out into the daylight, however, she grew accustomed to it, "but she lifted her feet high when she walked."[80] Man, who is so curious about everything, comments Linnaeus, has, strangely enough, left the troglodytes in their darkness. "It would also be a worthy subject for a philosopher to converse for a few days with one of these and to elicit from them how far their intelligence compares with that of man, so as properly to mark out the difference between man and beast." This meeting would be of value to the naturalist, that is, Linnaeus, since despite his efforts he has not succeeded in placing the troglodyte in the simian genus. Such a rarity could easily be obtained by a king "whose wishes to perform a whole nation does compete."

Fuller information had already been anticipated from England about the matter, Linnaeus wrote in a commentary on *Systema Naturae*, and these expectations no doubt inspired his dissertation.[81] Early in 1758 he somehow learned of a very unusual show in London, and he wrote to his friend on the spot, John Ellis, for further details. His interest grew through a letter from Pehr Bierchén, a pupil who was visiting in the course of his studies, to Daniel Solander, who forwarded a copy. The letter tells of a ten-year-old girl (other sources give the age as fourteen) from Jamaica, wholly white, but with negroid features, having pale yellow eyes turned to a curious position as if squinting, and unable to tolerate daylight, although seeing better in the dark.[82] Linnaeus was more than usually enthusiastic; he had never been so delighted by a letter, wishing to hug and kiss Bierchén for every word. The new human could indeed have been described from *Systema Naturae*, so well does every "point" agree. But he wants to know more. Examine particularly, he urged Bierchén, the genitalia (*nymphae* and *clitoris*), whether she speaks gutturally, whether the eye has the characteristic eyelid (*membrana nictitans*), whether the big toe is not larger than ours, whether the caudal vertebrae are larger, the buttocks, too, also the extent of her reason—Linnaeus piles on the questions quite unsystematically. Bierchén is promised membership in the Society of Science at Uppsala for a description. His journey has already provided results

80. Kiöping (1667), 123–124.
81. *Svenska Mercurius*, April 1758, 1273.
82. Linnaeus to Ellis 8 Feb. 1758, *Correspondence* 1, 88–89; Linnean Society, London, Ms. Misc. Authors A–D, excerpt from letter Bierchén to D. Solander.

enough, "so important is this matter," Linnaeus declares ecstatically. If the owner is willing to sell this treasure, Linnaeus asks him to name a price, and Edwards is to be persuaded to help with an illustration.[83] But when the answer arrived, it was a disappointment. Bierchén had visited the girl twice and compared her with Linnaeus's description of the troglodyte, but without being able to confirm the correspondence. True, her keeper had forbidden an examination of the private parts on both occasions, despite being offered a handsome consideration; tests showed, however, that the girl could not see well enough to read in total darkness.[84] At about the same time John Ellis gave his frank but equally negative reply. There is not so much as a word in the *Anthropomorpha* dissertation of what was to have been its showpiece.

But Linnaeus did not allow himself to become despondent. The plea for royal assistance was eventually answered. Claes Grill of the Swedish East India Company informed Linnaeus in 1764 that orders to obtain a specimen of the creature concerned had been issued from Gothenburg, obviously through the queen. For three years efforts were made to meet the wishes of Linnaeus.[85] The troglodyte hunt yielded no results, of course. A few years later (1772) an unequivocally negative answer followed from J. G. König, a doctor and natural historian at the Dano-German mission station at Tranquebar on the east coast of India and a frequent correspondent. Troglodytes, or "cockroaches," are usually born as such, but of black parents, he said, and only seldom were normal at birth. Their characteristics are undoubtedly the result of some disease. A man of this kind, who had recently married, had promised to inform König of the nature of the offspring.[86] What became of this case is not known, nor is the reaction of Linnaeus, but there is nothing to indicate that he might eventually have altered his views on the existence of a second human species.

To recapitulate the classificatory side: in the 1758 and 1766 editions of *Systema Naturae*, Linnaeus includes *Homo sapiens* (*diurnus*), and in addition *Homo troglodytes* (*nocturnus*). *Homo caudatus* (*Lucifer*) is mentioned in a footnote and does not enjoy the same taxonomical status, although it is marked in the author's copy as a third human species. It is also treated as such in the *Anthropomorpha* dissertation, while earlier, in the *Paradoxa* group, the same form has been clearly assigned to the simian genus. The apes, which Linnaeus really sees as only *one* species called *Simia satyrus*,

83. Linnaeus to Bierchén, no date, *Bref och Skrifvelser* I:3, 210–211.

84. Bierchén to Linnaeus 14 June 1758, ibid., 208 ff.

85. C. Grill to Linnaeus 17 Dec. 1764, *Bref och Skrifvelser* I:6, 225–226. Cf. J. Beckmann, *Schwedische Reise in den Jahren 1765–66*, ed. T. Fries (Uppsala, 1911), 111–112.

86. J. G. König to Linnaeus 22 Feb. 1772 in Linnean Society, London, *Letters* VIII: 174–175.

are clearly separated from man as far as classification is concerned, but the distinction is primarily nominal.

Linnaeus even went so far as to introduce a fourth human species, *Homo lar*, but this one was also quickly dismissed from scientific discussion. We find it among a series of other supplements in *Mantissa altera* (1771). *Homo lar* is said to be a native of Coromandel, Malacca, the Moluccas, and the forests of Bengal, and is described as "tailless, walking upright, and of human height."[87] Linnaeus was aware of the two recent descriptions of the creature: by Stephen de Vismes in *Philosophical Transactions* (1769), and by Buffon two years earlier. (This is, incidentally, one of the very few—only two, it would seem—occasions on which Linnaeus mentions his adversary in print.) When comparison is made with the sources, the classification becomes even more remarkable. Buffon does not claim anthropoid status for his "gibbon"—the name soon gained currency—which is said rather to be an intermediate form between tailless monkeys (*singes*) and baboons. Nor do the illustrations make an anthropomorphic impression.[88] Moreover, in the same volume of *Histoire Naturelle*, Buffon dismisses the troglodyte, not without sarcasm, as a misidentified orang-outang. The far less impressive description and illustration by de Vismes do not give any cause to associate the species with man, either, with the possible exception of the observation that "Golok or wild people are thought to be originally a mixture with the human kind having no tails."[89] But Linnaeus persevered. He had dispelled the mystery surrounding the designation "man" in 1735, and he continued in the same vein. *Homo sapiens* was only one of several other human species of unknown character. To him the evidence seemed perfectly clear.

The Mythical Beings Explained

The reality behind *Homo caudatus* and *Homo troglodytes* is hardly difficult to discern: in the former case, quite simply a species of ape, a black baboon, for example, or possibly people, wearing animal skins either for reasons of ritual or to terrify visitors; in the latter, albinos together with confused details of the higher apes. The troglodyte has most frequently been explained as a misidentification of the orang-outang, as Linnaeus gives this synonym in *Systema Naturae* with a reference to Bondt, but here it is Bondt who is responsible for the confusion, whereas Linnaeus is merely listing the

87. *Mantissa altera* (Holmiae, 1771), appendix, 521.
88. Buffon, *Histoire Naturelle* 14, 92–108, tab. 2–6; 45–46. Linnaeus is also referring to Buffon in *Prolepsis Plantarum* (1763), c. 1.
89. S. de Visme, "Description of a Singular Species of Monkeys without Tails, Found in the Interior Parts of Bengal," *Philosophical Transactions* 49 (1769).

various designations that have been used. One synonym requires immediate explanation: "cockroach" presumably refers to the fact that the insect of the same name is active nocturnally. It is obviously a pejorative term, and may contain the origin of the custom (or the stock phrase) mentioned by Kiöping when he speaks of these people as being "exterminated as vermin"; Kiöping's is actually the first record of the sobriquet. As for the social status of albinos, it may be added that according to Cornelius de Pauw the emperors of Java traditionally welcomed these frail creatures "in order to win favor with the Gods."[90]

Linnaeus's troglodyte can, in fact, be traced to one particular episode. The source freely used by Dalin, although without acknowledgment, is none other than Voltaire's description of a little albino Negro, shown in Paris in 1744. From this Linnaeus has unknowingly taken his information about the appearance of the eyes and other details, which do not require a lengthy discussion here. These people, says Voltaire, dwell principally in Loango (Congo); they live no longer than twenty-five years, and their characteristics should not be interpreted as a disease—he can testify to this after seeing the boy at the Hotel de Bretagne. Their existence has been disputed, he continues, but no doubt there are even more human types still unknown to us. Such red-eyed beings see things differently from the way we do, so if there is a Newton among them, he will be able to develop another theory of optics. Their view of their former greatness provokes typically Voltairean comments on the incurable arrogance and foolishness of man.[91]

This case is dealt with at greater length by Maupertuis in his *Venus Physique* (1746). The work is inspired by the same remarkable boy, even though it does contain a good deal else. The boy is stated quite definitely to be born of black parents, but we also learn that there are supposedly whole races of similar beings in Senegal. Maupertuis's interest in genetic matters is evident from a note, that modifications in nature never or hardly ever go from white to black, but occur in the opposite direction, as in the present case.[92] Accordingly, interest in albinos long focused on non-European and, in particular, on negroid cases, which were not associated with albinism in the white race. There was also no inclination, initially, to draw comparisons with similar cases in the animal kingdom. Maupertuis does make a passing reference to white ravens, but Linnaeus never makes such an association. The phenomenon was thus seen, not as having universal validity,

90. C. de Pauw, *Recherches Philosophiques sur les Americains*, nouv. ed., 2 (Berlin, 1772), 17.

91. Voltaire, "Relation touchant un maure blanc," *Oeuvres* 6 (Amsterdam, 1745), 238 ff.

92. Maupertuis, *Venus Physique* (La Haye, 1746), 135 ff.

but as restricted to a particular group or species. Buffon, however, had originally (1750) proposed "degeneration" as the explanation, and later (1777) he gave a detailed exposition of a disease theory, accompanied by good illustrations of piebald Negroes (*nègres piés*). This theory implied that albinism occurs in all peoples.[93] De Pauw, furthermore, opposed the Linnaean view with the simple question of whether any traveler had ever found more than ten such individuals at the same time. But the man who had definitively solved the riddle of the troglodyte was Johann Friedrich Blumenbach in Göttingen, who had come to the conclusion, from the reports of the Tranquebar mission and from other evidence, that this peculiarity was caused by a disease. There were pointers to some form of leprosy, a theory which was not altogether new and which proved to be a persistent one; *blafards,* troglodytes, or whatever they might be called, belonged quite simply to the realm of pathology, not natural history, he decided.[94] Nevertheless, the name "cockroaches" was to occur until the end of the century and also to be applied to European albinos, several of which were described scientifically within a few years.

A similar explanation could also apply in part to the tailed man.[95] An atavistic extension of the caudal vertebra does occur in rare cases and is recorded in earlier medical literature. The sixteenth and seventeenth centuries are a great period for an interest in monstrosities in general, unfortunate "freaks" being taken from town to town to show off their unusual peculiarities. A much-discussed curiosity of this nature was the "porcupine man," whose civil name was Edward Lambert, who was born in 1710 and described in *Philosophical Transactions* and George Edwards's volume of prints. Lambert's skin was covered with countless little blackish spikes that were shed in the winter. He had six children, all of whom inherited the same characteristic, but only one survived. Another report from 1800, arising in connection with the exhibition of younger descendants, states that the trait was passed down on the male side only.[96] Edwards repeats a comment from an earlier description to the effect that a whole race with skin of this kind could propagate themselves and, if their origin were forgotten, be regarded as a separate species.

Why did Linnaeus not regard the troglodyte and the tailed man as individual, more or less monstrous variations to be consigned to *Homo*

93. Buffon, *Histoire Naturelle* 4: 499 ff.; 14: 45–46; Suppl. 4, 555–578.
94. J. F. Blumenbach, *De Generis Humani Varietate Nativa Liber* (Goettingae, 1776), 77–91. Cf. K. Pearson, E. Nettleship, and C. H. Usher, *A Monograph on Albinism in Man* 1–3 (London, 1911–1913).
95. Cf. M. Bartels, "Die geschwänzten Menschen," in *Archiv für Anthropologie* 15 (1884).
96. Edwards, *Gleanings*, 3 ff.; W. G. Tilesius, *Ausfürliche Beschreibung der beiden sog. Stackelschweinmenschen* (Altenburg, 1802).

monstrosus, the miscellaneous group for diverse abnormal variations which he had created in *Systema Naturae?* Why did he make species of them? Why did he take the trouble to include such stories from notoriously unreliable literature? There are many answers: one is the eternal attraction of singular things; moreover, these creatures fit his idea of the chain of being; and finally, he also felt compelled to follow the principles of his science, wherever they might lead.

The troglodyte had indeed taken its name from classical authors; *Systema Naturae* really harks back to Pliny. What the ancients had to relate could not simply be dismissed, though it should possibly be reinterpreted. Pliny places the troglodyte in the interior of Africa, beyond the desert and beyond the "white Ethiopians" (*leucae ethiopes*). It is not clear to whom he is referring, unless by the white Ethiopians he means the non-negroid inhabitants of North Africa, or some mixed race. They are said by Pliny to dig holes to live in, to live on snakemeat, and to have a hissing voice but no power of speech. The singular visual faculty may have a model (or a parallel) in another passage in *Naturalis Historia* dealing with an ethnic group in Albania, grey-eyed and bald-headed, it is true, but with better eyesight by night than by day. Pliny has also heard of troglodytes elsewhere; he finds them in Arabia, in India, and north of the Danube, and they are known to hunt elephants and to trade in spices.[97] In other words, he is referring, not to a specific people, but rather to peoples with a similar way of life. The sheer volume of such reports gave these fabulous beings a footing in the material world, however the individual items of information may have been regarded. And much later, the highly esteemed authors told of tailed man. Marco Polo asserted that the majority of the population of the kingdom of Lambri (Sumatra) had tails, but that they lived in the hills rather than in towns. No less a personage than William Harvey quotes a doctor who had returned from the East Indies with the report that a tailed human genus was living in the mountain regions of Borneo. He had himself seen a girl who had been captured. She had a thick fleshy tail curving inward between her buttocks and hiding her anus and pudenda.[98] Other travelers down until the eighteenth century, such as Carreri and Stryus, testified to the existence of similar races in the Philippines and in Formosa. The rumor of men with tails in the Asian interior was later spread by Johan Peter Falck, the unfortunate Linnaean who later took his own life in Kazan.[99] And Falck was generally a scrupulous reporter.

By virtue of Linnaeus's references, Nils Matsson Kiöping has achieved a

---

97. Pliny, *Naturalis Historia* V: 43–45; VI: 154; VII: 23; XII: 87.

98. W. Harvey, *Exercitationes de Generatione Animalium* (Londini, 1651), 10.

99. J. P. Falck, *Beyträge zur topographischen Kenntnis des russischen Reichs* 3 (Petersburg, 1786), 525.

certain international renown. After having been employed by the Dutch East India Company in the years 1648–1656, during which time he made several trips to the East Indies, Kiöping returned to his native land, and in 1667 he published an edited description of his experiences from Count Per Brahe's presses at Visingsborg.[100] For a long time this was almost the only work of its kind in Swedish literature, and it was frequently quoted. It was reprinted in 1674, in 1743, and twice more before the close of the eighteenth century, which indicates an unusual popularity. Kiöping's reports have been dismissed as mendacious, but at times, as in the story of the perpetually hovering legless bird of paradise, he weighs his information carefully. This is true also, for example, of his treatment of the notion that the chameleon lives purely on air, and of his doubtful remarks about the common picture of the "elephant master" (i.e., Dürer's famous reproduction of a rhinoceros, of which innumerable versions were circulated). Without being a trained natural historian, Kiöping impresses as a good observer with a somewhat Linnaean receptivity for nature's variety. Copious notes from his student years show that Linnaeus had been captivated by these travels at an early age, and in answer to a question about men with tails, Linnaeus wrote to Lord Monboddo that while Kiöping in his simple manner might seem to have rather a lot to relate about animals and plants, all of it is carefully and reliably presented and, moreover, confirmed by contemporary natural historians.[101]

It is not always possible to see clearly what the original source has meant after an account has been recast by various intermediaries. Illustrations were particularly difficult to pass judgment upon. Linnaeus's plate showing the four *Anthropomorpha,* which quickly became well known and was later frequently reproduced, is an excellent example of this simple truth, particularly as far as *Homo caudatus* is concerned, and of the way in which the roots of these accounts may be traced back to the Middle Ages. Linnaeus says that he has found the figure of the man with a tail only in Aldrovandi's work, where the model is a specimen from the East Indies. But the reproduction can, in fact, be found in the *Historia Animalium* by Aldrovandi's predecessor Gesner, which contains another reference, namely, to Bernhard von Breydenbach's description of his pilgrimages to the Holy Land, published back in 1486! In a large plate the old monk presents a variety of animals, such as the giraffe, camel, unicorn, a pair of long-eared goats, a salamander, "cocodrillus" (the Nile monitor)—pictures which

100. Cf. S. Almquist, "Nils Matsson Kiöping och hans mecenat," *Lychnos* (1965–1966).

101. [Lord Monboddo], *Of the Origin and Progress of Language*, 2nd ed., 1 (Edinburgh, 1774), 260. Linnaeus's excerpts are in his *Manuscripta Medica* (Linnean Society, London).

formed the first printed collection of zoological illustrations, and which were accepted almost without question for several centuries—and also this tailed animal, which Breydenbach has seen beside the Red Sea, but whose name he says he does not know. From the details we understand that it is a hamadryas baboon, which three centuries later has been elevated to a man under the name *Homo caudatus*.[102] It is difficult to imagine better evidence for the perplexity surrounding the situation with regard to sources in early anthropology.

Of course, creatures of this sort had an important function to fulfill in conceptions of the coherence of nature and the chain of being. Creation was so infinitely varied; even the gap below man had to be filled in some way. The connection from the animals up to man was the ultimate proof that the chain would hold. Linnaeus was far from indifferent to this aspect; the troglodyte was only a short step from our species, and, in turn, had its gradations. The eighteenth century looked upon these phenomena as something more than curiosities. In *Vue Philosophique sur la Gradation de l'Etre* (1768), for example, Jean Baptiste Robinet shows a predilection for mermaids based on philosophical considerations. Robinet carries to absurd lengths the hypothesis that the manifold forms of nature are only variations on a single prototype, which has found its highest expression in man. He finds human traits everywhere—anthropomorphization has seldom been taken so far as here: everything down to stones and plants bears our imprint in some way, even various marine creatures, which Linnaeus was not alone in mistaking for semi-humans.[103] If we look further ahead, it is, of course, no coincidence that the most emphatic critic of the idea of anthropomorphic creatures, namely, Blumenbach, was also strongly opposed to the idea of a chain of being.

Finally, reasons of general philosophy could not be enough for Linnaeus; he had to note and assess information from the point of view of natural history. The literature gave data relating to the appearance of the eye, the teeth, and the sex organs, which had to be looked on as the characteristics that distinguish the species. The nictitating membrane of the troglodyte was particularly worthy of note, whereas according to taxonomic rules the whiteness ought not to play a decisive part. Recent travelers confirmed the existence of the fabled creatures mentioned by Pliny and others, and these creatures, or their counterparts, could no longer be left out of the great natural inventory that was in progress. Linnaeus was the arbiter of such

102. Cf. H. W. Davies, *Bernhard von Breydenbach and His Journey to the Holy Land 1483–1484. A Bibliography* (London, 1911), pl. 42. The connection is observed by Blumenbach (op. cit., 94–95).

103. J. B. Robinet, *Vue philosophique de la gradation des formes de l'être* (Amsterdam, 1768), 106–141 (Mermaids), 141 ff. (Orang-outang), 160–167 (Tailed Man).

questions, objective in reading the texts of the case, and consistent in his conclusions. He little suspected that posterity would regard the novelties which he presented as outmoded and belonging to a world other than that of reality.

Concluding Remarks: "Two Mental Habits"

Apart from what were in themselves unusually troublesome problems of identification and synonymy, the matter of man's classification does not seem to have been any real problem for Linnaeus. He brought man into the animal kingdom without hesitation; new material was absorbed and used to underline the fact that man is a part of natural history. But this isolated act in an enormous volume of work illustrates both Linnaeus's outlook on nature and his view of civilization, apart, of course, from something of his everyday toil.

We are too often content to see in Linnaeus a craftsman working with limited perspectives. He was a taxonomist in botany and zoology, and somewhat narrow-minded. But it is clear that he was far from being un-affected by contemporary themes of natural philosophy. More than a glimpse of his interest in the cherished idea of nature as a ladder or a chain has been seen in the discussion of the half-humans to which he gave cre-dence. Similar examples of this way of seeing things could be found in Linnaeus's treatment of other frontier areas of nature, entirely as parts of the world of learning. Mention must also be made of an unwillingness to compromise. *Homo troglodytes* shows not only Linnaeus's belief in inter-mediate organisms in nature, but also his confidence in his principles, in this case in those of his mammalian taxonomy, which led him to perceive the troglodyte as a separate species and not merely as a variety of *Homo sapiens*. In his well-known criticisms of the Linnaean method, Buffon might have noted that this example alone is sufficient to show its ar-tificiality, whereas Linnaeus appears rather to have considered his ar-rangement in this and similar cases to be natural insofar as it did justice to the scale, or chain, of nature. One recalls the comment of A. O. Lovejoy: "There are not many differences in mental habit other than that between the habit of thinking in discrete, well-defined class concepts and that of thinking in terms of continuity, of infinitely delicate shadings-off of every-thing into something else, of the overlapping of essences, so that the whole notion of species comes to seem an artifice of thought and not truly applica-ble to the fluency, the, so to say, universal overlappingness of the real world."[104] These two types of "mental habit" may, however, be found in

104. A. O. Lovejoy, *The Great Chain of Being* (1936) (New York, 1965), 57.

one and the same person. One example is Aristotle, who inspired Lovejoy's comment, and another, on closer consideration, appears to be Aristotle's pupil Linnaeus.

The implication of Linnaeus's classification for man is undoubtedly a demotion. Linnaeus carries it out with a certain pleasure, and without hesitation. In various contexts he emphasizes the deranged state of man's reason and his present general wretchedness, and he is also equally inclined to point out the wisdom of the apes and the sound regimen of animals. Even if man is not exactly dethroned from his classic place as the lord of the universe, the intention is, nevertheless, to warn our species against arrogance and pride. Biologically, man belongs to the animal kingdom, and he should order his life accordingly. The introduction of further human species only underlines the same moral lesson. Seen in this light, the apes, tailed man, the troglodyte, and the various unknown human races are welcome arguments in the sometimes biting commentaries of Linnaeus on his society and his times, a theme which we shall not go into more deeply here. He is a critic of civilization as much as a natural historian when he gives man the name *Homo sapiens*.

It is these aspects, the understanding of the biological relation between man and nature, and the view of man's historical degeneration, that caused Linnaeus to take such a great interest in the question of man's classification—not uncertainty as to the point at issue, nor any predilection for the subtleties of philosophy. He knew that this was the most important case in his whole classification of nature, and that its conclusion had implications beyond the field of pure natural history. As a contribution to cultural criticism, Linnaeus's classification of man is not a little polemical; it is, in fact, his subjective assumption of a stance, rather than a mechanical piece of craftsmanship. And, of course, it may be asked, after all, whether it is ever possible to deal with man and man's place in nature objectively and without a good measure of one's own personality.

Works of Linnaeus Mentioned

Index

197

Designer: Marilyn Perry
Compositor: Computer Typesetting Services, Inc.
Printer: Thomson-Shore, Inc.
Binder: John H. Dekker & Sons
Text: 10/12 Baskerville
Display: Baskerville